W9-BXA-165

Before the
Convention

Before the Convention

Strategies and Choices in Presidential Nomination Campaigns

John H. Aldrich

The University of Chicago Press

Chicago and London

John H. Aldrich is associate professor of
political science at Michigan State University.

The University of Chicago Press, Chicago 60637
The University of Chicago Press, Ltd., London

© 1980 by The University of Chicago
All rights reserved. Published 1980
Printed in the United States of America
87 86 85 84 83 82 81 80   5 4 3 2 1

Library of Congress Cataloging in Publication Data

Aldrich, John Herbert, 1947–
  Before the convention.

  Includes bibliographical references and index.
  1. Presidents—United States—Nomination.
2. Primaries—United States. I. Title.
JK521.A42   324.5′0973   79-27752
ISBN 0-226-01269-7
ISBN 0-226-01270-0 pbk.

To Cindy

Contents

Figures

Tables

Preface

The research that led to this book is my attempt to explain the complex process of campaigning for a major party presidential nomination. To explain a political phenomenon requires generating principles that can then be combined with the specific features of the particular instance. My theoretical orientation is drawn from the view of political man as a rational actor. Therefore, I have modeled various aspects of the presidential nomination campaign in an attempt to produce the necessary general principles. (I have also borrowed freely from the work of others when it seemed relevant). I have reported here only the basic notions of some models and their general principles, i.e., derived propositions. Those interested in the more formal effort should consult the sources cited.

The particular instance in this book is, by and large, the 1976 campaign for the presidential nomination. Many individuals and organizations associated with the 1976 campaigns have supported this research. Each of the declared candidates' organizations willingly assisted me, sending position papers, daily itineraries, etc. Virtually all state party organizations, the two national party committees, and many state governments tracked down whatever data were available. A special word of thanks is owed the staff of the Federal Election Commission, who were helpful, prompt, and efficient.

This research was supported by a grant from the National Science Foundation. Richard Dawson and Gerald Wright, the past and present political science directors, did their best to adapt the agency's policies to my particular needs and problems. Charles Cnudde, chair of the Political Science Department, helped marshall the support of the department, the college, and Michigan State University for this project. Katherine Lehman advised Chuck and me about what could be done and how to do it. My research benefited from the College of Social Science's College Scholar Program and All-University Research Grants. The National Science Foundation and Michigan State University bear no responsibility for the analysis reported in this book.

The most consequential assistance came from the intellectual challenges and ideas of many political scientists. John Kessel instilled in me a continuing interest in politics in general and in presidential nominations in particular. William Riker refined my interests and skills, most of all by demonstrating the importance of approaching the political world as the process resulting from the choices of rational actors.

Even a partial listing of colleagues who critiqued parts of this project is lengthy. Among them are Paul Abramson, Steven Brams, John Ferejohn, Morris Fiorina, John Kessel, Richard Niemi, Charles Ostrom, Benjamin Page, Barbara Salert, John Sprague, Kenneth Shepsle, and Mark Winer. Robert Axelrod, John Chamberlin, and Michael Cohen, at the Institute for Public Policy Studies, University of Michigan, made space, scholarly exchange, and solitude (rarely) available.

The notion of attempting this research originated in the office of my friend and colleague, David Rohde. In early January 1976, he claimed that primaries and caucuses were unpredictable. He may still be right.

Two others who deserve special thanks are Michael Gant and Dennis Simon. At the beginning, they were students and my assistants. As such, they willingly gathered and codified diverse data and helped analyze them. Now these two are my peers.

For technical and clerical assistance in completing the manuscript, I thank Karen Albrecht, Chris DeLosh, Pat Everett, Donna Reid, and Iris Richardson.

Cynthia and David, my wife and son, demonstrated the importance of love, support, and understanding. To them I will be ever grateful.

1 The Problem and the Approach

Candidates for president of the United States embark on a long and difficult campaign that may stretch over two or even four years and that consumes the bulk of their attention and effort for at least a full year. Metaphors used to describe the nature of this campaign such as "marathon" and "torture trail," symbolize the enormity of the quest for our highest office.

Presidential campaigns can be divided into two distinct phases, the nomination and the general election campaigns. Of these, the campaign for the nomination is the longer but less well understood. Yet this phase is the screening device that filters out all but one individual per party. As Peabody, Orenstein, and Rohde put it, "many are called but few are chosen."[1] The importance of narrowing the field of presidential contenders from five, ten, or even more hopefuls to precisely two can hardly be overstated. And when it has been done, the citizen is left with the narrowest possible range of policy positions, leadership characteristics, and the like, from which to choose in the general election. Therefore, it is crucial to understand how the filter of nomination politics works.

How are these two chosen from the many? Perhaps even more important, why were so many unsuccessful? Are there biases in the filter that influence the type of man nominated? If so, what are they? Only if we understand who succeeds and who fails in nomination campaigns is it possible to understand how we choose our presidents and what sort of leaders we elect. And only if we understand how candidates campaign for the nomination can we understand who succeeds and who fails.

This book is about nomination campaigns, but only about that portion of the campaign that precedes the national party conventions and the balloting. That is, I am writing about the preconvention campaign period, from January through June or July of the election year. This limitation is not severe. Later in this chapter and throughout this book, it is argued that our nomination system, as currently constituted, has made this preconvention period the single most important filtering process. The institutions that most effectively narrow our range of choice are the presidential primary and the state caucus.

The point of view taken here is of the candidates as decision makers. How and why do they decide to become active candidates? What sorts of strategies are open to them? How do they obtain money, publicity, popular support, and votes at a national convention? Is there a time dynamic or "momentum" as it is called popularly? If so, what effect does it have on the various competitors? Where do candidates choose to compete against others, and when do they decide to let others carry the campaign? How do candidates use public policy as a strategic tool? How does their treatment of issues vary during the campaign? What, in short, is the nature of decision making in this competitive environment, and why do candidates compete as they do?

Three central premises underly this book. The first is that the institution of party nominations—the rules, laws, procedures, and norms that describe how presidential hopefuls become party nominees—plays a major role in structuring the politics of nominations and, consequently, in the behavior of candidates and the outcome of their campaigns.

The methods of selecting nominees have evolved substantially over time, and at a quickened pace in recent years. The process has been reformed to such an extent that, for the first time in our history, candidates for the nomination are campaigning directly to the general public rather than to party leaders. Until very recently, campaigns for the presidential nomination were directed to the élite of the political parties. The public was not ignored in this process, to be sure. Demonstrated popular appeal was always useful in convincing party figures that the candidate was a force to be reckoned with, but it was not in itself a direct route to the nomination. By 1976, however, if not earlier, the nomination was being won—and more often lost—by direct appeals to the electorate. By 1976, that is, the balance of influence was tipped from the political élite that had held it historically to the mass of the electorate.

The second central premise of this book is that presidential candidates are rational political actors who have well defined preferences and who act so as to maximize their chances of realizing those preferences. Models of rational choice are becoming increasingly popular among political scientists. These models, however, remain controversial. Well-reasoned criticisms ordinarily attack the basic assumptions of these models. In this study, many of these criticisms will be minimized. For example, candidates for the presidency *do* know what they want. The decision to campaign *is* of major importance to them. They expend huge amounts of time, energy, and money to become informed about pertinent matters. They come as close as possible to being the literal calculators that these models presume. In short, if anyone makes rational choices, they do.

The third premise is that nomination campaigns can not be understood properly in anything but dynamic terms. They occur over a relatively long period of time. Jimmy Carter's campaign, for example, can be traced back to 1972. Virtually all serious contenders begin to make serious plans two years or more before the first primary. Most of the action is concentrated in the election year, of course. Even so, this period of thirty or more weeks of active campaigning is eight to ten times longer than the mandated length of British national election campaigns. The very length of the campaign suffices to indicate that time plays a crucial role. The rise of such candidates as Carter in 1976 and George McGovern in 1972 and the fall of such front runners as Edmund Muskie in 1972 make the importance of the dynamic element all the clearer.

I propose, in this book, to offer a theory that can explain the actions of candidates in preconvention presidential campaigns. The focus is on the questions of why candidates act as they do and why some succeed but most falter. In the next chapter, for example, I examine who runs for the presidential nominations—not in order to describe who chooses to run for the nomination but to explain why certain candidates did and why other potential candidates did not. The presumption is that a relatively small number of assumptions can be used to generate predictions about behavior. These deductions, combined with the relevant circumstances of a specific situation, can then be tested against the actual behavior of relevant actors.

Empirical observation, in the absence of a theoretical base, is at best descriptive. It tells one what happened, but not why it has the pattern one perceives. Theoretical analysis, in the absence of empirical testing, has a framework more noteworthy for its logical or mathematical elegance than for its utility in generating insights into the real world. The first exercise has been described as "data dredging," the second as building "elegant models of irrelevant universes." My purpose is to try to understand what I believe to be a problem of major importance. This understanding cannot be achieved merely by observation, nor can it be attained by the manipulation of abstract symbols. Real insight can be gained only by their combination.

The data for this exercise are drawn from several elections. For the most part, however, they come from just one: the 1976 nomination campaigns. It happens that the two nomination campaigns of 1976 are particularly useful. Both nominations were vigorously contested. Few foresaw the dramatic rise of Jimmy Carter from relative obscurity to first-ballot victory at the Democratic National Convention. More may have foreseen Gerald Ford's victory, but all must have had doubts as the Republican campaign unfolded. At times it appeared that Ronald Reagan, not the incumbent, would be the nominee, and at the end it was a remarkably close affair.

Although the two campaigns were hotly contested, they differed in important ways. The Republican campaign was a two-candidate contest from beginning to end. Moreover, the contest was close from January through the first and final ballot in August. The Democratic campaign was much more complex. More than a dozen hopefuls were considered major candidates during the winter and spring of 1976. Several more figures played major roles by their presence—and sometimes by their absence. While the Republican campaign was close throughout, the Democratic campaign was volatile, full of twists and turns, of rises and falls. Thus, the two campaigns were somewhat like the end-points of two continua: a small number of actors in a relatively stable competitive balance and a large number of competitors in a most unstable race. The challenge is to provide a coherent and unified account of two quite different campaigns.

In the remainder of this chapter, I shall describe the evolution of the presidential nomination process and develop the basic notions of the model of rational choice.

The Structure of Presidential Elections

The American political system was founded as a representative democracy. Eighteenth-century America was too large to admit of a direct democracy, and there is little evidence to suggest that the Founding Fathers would have desired one even were it feasible. James Madison made it clear that in his view of the Republic, the public had one major role: to select the political leaders who would develop, administer, and adjudicate public policy. Votes were to be cast for men, not for policies. In consequence, the decision to cast one's sole vote must represent a selection of a complex bundle of characteristics. The citizen votes for an individual who has attractive leadership characteristics as well as— perhaps even instead of—a well articulated set of policies. Initially, of course, citizens were entrusted only to select those whom John Adams called the "most wise and good." These few, selected as members of the Electoral College, were those who were to select the president.

The Rise of Political Parties

The Founders did not foresee the rapid emergence of political parties in the United States. Indeed, their concern with the danger of faction was presented in more temperate language by Madison in *Federalist #10* than by most other Founders.[2] Yet many of these very same men were drawn into the formation of the two factions that became the basis of the two-party system. While it is important that the parties crystallized over sharp ideological and policy differences, it is equally important that the political parties, once formed, had major consequences that transcended policy differences, *per se*.

It is hard to understate the importance of the two-party system and its nominations in the structuring of presidential elections. Perhaps most important, the reduction of the number of feasible candidates to precisely two is a major simplification. The standard line that anyone can grow up to be president may be true, but it is true only if one grows up to be a major party nominee. On the one hand, the average voter is asked to make a straightforward decision—to choose one alternative out of two. Barring an exact tie, one candidate will win by a majority. In multiparty systems, one-party majorities are the exception and parliamentary majorities are usually obtained through coalitions negotiated after the election. In consequence, the voter's decision in a two-party election is not only simpler, it is also more directly related to the selection of the chief executive.

On the other hand, American voters are presented with candidates representing highly complex packages, and only two of many possible packages are presented. Thus the individual citizen may be faced with a choice that inadequately reflects his or her preference. One candidate might be an economic and social liberal, and the other might be a conservative in both senses. A citizen who is conservative about economics but liberal about social issues might find neither candidate satisfactory. A liberal voter might consider the liberal candidate a poor leader. When there are only two choices, there is precious little room for shades of opinion. If the choice is between two highly complex alternatives in the general election, the obvious and important first question is, quite simply, How were these two candidates chosen in the first place?

National Party Conventions

Political parties achieved their nomination power in 1804, the date marking the first election when the parties coordinated their support of both a presidential and vice-presidential candidate, as made possible by the Twelfth Amendment. Between 1800 and 1824, party nominees were selected by the congressional caucus. The congressional delegation of a party would simply get together sometime during the election year and, sometimes not so simply, agree on the party's presidential and vice-presidential candidates.[3]

By 1824, however, the congressional caucus was being criticized as an oligarchy that imposed its preferences without regard to opinion in the nation at large: a problem compounded by the existence of only the Democrat-Republican (today's Democratic) Party. "King Caucus," as it was called derisively, chose Secretary of the Treasury William H. Crawford as its presidential nominee for the 1824 election. With the nominations of their respective state legislatures, such other aspirants as John Quincy Adams, Andrew Jackson, John C. Calhoun, and Henry Clay ran in opposition to Crawford. When Adams eventually won the confusing and divisive election, "King Caucus" was dead. State legislalatures also nominated the candidates in 1828, but the nation-in-the-making required a more national procedure.

The first true national party convention was held in 1831 by the Anti-Mason Party, and the Democrats followed suit in 1832. Since that time, all presidents have been nominated by their party's national convention. It has become virtually, if not logically, necessary to obtain a major party nomination to win the presidency.

Political parties in the United States are not accurately described as "national" organizations. Except for having an administrative structure, the political parties act as a national entity but once every four years. At best, parties in this country are federal structures: the preponderance of power is located at the state or even local level. Appeals for party unity are by no means idle rhetoric. National conventions have limited and usually well-defined purposes. They verify the credentials of delegates attending the conventions, formulate a national party platform that may bind the presidential and vice-presidential nominees on occasion but has even less effect on other elected officials of that party, select the candidates for the only two offices with a national constituency, and make the rules that are to govern the national party four years hence.

Even though national conventions had limited purposes, they became subject to much the same criticisms as "King Caucus." The mass electorate had little, if any, role in selecting delegates to the conventions. The preferences of the party-in-the-electorate were represented only to the extent that the delegates (often elected or party organizational leaders) chose to be sensitive to them. By the turn of the twentieth century, national party conventions were open to the same antidemocratic charges that led to the downfall of the congressional caucus and the rise of the convention.

Presidential Primaries

The progressive movement of the early-twentieth century proposed wide-ranging reforms to remove political power from the hands of the "bosses" and put it in the hands of the people as a whole. This democratic thrust led, among other things, to reforms of nominating procedures. The removal of the control of nominations from the bosses, it was felt, could make elected officials more independent of political machines and more attuned to the wishes of the public. The electorate could exercise vastly greater control over government if it could choose the nominees of the two parties. To help correct the antidemocratic bias in party conventions, progressives proposed the primary election.

The first law permitting a presidential primary was enacted in Florida in 1901.[4] Voters in the primary could choose among individuals desiring to become delegates to the national party convention. There was no provision by which voters could express their preference for a presidential nominee, however. Wisconsin (in 1905) and Pennsylvania (in 1906) also legislated presidential primaries into existence. Neither included any binding provision that enabled citizens to express their presidential preferences. Pennsylvania's law permitted those aspiring to become delegates to indicate their presidential preference on the primary ballot, but no candidate exercised this option in 1908. Oregon (in 1910) passed the first primary law that permitted the voters to express a presidential preference that was binding on the delegates. By 1916, 26 states had some form of presidential primary.

The presidential primary marks the first point at which the mass of the electorate had a significant and direct influence on party nominations. It was therefore to be expected that, for the first time, candidates for the presidential nomination would appeal directly to the public. Theodore Roosevelt did just that in 1912, entering 12 Republican primaries and defeating the incumbent President William Taft in 9. Roosevelt lost but one primary to Taft and two others to progressive Republican Senator Robert La Follette. But he lost the nomination to Taft.

Recent Reforms

The presidential primary went into decline during the twenties, thirties, and forties, when many states repealed their primary laws. It has enjoyed a resurgence since then. In 1976, more than 70% of each party's delegates were selected in 30 primaries. This, combined with the growth of the national media, made it necessary for candidates for the presidential nomination to conduct their campaigns in public—and to appeal to the public.

One reason for the movement of campaigns for the nomination from "smoke-filled rooms" to the stump and the nightly news is the increased proportion of convention delegates selected in primaries. The Democratic Party, in particular, has undergone extensive reforms since 1968. A number of these reforms made the state primary a more important influence on the state's delegation. For example, new rules encouraged primaries that legally bind successful delegates to vote in accordance with the voters' expressed preference for a presidential candidate (details can be found in chapter 3). These reforms affected Republican primaries as well, because the laws governing a state's primary are enacted by state legislation, ensuring at least a modicum of uniformity. The Democrats also reformed their remaining caucus procedures to encourage greater responsiveness to the states' party members. State caucuses in the Democratic Party are more primary-like in this regard, a feature not shared by the opposition party.[5]

Another kind of change has made the preconvention campaigns more influential in the selection of presidential nominees. The growth of the mass media of communication has been noted already. Most media have become more nationally oriented and are focusing more attention on state primaries and caucuses. Before 1920, there was no radio broadcasting of national importance. The rise of television came even later. Newspapers have become much more nationally focused and nonpartisan. An increasingly large number of newspapers attach reporters to the preconvention campaign. Others have access to national wire services such as the Associated Press and United Press International, and to syndicated news services such as the *New York Times* and the *Washington Post* provide. News weeklies like *Time* and *Newsweek* fall in the same pattern. What these technological advances do is bring the day-to-day campaign activities of the individual candidates home to the public. At the same time, the candidates tailor their campaigns to the limitations and incentives of the media. It is now feasible, or at least much easier, for a candidate to circumvent party organizations and appeal directly to voters in primaries—and, of course, the primaries are selecting an ever larger proportion of the delegates.

The advent of public-opinion polling—such as the Gallup and Harris Polls and the polling agencies available for hire by individual candidates —serves to make both the candidates and the media more aware of public preferences, perceptions of candidates, and expected voter response. Public popularity has become a valuable resource to the candidates as they argue that they best represent the party and/or that they are electable. As we shall see later, opinion polls are both responsive to and in part responsible for the ebb and flow of a candidate's fortunes and the outcome of specific primaries.

A final class of factors that has moved the action from the national convention to the public at large is the weakening of the party organization. The reforms of the Progressive Era and of subsequent decades broke the hold of political bosses in most areas of the country. As a result, few remain who can control and hence "deliver" large blocs of delegates to whichever candidate offers the most. The general decline of the organizational strength of party and loyalty to it is well documented.[6] By implication, individual candidates and their personal organizations have become more effective in nomination politics, and the party "regulars" have become less influential.

This complex of forces may be good or bad for the Republic. However one evaluates these changes, it is not hard to come to the conclusion that the thrust of these reforms, technical advances, and structural changes has led to a substantially greater democratization of nomination politics. For good or ill, the public plays a much larger role in the selection of party nominees than it did even a decade ago. Nomination conventions no longer bring together party chieftans to decide, on the convention floor or in its accompanying "smoke-filled rooms," who will carry the party's standard. With increasing frequency, it is the candidates themselves and their personal organizations that carry or lose the day. They do so, moreover, with increasing regularity before the convention even convenes. The last convention that exceeded a single ballot was in 1952. Party leaders have not been in complete control of nominations for many years. The balance has been tipped. The nomination campaign is waged in public and is an appeal to the public. Delegates to conventions play an ever-shrinking role in the decisions about which presidential nominees are chosen. The central actors have become the electorate and the candidates themselves.

Until recently, primaries were used less often for winning delegates in a state than as bargaining chips by the candidates. In 1960, John Kennedy was criticized as young, inexperienced, and Catholic, all of which, it was speculated, were political liabilities. His defeat of Hubert Humphrey in the Wisconsin and West Virginia primaries that year helped convince such Democratic leaders as Mayor Richard Daley of Chicago and Governor David Lawrence of Pennsylvania that he was able to win votes. His nomination symbolized the tipping of the balance of power from party to electorate. It was the first nomination in which primary victories were undeniably the keystone of success. Since that time, only Humphrey (in 1968) has been able to win the nomination without "going the primary route."

John Kennedy's use of the primary marks a symbolic change only, because he did not win the nomination in spite of the party regulars but because of them. Humphrey's nomination in 1968 marks another turning point. Senator Eugene McCarthy's campaign for the 1968 Democratic nomination had the end of President Lyndon Johnson's Vietnam policy as its central goal. McCarthy's surprisingly strong showing in the New Hampshire primary helped prod Johnson to retire and encouraged Senator Robert Kennedy to enter the race. After Johnson withdrew, Vice President Humphrey became the administration's (and the party regulars') candidate. Humphrey chose not to enter any primaries or make a public campaign, but relied instead on party organizations and Johnson's powerful, if somewhat untamed, leadership. He was aided in his quest by the support of the bulk of the one-third of the national convention delegates who were selected in 1967, well before the tumultuous events of 1968. With Kennedy's assassination after the California primary, Humphrey was able to win the nomination. His victory, however, was pyrrhic. McCarthy, who ultimately failed, was nevertheless the first candidate who "went over the heads of party" to the public (a phrase that now seems dated) and who materially affected the course of the campaign.

The Democratic National Convention of 1968 was a turbulent affair. Protests, demonstrations, and riots in the streets of Chicago accompanied bitter debates, power struggles, and even arrests on the convention floor. Large groups of delegates felt that the power of party bosses was being used to circumvent the will of the people. The bitter feelings engendered on all sides sealed the fate of party leaders as the central point of influence in selecting presidential nominees.

Out of the experiences of 1968 grew a series of reform efforts within the Democratic Party. A commission was established to propose new rules for nominations. It was first chaired by Senator George McGovern, who was succeeded by Rep. Donald Fraser when McGovern decided to seek the 1972 presidential nomination. Since that time, there has been some commission or other in the Democratic Party continuously seeking the appropriate means of selecting its national nominees. The McGovern-Fraser Commission, which set rules for the 1972 convention, was followed by the Mikulski Commission, whose rules applied to the 1976 convention. It was succeeded by the Winograd Commission, whose task was to establish procedures for 1980. The end product of these various committees (detailed in chapters 3 and 8) was the virtual requirement that any serious candidate has to confront the Democratic electorate actively and repeatedly. (I should point out here that Mc-

Govern's close understanding of the new rules provided him with greater information than most other candidates and undoubtedly provided him an important advantage, in a sense completely consistent with one of the central themes of this book. It should also be noted that the various Democratic reform committees had broader mandates than discussed here.)

Thus, the nominating system of 1976 bears little resemblance to that of 1796. The system of 1976 is far more democratic than ever before. Nonetheless, the national convention remains, and it remains possible that convention delegates will be called upon to select a nominee who was not in effect selected in the preconvention campaign. The circumstances under which this could occur, however, are much more limited than even a decade ago. It could happen, it would seem, any time there are several candidates for the nomination and, thus, the preconvention campaign could be indecisive, failing to generate majority support for one candidate. A deadlocked convention would then be free to select whatever nominee the delegates prefer. Since most contested nomination campaigns in recent history have involved many hopefuls, it would seem that the argument that the electorate has become the central audience has little force. Granted, the 1972 and 1976 Democratic campaigns began with crowded fields, yet they narrowed quickly and a first-ballot victor was selected well before the convention was gaveled open. It can be argued that these two examples are exceptional cases based on exceptional circumstances. If so, it might appear that a small, rather unrepresentative, group of party leaders retains basic power over nominations anytime there is a divided party. In chapter 5, I argue that the 1972 and 1976 campaigns were not at all unusual. Even in (perhaps especially in) crowded fields, the nominating system as currently constituted sets the stage for dynamic forces in the public campaign that will lead to one-ballot conventions more often than not. The public campaign is indeed the campaign that generates most presidential nominees.

Rational Choice

The argument, so far, has been focused on the role of the public versus the role of convention delegates and party leaders. The question has been, Who is the audience of the campaign for the nomination? Whether it be the party or the public, it is but the audience. It is the candidates for the nomination who hold center stage. The candidates, then, should be the central focus of any attempt to understand nomination politics, and they will be of central concern throughout the remainder of this book.

If the major effort is to understand the candidates' behavior, I must make clear at the outset just what I believe about the candidates. The second central premise of this book is that the candidates are rational political actors. While the full scope of this assumption will be revealed throughout the book, the basic idea of and the essential elements of rational choice can be outlined briefly.

The central idea underlying the concept of rational choice is that the behavior of the rational actor is goal-directed. A prerequisite for purposive behavior is that the actor must have a clearly defined set of goals in mind. The notion of goal-directed behavior presumes only that the individual has goals. The goals may be consequential or trivial, admirable or abhorrent. For the exercise of rational choice modeling, these distinctions do not matter. What matters, simply, is that the individual chooses actions that will help attain these goals. Rational choice, thus, is the selection of appropriate means to attain desired ends. Those seeking to understand an individual's behavior must take the chosen ends as given.

A great deal of the controversy over the concept of rational choice concerns precisely this point. Do individuals have clearly articulated goals, at least as defined in specific assumptions in the model? Even if they do, have we, as scientists attempting to understand their behavior, successfully captured their goals in our models?

Controversy over goals of presidential candidates cannot be dismissed lightly. Yet such actors are as likely as any others to have well-defined goals. Many writers have assumed that candidates share one simple goal: to win. Such a simplification misses much of the subtleties of the candidates and their behavior. Even so, a great deal of progress can be made with even this simplest of all posited goals. In the next chapter, the candidates' goals will be considered at some length. I shall argue, for example, that candidates have policy goals, and others, in addition to the goal of victory. While goals other than winning impose constraints on candidates, I shall argue that doing well in the electorate furthers most other goals under broad sets of circumstances.

A second type of controversy over the use of rational choice models in political science has to do with information. In any interesting and hence complex choice situation, the rational actor may need a substantial amount of information. Becoming fully informed about even such a relatively straightforward choice as whether or not to buy a car is time-consuming. Moreover, each automobile has a variety of character-istics: looks, performance, efficiency, cost, and the like. Rarely does one type of car seem best in all ways. Rather, all require some tradeoffs: trading power for safety devices, size for better gas mileage, and so forth. Any interesting political choice is much more complex. In par-ticular, the competitive nature of a political campaign means that the campaigners must have a great deal of information about their oppo-nents' goals and choices of action.

The failure of actors to obtain full information lessens the plausibil-ity of rational choice models that are based on the assumption that the actors have full information, and we shall see instances in which can-didates erred because of incomplete information. For example, Ford's campaign in North Carolina was based on insufficient information, as admitted by his own staff. This problem is discussed again in chapter 6. Candidates do, however, make a concerted effort to acquire the full-est possible information about the nominating system and its rules and norms, about their opponents, and about the consequences of their ac-tions. While, as in all modeling, the assumptions made here are simpli-fications of the actual decision making, it seems reasonable to assume that candidates and their staffs make calculations not unlike those mod-eled here.

If the basic concept of rational choice is purposive behavior, there are a number of elements that define and structure the setting of deci-sion making.[7] The elements of individual choice include the following. First, the set of all logically possible outcomes must be specified. The degree of precision with which outcomes must be specified varies with the context, purpose, and time-frame of the analysis. One pair of out-comes here would be that the candidate wins the nomination or does not. There are, however, different ways of winning or losing. A candi-date who narrowly loses the presidential nomination might be in line for the vice-presidential nomination, or improve the chance of winning the presidential nomination four or eight years later. Winning a close race for the presidential nomination, on the other hand, might decrease the odds of winning the general election. Therefore, we might want to define the outcome by how many delegate votes a candidate wins, or refine them in some other manner. This point becomes particularly rele-vant when we focus on the outcome of specific primaries. Outcomes also may be defined as more complex bundles, e.g., win the nomination *and* adopt preferred policy positions.

The next part of the concept of rational choice involves the individual's goals; specifically, how the individual values the different outcomes. A utility function is used to evaluate the individual decision maker's goals. Depending upon the particular purposes involved, the nature and strength of the assumptions necessary to generate a utility function varies.[8]

The simplest form of a utility function is a preference order: an ordinal utility function. This makes it possible to rank outcomes in terms of preference, but it is impossible to say how much one alternative is preferred to another. The key assumptions underlying an ordinal utility function are comparability and transitivity. Comparability means that a person can compare any two outcomes. One either prefers the first to the second, or the second to the first, or is indifferent. Transitivity enables these preferences to be extended from pairs to the full set of outcomes. If a candidate prefers outcome a to b and outcome b to c, then transitivity requires that a be preferred to c. Preferences are based solely on the values and tastes of the decision maker.

The next level of complexity of relevance is an interval, or cardinal utility function. As I have observed, an ordinal utility function does not permit one to say how much an individual prefers outcome a to outcome b, or whether the difference between a and b seems greater than that between b and c. A cardinal utility function assumes that such evaluations can be made. To establish cardinality, differences in preference are given numerical values. If outcome a is given a utility index number of 4, b is given 0, and c is assigned -2, then the difference between a and b is twice that between b and c. While the relative magnitudes are meaningful, the absolute numbers are not. The method is analogous to temperature scales; whether ice freezes at $0°$ or $32°$ depends not on some absolute magnitude of temperature, but on whether one is using Celsius or Fahrenheit as the cardinal scale.

The assumptions underlying cardinal utility functions are more complex and controversial and are ably reviewed elsewhere.[9] Here, it is assumed that candidates can be modeled as having a cardinal utility function defined over the set of outcomes.

The third ingredient of the individual decision-making setting is the set of actions or behaviors open to the candidate. A citizen in a general election can vote for the Republican, the Democrat, some minor party candidate, or can abstain. A candidate can enter a primary or fail to contest it. A candidate can issue a position paper now, later, or never.

It is this sort of observed, manifest behavior that we can study, predict, and explain, along with its consequences.

A mere listing or alternative actions open to the candidates is insufficient. There must be some known or hypothesized connection between an act and one or more outcomes. The central assumption underlying the rational choice theory is that the behavior is directed toward a desired outcome. If the decision maker has absolutely no idea of the consequences of an act, the choice of acts cannot be goal oriented.

The strength and clarity of this connection between act and outcome vary. The act of purchasing an object leads directly to the possession of that object (and, of course, it is the purchaser's utility function that determines the desirability of that object compared to its price and to other obtainable goods compared to their prices). This situation is termed decision making under certainty, because the act leads to the outcome for certain.[10]

Most social situations are not well described as decision making under certainty. Even some purchases do not fit this model. For example, purchasing a lottery ticket is considered decision making under risk. The goal, or desired outcome, is to win the lottery and its accompanying prize. But purchasing a ticket leads directly to two sets of outcomes, not one. The more common outcome is that the ticket is not a winner, in which case the outcome is the loss of the purchase price of the ticket. Someone, somewhere, however, does buy a winning ticket. The outcome for the lucky individual, then, is the prize less the cost of the ticket. The decision making is made under risky conditions if the probability of the ticket being a winner is known.

Still, even risk does not describe most social situations. For example, Ronald Reagan may have known that if Gerald Ford did not run against him in the Pennsylvania primary, Reagan would win many delegates. Reagan knew that he would win few if his opponent contested the primary. He even may have been able to make precise calculations of few and many. He also preferred more delegates to less. What Reagan might *not* have been able to calculate was the probability that Ford would contest the primary and, therefore, the probability of the several outcomes following from the decision to enter. The outcomes, thus, are conditional on the actions of both candidates, not on either one alone.

In decision making under uncertainty, the outcomes are known and they are valued to the individual. The available actions are known as well, but it is impossible to specify a single outcome each will lead to or the probability distributions over the sets of outcomes they lead to.

When the uncertainty is due to opposing rational actors, the theory of games can be used to explain behavior. In other circumstances, decision-making procedures not used in this book can be employed.[11]

To this point, nothing has been said about rationality. Once the set of outcomes, the utility function, the possible actions, and their connection to outcomes have been specified, rational choice follows. The assumption is simply this: the individual will choose that act that leads to the (set of) outcomes(s) from which the greatest utility is derived. Rational choice, that is, is goal-directed behavior.

The general statement of the axiom of rational choice is misleading, for there are actually many rational choice assumptions. In decision making under certainty, a rational choice is simply the selection of the action that yields the most desired outcome. In particular, it is assumed that a rational chooser is a utility maximizer, maximizing the net benefit (i.e., benefit less cost).

A rational choice in decision making under risk usually (but not always) is assumed to be one that maximizes expected utility. For example, the probability of winning the lottery is multiplied by the utility of the prize to yield the expected benefit of buying a ticket. The net expected utility of that ticket, then, is the difference between expected benefit and cost. If the net expected utility of the purchase exceeds the net expected utility of not buying it, then a rational expected utility maximizer will buy the ticket. If not, he or she will not.

The game theoretic versions of decision making under uncertainty are designed to account for competitive behavior and strategic interaction. As such, they are quite complex, but they promise to be especially useful in many political situations, including nomination campaigns. A game theoretic model is used to analyze the problem of *where* to compete (in chapter 6) and *how* to compete, at least in terms of policy (in chapter 7). The technical difficulties of using such models have plagued game theorists since its foundations. Although applications are increasing, most are based on the general reasoning of game theory, rather than being literal applications. The difficulties encountered in the attempt to extend the model from the two-candidate Republican to the multicandidate Democratic campaign (see chapter 6) illustrate the difficulties of applying the theory but also show the value of the reasoning.

The Institutional Context

The most impressive body of rational choice literature is social choice theory. The core of social choice theory is Kenneth Arrow's general possibility theorem. Arrow abstracted the famous "paradox of voting" to a more general and fundamental level.[12]

The paradox is simply this. Suppose there are three individuals, I, II, and III, and three outcomes, a, b, and c. Suppose further that the three individuals have well defined ordinal utility functions: I's being a, b, c; II's *being b, c, a*; and III's being c, a, b, all in the order listed. If these three alternatives are voted on in pairs, the outcome of the votes is cyclical. That is, a defeats b, b defeats c, and c defeats a (in violation of transitivity), if all vote their preferences sincerely. Although all the individuals involved have well-defined and consistent preferences, the choices made by this small society are neither well-defined nor consistent. Perhaps a "better" social choice would be the one within any pair that defeats its alternative. But while a defeats b, a is not the best alternative because c defeats it. But c is not best either, because b defeats it. And b cannot be best because a defeats it. But . . . And so on, infinitely and cyclically.

Arrow's theorem demonstrated that any method of aggregation of even well-defined preferences that satisfies a few apparently innocuous conditions—be it voting, the market place, or whatever—may reveal the same sort of inconsistency so long as there are at least two members in the society and at least three possible choices. What he proved, is that virtually any non-dictatorial method of selection, in any society, can be incoherent no matter how coherent its members. The generality of this theorem and the ensuing social choice theory is that it applies to nearly every social institution. Pure social choice theory, then, is the study of choice independent of most institutional structure. The subsequent, voluminous literature on social choice can be summarized best by saying that it reaffirms the perniciousness of Arrow's basic result.

While incoherence may be a fact of life in institution-free studies of social choice, actual choices are made within specific institutions, and specific institutional arrangements may reestablish (apparent) coherence.[13] Dictatorial methods of making social choices are an obvious example.

Political parties in the United States are another example. The reduction of the set of alternatives to precisely two presidential candidates in most general elections eliminates the paradox of voting and its more general counterpart. Thus, political parties play a crucial theoretical as well as practical role in structuring elections and their outcome. Bjurulf and Niemi argue that even in multiparty legislatures, there is a strong tendency to reduce the set of choices to two. That is, the possibility of voting-type paradoxes is of sufficient concern to encourage the development of formal or informal institutional structures that have the effect of limiting if not eliminating, the manifest consequences of paradoxical preference configurations.[14]

The institutional setting of individual and social choice plays a far greater role than merely limiting the set of feasible outcomes, important though this role may be. One of the major themes of this book is how the complex institutional arrangements of the preconvention campaign impinge on the choices of individual candidates and, ultimately, on the choices made by our society. In the next chapter, for example, it will be seen that the "opportunity structure" of political offices in the United States exerts a tremendous force on the candidates' decision about whether or not to run for the presidency. The third chapter contains a description of how the candidates' resources are influenced by the complex interaction of financial regulations, state procedures for selecting delegates, and the news media. In the fifth chapter, many of these same institutional structures are examined in terms of their role in generating dynamic forces. In the sixth chapter, there is a discussion of how candidates decide which primaries to contest, in part as a function of institutional arrangements, and in the seventh chapter many of the above aspects of structure are shown to impinge on the candidates' policy positions. In short, preconvention campaign politics are politics embedded in a highly unusual institutional context. It should not be surprising that political choices, both individual and social, are understandable only in their institutional context.

The Plan of the Book

The rest of this book is an attempt to explain the workings of the complex process by which presidential hopefuls attempt to become major party presidential nominees. I have already explained that the theme of the institutional context in which political choice is made pervades this work. In addition, each chapter has been focused on a particular aspect of the presidential nominating campaign.

Chapter 2 is an examination of the motivations of the candidates and of how they came to decide to run for the presidency while many others did not. Many may be called to run, but many, many more are screened out or screen themselves out of contention long before the visible campaign commences. The set of candidates who choose to campaign for the nomination is in no sense typical of the entire population. Some sense of how the general structure of our political institutions creates a set of possible nominees, one that is quite atypical, is crucial to understanding the nature of the competition.

Chapter 3 is an overview of the complex maze of procedures, regulations, and norms that govern the politics of nomination. This chapter also provides a first look at the resources the candidates acquire and expend in the preconvention campaign. These two topics are not at all independent. Money, for example, is a resource that candidates need in large quantities and that they expend judiciously and purposefully. At the same time, extensive financial regulations create one of the major mazes that candidates must run. Another example: the nomination campaign is a national effort that must be waged in fifty individual states. Each state has a unique procedure for selecting delegates. Even though a presidential primary may have important national implications, its basic purpose is to select the delegates from that state. A national campaign, therefore, is an aggregation of fifty state-by-state contests. Where candidates go and where they expend their resources, then, is governed by idiosyncratic state procedures. The national media, as another example, provide a series of norms that affect the candidates' behavior but are also a crucial resource.

Chapter 4 completes the basic scenario. The individual citizen as potential participator is examined in this chapter. The decision to participate or not is affected by the decision about whom to support. Thus, both turnout and the results of voting in primaries and in caucuses are discussed.

In chapter 5, I argue that there are crucial dynamic, or time-related, forces in preconvention campaigns. There is also a close relationship between the gathering and expenditures of resources and the outcome of primaries and caucuses as the campaign progresses. The explosive phenomenon of momentum that many claim explains (or at least describes) the successes of McGovern in 1972 and Carter in 1976 illustrates the importance of dynamic elements. Precisely what these are, how resources and the acquisition of delegates are intertwined, why some "take off" while others do not is analyzed in this chapter.

Given the power of these dynamic forces, rational candidates respond to them and try to manipulate them to their advantage. One aspect of this attempt, *where* the candidate chooses to compete, is the subject of chapter 6. Candidates seeking the nomination by competing actively for delegates in primary and caucus states must attempt to forge a winning coalition in some manner. At some point, they must "lay their candidacies on the line" and subject themselves to a public test against their competitors. Just where they choose to do so and how they come to that decision is analyzed by means of game theory.

The seventh chapter is an examination of the nature of policy competition. The sorts of questions considered include: What positions do candidates take? How do these evolve and how do they vary from one state primary or caucus to the next? Under what conditions are rational candidates clear or ambiguous on issues? How do they decide which issues to discuss and which to deemphasize in their rhetoric? What sorts of constraints are there on the candidates? What are the consequences of these decisions for the nomination and for the general election?

The last chapter is an attempt to draw these various aspects together into a unified theory of nomination campaigns. There is also an attempt to draw lessons from this theory. What sort of individual becomes the presidential nominee? What effect, if any, does the nomination system have on the president, once in office? What effect would reforms of the system, be they planned, proposed for the immediate future, or possible in the longer run, have on presidential campaigns? How are executive procedures and public policy in the United States shaped by this "first season" of presidential politics?[15]

We must begin this story at the beginning. Potential presidents begin to run for this highest office shortly after the incumbent has been sworn into office four years earlier. A presidential campaign rests on a complex organization, requiring vast resources, and it must rest as well on a plan. Much of this precampaign maneuvering occurs outside of the light of public scrutiny. A candidate's commitment to run, however, must be made early, and in view of at least the attentive public. It is a decision not to be made lightly, for by January of an election year, that commitment will cost the candidate dearly. Who runs, and why do they do it? That is the first question.

2 Who Runs for the Presidency and Why

Any child may grow up to be president of the United States, or so we are told. Judging by the large number of presidential candidates and hopefuls in most election years, the adage would seem to contain a grain of truth. Of course, it is not true that *anyone* who is eligible will actually seek the presidential nomination of a major party. There are two basic reasons for the narrow spectrum from which presidential aspirants are drawn. First, not everyone wants to be president. Second, not everyone who wants to be president has a real chance of being nominated. The purpose of this chapter is to amplify on these two points and their relationship.

Assuming that the constitutional criteria of eligibility are satisfied, anyone *can* run for the presidency. The decision to run is voluntary. Yet few do, and these few who do are atypical of the general population. The essential argument of this chapter is that the nature of our political system encourages certain types of individuals to run for the presidency and discourages others. The implication is that only individuals with certain characteristics will choose to make a serious run for the nomination. Consequently, just what types of individuals have the desire and a realistic opportunity to become president is a function of the nature of our political institutions. At the same time, the decision to run is a choice made freely by the individual and, therefore, can be explained by rational decision-making models. In this chapter, I attempt to account for the decision to run for a presidential nomination by studying the nature of choice in an institutional context.

Same General Constraints

The Constitution mandates that only natural-born citizens of thirty-five and over may be chosen president. In practice, there are many other conditions that are crucial.

The most important constraint is that the individual must be identified with one of the two major. parties and, indeed, must be chosen as its nominee. This constraint is very real, because it narrows the focus of politics substantially. Socialist Party nominees like Eugene Debs or Norman Thomas could not have expected to become president. At best, any third-party candidacies can affect public policy only by influencing Republicans or Democrats. Even being a party member may not be a sufficient qualification. It was questionable that the Democratic Party would have endorsed a long-time Democrat like George Wallace, whose policy positions were at odds with the bulk of established Democratic leaders and with party tradition.

The major exception to the requirement of being a well-known partisan of long standing and experience is the military leader. Successful generals like Dwight Eisenhower may be perceived as attractive candidates because of their leadership experience as well as their popular appeal. The subordination of the military to the body politic in the United States implies that one should not expect a military leader to have partisan political experience. Both parties may simultaneously seek to attract a popular military figure like Eisenhower to their fold.

There are other constraints imposed by the more general social system. Historically, the presidency has been reserved for the white, male Protestant. The breaking of these constraints that have to do with status comes but slowly. In 1928, Al Smith became the first major party nominee who was Catholic. His overwhelming defeat reestablished the importance of Protestantism until 1960. Kennedy's victory in that election changed the constraints to white, male Christian.

These constraints are not unchangeable. However, they are a major hurdle. It will require unusual and favorable circumstance before a female, a black, an Oriental, or a Jew can become a viable major party

candidate. While blacks and women have run for major party nominations, circumstances have not been favorable enough for them to make
a strong showing. Kennedy's success suggests that once one member of
a social category has surmounted that hurdle successfully, the liability
of that characteristic is greatly reduced, if not eliminated completely.
Catholicism, for example, seems totally irrelevant today. Presumably,
the first successful woman, black, or Jew will open the presidency to
others of the same group.

A final but very important type of general constraint is more directly
political. Extreme or highly unusual political beliefs are major liabilities.
The reason most third-party candidates have so little chance to become
president is that third parties generally espouse quite different political
philosophies. Individuals out of the mainstream of political thought,
typically as measured by the range of beliefs espoused by the Republican or Democratic parties, will not be able to attain the support either
of party regulars or of the public.

The nature of extreme or unusual political beliefs is neither precisely
definable nor constant. There is some extreme point on the continuum
that is beyond what the party and the electorate will tolerate. Yet, there
is no necessary, precise dividing line. Philosophies wholly other than
the traditional liberalism of our American system, such as avowed com-
munism or facism, are clearly beyond the pale. Advocacy of specific
policies that sound, say, socialistic may or may not be. Our political
parties admit of substantial diversity of opinion. Nonetheless, an acceptable but relatively extreme candidate has liabilities, both in attaining the
nomination and in winning the general election. The divisiveness of the
nominations of Barry Goldwater and George McGovern, and their overwhelming rejection by the electorate in the fall, illustrate the extent of
these hurdles for even relatively mild extremists.

What is extreme is defined by party and public belief. The definition,
therefore, changes as beliefs change. What today sounds extremely conservative would have been considered radical beyond comprehension in
nineteenth-century America. The beliefs of the public and the parties,
then, impose substantial constraints, conserving the status quo to the
extent of ruling out advocacy of radical change in all but the most unusual circumstances. Change, that is, can come no faster than partisans
and the public will allow.

These sorts of constraints form a general background from which
most serious candidates emerge. The more specific institutional context,

in combination with the decision-making context, imposes more specific criteria for potential candidates. It is to the decision-making problem that we now turn.

Ambition Theory

Joseph Schlesinger began his classic study of political career patterns by stating, "Ambition lies at the heart of politics. Politics thrive on the hope of preferment and the drive for office."[1] His study emphasized the interaction of ambition with the "opportunity structure," or the way the organization of political offices shapes the choices open to an individual at any given time. Thus, ambition theory is designed precisely to answer the questions posed in this chapter: Who runs for office and why?

Schlesinger created a threefold categorization of ambition. Of relevance here is the third type: a politician who holds one office but seeks to obtain another regarded as more desirable is referred to as having progressive ambition.

His theory assumes that the various elective offices can be ordered (at least partially) on the basis of their "attractiveness," and that all share the same conception of relative attractiveness. These assumptions appear to hold true. The euphemism "higher office," for example, is meaningful to most politicians and nonpoliticians alike. The U.S. presidency is considered the ultimately desirable political office. Therefore, in virtually all instances, a candidate for the presidency has (or suffers from) progressive ambition.

David Rohde has developed a theory of progressive ambition that amplifies and extends Schlesinger's and might be called the calculus of candidacy.[2] His basic assumptions, as translated into our context, include the following.

First, it is possible to identify the set of politicians desiring to become the president (i.e., those who possess the relevant form of progressive ambition). Because he was studying the decision of U.S. representatives to run for the Senate or state governorship, he assumed that almost all members of Congress would prefer to be senators or governors if they could do so without cost or risk. Thus, he assumed that all members of Congress have progressive ambition. What distinguishes those who seek higher office, then, is the calculation of the costs and/or risks involved. Identifying the set of politicians who desire to become president is more difficult, but I assume initially that almost all elected officials (and some others) are progressively ambitious and would take the office of president if it were offered without cost or risk. This implies that the categorization of types of ambition is the result of circumstances that affect the costs and risks. Gerald Ford, in his oft-stated desire to remain in the House of Representatives and become its speaker, was a classic instance of ambition that is not progressive. Changed circumstances led Ford to change that apparently lifelong ambition and to desire the presidency.

Second, Rohde assumes, as I do, that politicians are rational. The meaning of rationality was described in chapter 1. However, he also assumes that the nature of the rational choice is the comparison of two specific alternatives. The particular alternatives, in this book, are that a politician runs for the presidency or chooses to remain in the presently held office, which may or may not entail running for reelection. The possible outcomes, then, are that the candidate is elected president, that no office is held after the election, or that the current office is retained. Obviously, this is a simplification. A representative, for example, might have the following choices: running for the House again, for a Senate seat, for the governorship, or for the presidency, or even retiring from public life. A senator might be up for reelection or might not have to stand for two or four years. Different calculations would apply in these different circumstances. On the other hand, presidential hopefuls generally decide to try for the nomination from six months to three or four years before they must decide about campaigning for reelection. Moreover, if they run for the presidency, they generally have several months of campaigning in which to ascertain their chances for the nomination before foreclosing some other office. Therefore the simplification is not too severe.

The decision to run for the presidency is based upon an expected utility calculation of the sort described in chapter 1. The probability of winning the presidential nomination is multiplied by the value of that outcome, and so on for all possible outcomes. The sum of these calculations is the expected benefit of choosing to run. A similar calculation can be made for not running. The direct costs of the two possible choices must be subtracted from the expected benefits, to yield the expected utility of each action. The rational candidate, as an expected utility maximizer, chooses to run for president if that course of action provides the larger expected utility, and does not if it does not.

A third assumption concerns risk taking. Politics is a risky business by its very nature. Nonetheless, politicians, like all individuals, vary in the degree to which they like or abhor risky environments. Therefore, the risk takers among them are more likely to enter the especially risky environment of presidential elections—more so, at least, than those who display less appetite for risk taking.

This skeletal outline of the central elements of ambition theory gives us some idea of what is involved in a potential candidate's decision to run or not. Combined with the variety of contexts in which potential candidates are situated, it enables us to produce hypotheses about who chooses to run for president.

Who Runs for President?

Presidential candidates tend to emerge from a very few offices (see table 2.1).

This traditional concentration of presidential contenders became even greater after World War II. Senators and governors have accounted for 80 percent of the "serious" candidacies in the period from 1948 to 1972. The vice-presidency should be added to this list of offices. Although there have been only two serious candidacies from this office, that number is a large proportion of the available pool of vice presidents.

Presidential candidates in 1976 emerged from the same sources. There were two active Republicans, President Ford and former California Governor Reagan. A number of other Republicans were publicly considered potential candidates, although they never made a serious effort. Significantly, those so considered were the vice president (Rockefeller), a former governor and later a federal appointee (Connally), and a senator (Mathias, who briefly considered a third-party as well as a Republican candidacy). Two other senators (Baker and Percy) were considered newsworthy possible candidates early in the campaign.

Thirteen Democrats declared their candidacy for the presidency and initiated a nationally oriented, if sometimes brief, campaign. For purposes of this study, these thirteen individuals will be called "declared candidates" and will be those studied most closely. The distribution of these thirteen over the major categories of their last-held political offices is much like that found by Peabody, Ornstein, and Rohde (table 2.1). The group consisted of one U.S. representative (Morris Udall), four senators (Birch Bayh, Lloyd Bentsen, Frank Church, and Henry Jackson), one former senator (Fred Harris), three governors (Jerry Brown, Milton Shapp, and George Wallace), two former governors (Jimmy Carter

Table 2.1   Office Held by Major Contenders for the Presidency:
Two Major Parties, 1868–1972

Office and Period	Presidential Contenders at Convention[a]		Presidential Nominees		Presidential Contenders as Determined by Gallup Polls[b]	
	Percentage	No.	Percentage	No.	Percentage	No.
1868–1972						
U.S. representative	9.8	10	5.4	2		
U.S. senator	30.4	31	13.5	5		
Governor	28.4	29	37.9	14		
Federal appointee	13.7	14	13.5	5		
Vice-president	2.0	2	5.4	2		
Other and none	15.7	16	24.4	9		
Total	100.0	102	100.1	37		
1948–1972						
U.S. representative	.0	0	.0	0	1.4	1
U.S. senator	44.0	11	30.0	3	40.8	29
Governor	36.0	9	30.0	3	29.6	21
Federal appointee	4.0	1	.0	0	4.2	3
Vice-president	8.0	2	20.0	2	5.6	4
Other and none	8.0	2	20.0	2	18.3	13
Total	100.0	25	100.0	10	99.9	71

SOURCE: Robert L. Peabody, Norman J. Ornstein, and David W. Rohde, "The United States Senate as a Presidential Incubator: Many Are Called but Few Are Chosen," *Political Science Quarterly* 91 (Summer 1976): 242–43.

[a]Those who received 10% or more of the convention vote on any ballot. [b]A contender, as determined by Gallup polls, is one who was mentioned by at least 5% of sample identifying with that party.

and Terry Sanford), one former federal appointee (Sargent Shriver, who was, more recently, the 1972 vice-presidential candidate), and one who never held office (Ellen McCormack). The last candidate ran a "one-issue" campaign, a different type of candidacy that will be discussed later.

There were seven other people who were either thought to be possible Democratic candidates, at least very early in the campaign, or who undertook some sort of campaign. They were all senators (Hubert Humphrey, Ted Kennedy, Edmund Muskie, George McGovern, John Glenn, Adlai Stevenson, and Robert Byrd). Senator Walter Mondale also initiated an active campaign for the presidency. However, he withdrew in November 1974, more than a year before the first delegate was selected, citing the hardships of conducting a campaign for the presidential nomination and saying that he didn't have the "fire" in him to make the run. His concerns mesh well with the "calculus of candidacy" offered later in this chapter, even though, as we shall see, he was perfectly situated to run for the presidency in 1976 (with zero liabilities). However, he was not a proven "high risk taker" as we shall define that term, having been initially appointed to the Senate. Carter, when he was considering Mondale for the vice-presidency, said he "resented" Mondale's attitude toward campaigning, and remarked that Mondale's withdrawal was "the single most detrimental factor."[3] Details about the Democratic candidates may be found in table 2.2.

One interesting point about the table is the high percentage of candidates in 1976 who were no longer political officeholders. Their reduced costs and risks also meshes well with the general model of the calculus of candidacy.

Why They Run: The Situational Context

If it is true that politicians are progressively ambitious and desire the presidency in their heart of hearts, why do candidates come from so few offices? The answer is obvious. The three offices that provide most of the active candidacies are the most visible ones, short of the presidency itself. The assumption about ambition only states that most politicians prefer it to other offices. The *calculus of candidacy*, however, includes the costs of running for office, the probability of winning it, and the risks associated with the race. Clearly, our system of nominating presidents makes it important for a candidate to have at least some public recognition, and this recognition is concentrated in a small number of offices. Not only are senators, governors, and vice-presidents more widely known, but they look like strong contenders, in part because they already hold high office.

Schlesinger, in his initial statement of his theory about ambition, marshaled evidence for an "opportunity structure" consisting of a loose hierarchy of offices that ambitious politicians climb, generally one step at a time. The reason such an informal arrangement exists, of course, is that the probability of a candidate attaining the next higher office is generally substantially larger than the chance at an office farther up the opportunity structure. Furthermore, the next higher office often has an overlapping constituency. Therefore, the costs of gaining public recog-

Table 2.2   Office Held by Contenders for Presidential Nominations, 1976

Candidate	State	President	Vice-president	Governor	Senator	Representative	Other
Declared Democrats							
Bayh	IN				1963–		State representative, 1957–62
Bentsen	TX				1971–	1948–54	County judge, 1947–48
Brown	CA			1975–			
Carter	GA			1971–74			
Church	ID				1957–		
Harris	OK				1965–70		
Jackson	WA				1953–	1941–52	County prosecutor, 1939–40
McCormack	MA						
Sanford	NC			1961–64			
Shapp	PA			1971–			
Shriver	MD						Dir., Peace Corps; Office Economic Opportunity, 1961–67
Udall	AZ					1961–	
Wallace	AL			1963–66, 1971–			County attorney, 1953–54

Declared Republicans							
Ford	MI	1974–	1949–73			1973–74	
Reagan	CA				1967–75		
Possible Democrats							
Byrd	WV		1952–58	1958–			State representative, 1946–50; State senator, 1950–52
Glenn	OH			1974–			
Humphrey	MN			1949–64, 1971–		1965–68	Mayor, 1945–48
Kennedy	MS			1962–			
McGovern	SD		1957–60	1963–			Dir., Food for Peace, 1961–62; State representative, 1949–54
Muskie	ME			1959–	1955–58		
Stevenson	IL			1971–			State Supreme Court, 1957–58; State treasurer, 1967–70

nition, of extending the scope of the campaign, and so forth, are lower than the costs associated with a less overlapping electorate. One-step-at-a-time movement up the opportunity structure is related both to higher probability and to lower costs.

Peabody, Ornstein, and Rohde call running for president from offices near it in the opportunity structure, and from offices that have a relatively large constituency, running from a "strong electoral base." They note that the proportion of contenders in national conventions who ran from a strong electoral base has increased sharply.[4] From 1868 to 1888, only 17.6 percent had a strong base. This figure grew to 30.0 percent between 1892 and 1916, to 60.9 percent between 1920 and 1944, and to 88.0 percent in the postwar period. As we have seen, 1976 was no exception.

There are a number of reasons for this increase. Almost all, however, involve the increasing activity of the general population in the nominating process, and the decreasing control of the parties over it. The first surge of candidates with a strong electoral base coincided with the reforms of the progressive era and the resultant primary elections. Recent reforms have served to weaken further the hold of party regulars on their party's nominations. Similarly, the growth of mass media communication has made it possible for direct appeals to a national electorate to succeed. All these trends work to the advantage of a candidate with a strong, visible, and credible electoral base.

There is another historical trend that fleshes out the portrait more fully: that of the growing advantage of senators over governors. During most of the past century, governors were much the more successful presidential contenders. Only recently have senators equaled them. Gubernatorial advantages included administrative experience, control of state party organizations, and proven electoral success. The balance started to swing in favor of senators after their direct election in 1914. In addition, the growing importance of national government and legislation, the senator's role in foreign affairs, the decreased importance of state party organizations, the difficulties endemic to modern governors,[5] and the focus of the media on senators, who work in Washington, rather than on governors, who are less often in news centers, have enhanced the probability of a senator receiving the nomination.

The advantages of those who have a strong electoral base can be seen best, perhaps, in comparison to those who hold office that does not provide a strong base. Most U.S. representatives, for example, are not well known to the electorate. Achieving widespread recognition is expensive for them. Members of Congress must run for reelection every two years, including, therefore, every presidential election year. On the other hand, only one-third of the Senate and a decreasing number of governors must stand for reelection in any presidential election year. Standing for reelection increases the risks of running for the presidency, because incumbents may have to give up their current office. As I have noted, however, presidential hopefuls may be able to "test the presidential waters" before irrevocably foregoing their current office. Nonetheless, the *cost* of organizing two campaigns is greater than one. The costs are not just monetary. They include spreading one's staff and supporters over two campaigns, and a larger variety of organizational and decision costs. Further, running for more than one office increases the risk of seeking reelection, since it might tempt stronger opponents to campaign for the currently held office. Fewer presidential candidates should be expected to emerge from the set of those who are up for reelection than the set of those who are not, other things being equal.

In 1976, several active candidates, including Carter and Reagan, ran from no current electoral base at all. However, excepting only Shriver, the nonincumbents had recently held an office with a strong electoral base. All had the freedom to wage a full-time campaign without risking their positions. They had fewer day-to-day, job-related duties, and they were not subject to charges of neglecting their public responsibilities. These advantages, combined with their having recently held high office and having maintained their credibility, made it possible for them to campaign at less cost with a reasonably high probability of success. The recent reforms of the nomination process and the growth in the use of primaries may have created a system that fosters this sort of candidacy. Candidates free of other responsibilities can wage longer and more continuous campaigns than their office-holding peers.

These variations in structural features, in combination with the calculus of candidacy, can be cast in the form of five hypotheses:

1. More candidates will come from a strong electoral base. Candidates will tend to be senators or governors rather than representatives, etc.

2. Of those who hold no political office, most will have held an office with a strong electoral base as the immediately preceding office.

3. Of those holding no office, most will have left office under favorable circumstances (e.g., ineligibility to run again or voluntary retirement), rather than as a result of, say, an electoral defeat.

4. There will be fewer presidential candidates among those who have to stand for reelection to some other office than among those not up for reelection.

5. Of those who are up for reelection to a current office, there will be more candidates who can lose the presidential nomination and still run for reelection than those who must make the choice of office before the national convention selects its nominees.

An examination of the declared presidential candidates in 1976 supports these hypotheses. The data relevant to the first two hypotheses are summarized in table 2.3. Ford and Reagan, on the Republican side, fit the expected pattern well. The large number of Democratic candidates

Table 2.3 Electoral Base of Democratic Candidates for the Presidency, 1976

Prior Public Service	Percentage	Number	(Number)
U.S. representative	7.7	1	
Current			(1)
Former			(0)
U.S. senator	38.5	5	
Current			(4)
Former			(1)
Governor	38.5	5	
Current			(3)
Former			(2)
Federal appointee	7.7	1	
Current			(0)
Former			(1)
None	7.7	1	
Total	100.1	13	(12)

Summary of Electoral Base

	Percentage	Number	(Number)
Strong electoral base[a]	76.9	10	
Current			(7)
Former			(3)
No strong electoral base	23.1	3	(3)
Total	100.0	13	(13)

[a]Current or former governor or U.S. senator.

provides a better test. The first hypothesis concerns the emergence from a strong electoral base. The most recent position of ten of the thirteen declared candidates was senator or governor. One of the other three, Shriver, was the Democratic vice-presidential candidate in 1972, and thus has a somewhat ambiguous position with respect to the second hypothesis, and to the third as well.

Udall, another of the three to run from a less than strong electoral base, was the only representative to campaign seriously for the presidency in recent decades. The unusual circumstances surrounding his candidacy illustrate the exception that supports the general rule. Influential Democratic members of the House felt that at least one from their midst should mount a candidacy. Representatives Obey and Reuss (both D., Wisc.) drew up a list of seven House Democrats and two Republicans who seemed the most promising presidential candidates, and Udall headed the list. When he was approached early in 1974, he said, "I get hurt at home. I look silly as a fellow who takes himself too seriously. I'm not going to spend time and money on something that isn't going anywhere. Nobody's going to pay any attention to a House member."[6] Obey and Reuss talked him into reconsidering if they could obtain a petition in support for him signed by 10 percent of the House Democrats. They had names to spare, and his candidacy was initiated.

The only clear exception to the general rule, then, was Ellen McCormack, a housewife whose role as a one-issue—pro-life and anti-abortion —candidate suggests that her goal was to generate attention to, and thereby exert influence on, a specific aspect of public policy. Her candidacy was of a different type than the others, and I shall return to it later in this chapter, when advocacy is discussed.

The third hypothesis concerns only those candidates holding no political office in 1976, and the circumstances surrounding their retirement. Carter, as governor of Georgia from 1971 to 1974, was ineligible to run for a second consecutive term. At least one source says, "Like Rubin Askew of Florida, he was highly popular going into the 1974 election, and could easily have won a second term; unlike Askew, he was barred from running."[7] Sanford was a popular governor of North Carolina from 1961 to 1964, the first of the "new Southern" leaders, but ineligible for reelection in 1964. Since that time, he has held such positions as the presidency of Duke University, but no major elective or appointive office. However, he still left office under favorable circumstances. Harris was the only former senator. He won his Senate seat in a special election in 1964, a surprise victory. He won reelection in 1966 by a small, but larger, percentage of the vote. His liberalism was considered a major liability in 1972, at which point he decided to withdraw from the Senate race and campaign for the presidency. He was considered, at the time, a logical running mate for the front-running Muskie. Whether these circumstances are favorable or not is unclear. Presumably an actual defeat is worse than an expected one. Reagan, on the Republican side, retired from the governorship of California in clearly favorable circumstances. Thus, there is no evidence to contradict hypothesis 3, although there are ambiguous cases.

The data bearing on the last two hypotheses are summarized in table 2.4. Of the fifteen declared candidates for the presidential nomination, eleven were not eligible for reelection in 1976. President Ford was one of the other four. Congressman Udall was another. Senators Jackson and Bentsen, the remaining two, were able to run for renomination to the Senate after the Democratic presidential nomination was resolved, in line with the fifth hypothesis. The Washington senatorial primary took place more than two months after the Democratic convention. Jackson's petition to stand for reelection did not have to be filed before July 30, 1976, sixteen days after the national nominating convention. Bentsen

Table 2.4   Reelection Status of Declared Democratic Candidates for the Presidency, 1976

	Percentage	(Percentage)	Number	(Number)
Not standing for reelection	76.9		10	
Not an elected officeholder		(38.5)		(5)
Officeholder not up for reelection in 1976		(38.5)		(5)

Not eligible or voluntarily
    not standing for reelection
    in 1976
		(0.0)		(0)

Standing for reelection	23.1		3	
Able to run without giving up current office		(15.4)		(2)

Unable to stay in race through
    the nominating convention
    and still stand for current
    office
		(7.7)		(1)

Total	100.0	(100.0)	13	(13)

was under the "Johnson rule" in Texas. Johnson ran for president in 1960 and John Kennedy tapped him for vice president. The Texas legislature passed a statute enabling him to run for the vice-presidency and the Senate at the same time. He won both races. Bentsen, as beneficiary, was able to run for the presidency without giving up his Senate seat. Thus, all five hypotheses are supported strongly by the evidence.

The preceding analysis is retrospective. That is, the declared candidates in 1976 were examined to see if they possessed the characteristics that we expected. They did, but perhaps many other politicians shared similarly favorable circumstances. If so, why did some choose to run and not others? To look at this question, I will examine the set of all Democratic senators to see if those who ran for the presidency were distinctive.

There were sixty-two Democrats in the Senate in 1976. Twelve can be eliminated immediately on the grounds that they were either too young to be constitutionally eligible or too old (born in or before 1910) for the race. Senator Eagleton could hardly have been a serious candidate. He was George McGovern's first vice-presidential running mate in 1972 but was forced to withdraw when it was disclosed that he had been under psychiatric care. The attendant controversy destroyed his chance of becoming president in the forseeable future.

For the remaining forty-nine senators in 1976, we can count a number of "liabilities," factors that would make it less likely for them to run. We would expect, then, that those with the fewest liabilities would have been the most likely to run for president. The relevant liabilities seem to include the following.

1. *Youth.* Senators born between 1930 and 1940 were legally eligible to run but would have faced considerable difficulty in demonstrating sufficient experience and maturity. Thus, their likelihood of achieving the nomination was reduced.

2. *Length of service in the Senate.* First-term senators faced similar difficulties. Beyond that, their electoral base was less firm, their exposure less and, thus, the probability of successful candidacies lower.

3. *Very short service.* If an individual had been in the Senate for three years or less (usually elected in 1974), the previous considerations would have been even more handicapping.

4. *Region.* Carter's nomination was unexpected by most observers, in part because he was little known but also because he was from the

South. Johnson was the first politician from the "deep South" to be nominated for the presidency since the reconstruction. Being from the deep South (old Confederacy states) is considered a political liability.

5. *Reelection status.* Senators currently up for reelection were handicapped because the costs and risks of running for the presidency would have been increased.

6. *Renomination status.* Senators up for reelection who could not enter their state's senatorial primary if their campaign for the presidential nomination was still active could be forced to choose between their Senate seat and a chance at the presidential nomination. Senators in this category are those who had to file for their senatorial primary before the presidential nomination balloting (14 July 1976).

Let us score each of these liabilities −1 if it applied to a particular senator in 1976, and 0 if it did not. Their sum indicates the probable status of the senator's candidacy. There are thus forty-nine senators to consider. Their average score is −1.67 liabilities. Only four were active candidates: Bayh (0 liabilities), Bentsen (−3), Church (0), and Jackson (−1). The average for this group is −1.00. (Senator Bentsen's poor score reflects his being a first-term senator, from Texas, who was up for reelection.) Even so, this group of four had a substantially higher average score than the larger group of senators. The seven other possible candidates had an average score of −1.57, slightly more than the average of the entire set of senators. While they may have desired to run for the presidency, their opportunities were simply not very good. Senators who fell in neither category had an average score of −1.76. The tendency of candidates to emerge from those who were well situated within the opportunity structure can be seen in table 2.5.

Why They Run: The Risk Takers

I have demonstrated that those well situated in the opportunity structure were more likely to run for president in 1976 than those in less favorable circumstances. In a sense, they were lucky that circumstances were right. Relevant circumstances limited the set of likely candidates considerably, and most candidates emerged from this set. Nonetheless, there was another group of Senators who were also well situated. Can we go farther and assess why at least some of those did not choose to run for the nomination? Perhaps. The relationship between risk taking and the likelihood of running for higher office has not yet been considered.

The concept of risk taking involves an assumption quite different from my previous ones. Up to this point, the characteristics examined have been associated with the candidates' situational context. Risk taking is an attitude associated with an individual's personality and values. A risk taker is one who is more likely than others to enter hazardous or uncertain situations, i.e., select a risky alternative. There is probably no campaign more risky than the campaign for the presidency.

Rohde's hypothesis, my sixth, is:

If two individuals have similar opportunities to run for the presidency, and one is a risk taker while the other is not, the probability that the risk taker will run is higher.[8]

Rohde measured risk-taking attitudes of House members by examining their past behavior. In particular, he defined a risk taker by two criteria. House members were considered "high risk takers" if, when they *first* ran for the House, they challenged an incumbent in the primary or the general election. Representatives were also considered high risk takers if, when they *first* ran, there was no incumbent, but the other party had averaged 57 percent or more of the votes in the three preceding elections.

We shall extend these criteria somewhat. In this context, Democratic senators in 1976 will be considered high risk takers if:

Table 2.5   Liabilities of Potential Presidential
                   Candidates: Democratic Senators, 1976

Status of Candidate	Number of Liabilities						Num- ber
	0	1	2	3	4	5	
Declared	50.0%	25.0%	0	25.0%	0	0	4
Possible	14.3	28.6	42.9	14.3	0	0	7
Not running	18.4	26.3	23.7	23.7	5.3	2.6	38
Number	10	13	12	11	2	1	49

Excluded are Democratic senators too young or too old, as described in text; the liabilities are also described in text. Six liabilities would be possible if a senator was first elected in a special election and was up for reelection in 1976. No Democratic senator met those requirements.

1. In their *first* campaign for the Senate, they faced an incumbent in the primary or general election.

2. If, in the three elections for the Senate prior to their *first* senatorial campaign, the opposing party averaged 57 percent or more of the two-party vote.

3. If, prior to running for the Senate, the individual ran for the governorship or for Congress and *any* of the first two criteria held for either office.

Several points should be made. First, this evaluation of risk taking is an objective measure of a subjective attitude. A senator who never faced the risks described cannot be classified as a high risk taker. Second, a senator's attitude toward risk can change. Third, Rohde has established that many House members who run for the Senate are risk takers. Therefore, a large proportion of the Senate already consists of high risk takers.

The test of this hypothesis is reported in table 2.6. Of the forty-nine Democratic senators under consideration, nearly two-thirds (65.3%) were classified as high risk takers, and over half (53.1%) were so on the basis of their first senatorial campaign. All four declared candidates demonstrated a willingness to take risks in their first attempt to enter the Senate. Five of the seven potential candidates (71.4%) met the same criterion. Only 60.5% of the rest were high risk takers, by any of the criteria. (Conversely, about 40% of noncandidates, 30% of po-

Table 2.6   Percentage of Risk Takers among Democratic Senators, 1976

	Risk Taker in First Attempt at Senate	If Not Risk Taker for Senate, Risk Taker for Governor or House of Representatives	Not Risk Taker for Three Offices	No.
Declared candidates	100.0	0	0	4
Possible candidates	71.4	0	28.6	7
Former presidential candidates	(100)	(0)	(0)	(3)
Not former presidential candidates	(50)	(0)	(50)	(4)
Other Democratic senators	44.7	15.8	39.5	38
Number	26	6	17	49

tential candidates, and 0% of declared candidates were not proven risk takers.) Interestingly, of the seven potential candidates, the three who had previously been presidential candidates (Humphrey, McGovern, and Muskie) were all proven risk takers, and the other four remaining scored like the senators who had never run for the presidential nomination. Effectively, then, seven of seven current or former presidential candidates were risk takers, and little more than half of those who had never run an active presidential campaign demonstrated a high risk-taking disposition.[9]

The purpose of this section was to answer three questions: Who runs for the presidential nomination? Why do they? Why don't others? The central assumptions of the calculus of candidacy are that all politicians are rational, progressively ambitious individuals who would accept a higher office if offered to them without costs or risks. In practice, however, costs and risks vary. My examination of some of the variables demonstrated that most candidates emerge from a small group whose costs and risks are relatively low. Finally, a demonstrated willingness to enter high-risk situations further differentiates presidential candidates from those who start with similar opportunities.

The question of why candidates run has been answered in terms of costs and risks. I assumed that all politicians strongly desire the presidency and hence the presidential nomination. However, candidates have different reasons for placing a high value on the office. An understanding of these reasons may help account for their behavior in the campaign and, if elected, in office.

Why They Run: The Goals of Candidates

Much of the literature about the strategies that candidates follow in elections assumes that the primary motivation underlying their behavior is the desire to win the election. Therefore, the campaign strategies they pursue and the policies they advocate are designed to increase the candidates' appeal to the electorate. For example, Anthony Downs, in his classic study of the theory of elections, asserts:

> We assume that [the candidates, or Downs' party-as-team] act solely in order to attain the income, prestige, and power which come from being in office. Thus politicians in our model never seek office as a means of carrying out particular policies; their only goal is to reap

the rewards of holding office, *per se.* They treat policies purely as means to the attainment of their private ends, which they can reach only by being elected.

Upon this reasoning rests the fundamental hypothesis of our model: [candidates] formulate policies in order to win elections, rather than win elections in order to formulate policies.[10]

William Riker axiomatically ties rationality to winning. "What the rational political man wants, I believe, is to win," he says. The "politically rational man is the man who would rather win than lose, regardless of the particular stakes."[11] Joseph Schlesinger distinguishes between candidates as *"office seekers"* who desire the rewards of office, *per se,* and noncandidates as *"benefit seekers"* who want benefits derivable either from the control of office or in some way dependent upon the existence of the party."[12] Downs, Riker, or Schlesinger do not qualify winning in any way. Their argument is reflected in a sign hanging in Jeb Mc-Gruder's office when he was head of Nixon's 1972 reelection committee: "Winning in politics isn't everything, it is the only thing."

Clearly, the desire to become president "to attain the income, prestige, and power" of the office motivates most or all candidates. It is also a goal wholly consistent with progressive ambition. And if candidates "formulate policies in order to win elections, rather than win elections in order to formulate policies," this need not be viewed cynically. What the goal implies, of course, is that politicians are sensitive to the policy preferences of the electorate and attempt to adopt policies that are viewed favorably by a majority of the electorate. That, after all, is a basic premise of representative democracy. Nonetheless, office seeking is only one goal that candidates may have. Some, perhaps all, candidates have other goals, and the nature and extent of these other goals affects the strategies they pursue. In the following paragraphs, I attempt to present a unified account of office seeking and of these other goals.

Undoubtedly the most prominent goal of candidates is office seeking. To the office seeker, the value or utility of any given campaign strategy is simple: it is worth 1 if it wins the nomination, 0 if it does not. For the office-seeking candidate, winning *is* the only thing.

Of course, candidates rarely know *for sure* if a particular strategy will be winning or losing. In some cases, it may be possible to estimate the probability that a given strategy will be winning. If so, various goals based on office-seeking can be formulated via calculations of *expected*

utility. For example, a candidate may attempt to maximize the expected
number of delegate votes or work for the largest probability of attaining a majority of the delegates. Or, especially in a two-candidate campaign like the Reagan-Ford contest, the candidate may attempt to maximize the expected plurality of delegates.

In the most common situation, however, the effect of any strategy on
the candidate's fortunes depends on the strategies that the opponent or
opponents follow. Therefore, the situation is understood better by game
theory than via expected utility maximization. Chapter 6 contains such
an analysis.

The office-seeking goal is, like all assumptions, a simplification. The
adequacy of such simplifications depends in part on how inaccurate
they are. For some candidates, at all times, and for all candidates, at
some times, the simplification is severely inaccurate. It is simply untrue
that candidates formulate policies only to win elections. Policy positions
are formulated with at least two other goals in mind. Candidates are to
some extent *policy seekers*, attempting to influence public policy in this
country. At times, they may simply be *advocates*, speaking out on the
issues. In the first instance, the politician is like the Downsian citizen,
choosing between alternative policies. In the second instance, the politician is considering the benefits (and costs) of campaigning, per se.

Candidates adopt some policies because they believe they are best for
the country. They are like the citizens in Downs's and related "spatial
models of electoral competition." In these models the citizens and candidates are distinguished by their goals. Candidates want only votes,
while citizens base their evaluations of candidates exclusively on the
positions the candidates formulate to win votes. It is unrealistic, however, to assume that candidates do not have their own beliefs and opinions about policies. Indeed, all the evidence suggests that they have more
clear-cut and consistent policy preferences than most of the electorate.

My assumption is that candidates consider the issues and have a set
of optimal or "ideal" positions. This ideal set of positions consists of
the policies they would most like the country to follow. If everything
else were equal, a candidate would advocate this ideal package. Of
course, everything else is not equal. Therefore, a candidate examines
policy positions in terms of how they will help him achieve the nomination *and* in comparison to the positions he most prefers. In general,
the candidate must make some tradeoffs. A campaign strategy geared
to ideal positions may be a poor strategy for achieving the nomination.

The exact tradeoff depends upon the candidate-as-office-seeker's evaluation of the effect any two strategies would have on the chance for nomination and the candidate-as-policy-seeker's evaluation of the similarity between vote-getting policy positions and his ideal positions.

This second comparison, even when made by candidates concerned only with public policy, is incomplete. The candidates must consider the positions taken by their opponents. If, for example, a conservative candidate is challenging a very liberal opponent for the nomination, the difference .between their policies will be vast. A conservative candidate challenging a moderate or conservative opponent might find the opponent's policies relatively acceptable. Thus, candidates as policy-seekers must make a series of comparisons: what their ideal platform is, how that compares with what they can reasonably enunciate in public, and how these compare with the policies their opponents are likely to espouse.

The conventional view of the candidate as purely and simply an office seeker is incomplete because candidates do not always change their publicly pronounced positions as electoral circumstances dictate. Henry Jackson has been known as a consistent supporter of a strong national defense policy since he entered public life. Even though the public's attitude toward large defense budgets and new weapons systems has become less favorable, especially among Democrats, Jackson has maintained his position. It is equally hard to imagine Hubert Humphrey having changed his position on civil rights, Ronald Reagan on welfare, or George McGovern on Vietnam.

The point, of course, is not that candidates never change their positions on policy positions. The point is that they combine a set of personal beliefs with their evaluation of the effect of a position on their chances for the nomination. Often they are faced with difficult choices, and sometimes they change, modify, or deemphasize particular positions to increase the likelihood of winning the nomination or election. On the other hand, they do not always adopt policies designed solely to win the nomination. Perhaps the best example is Goldwater's vote against the 1964 civil rights bill. That vote cost him key support within his own party for both the nomination and the general election. Had he voted for the civil rights measure, he probably still would have been nominated and then defeated in the general election. Nonetheless, it is clear that his visible vote against the bill cost him votes. His decision cannot be explained by the assumption that he was purely an office seeker. His "extremism in the defense of liberty is no vice . . . moderation in the defense of justice is no virtue" acceptance speech was hardly calculated to maximize votes, either.

Ronald Reagan chose a different tactic. Early in the 1976 campaign, he proposed a major plan for welfare decentralization, moving many programs from federal to state or local control, a plan consistent with long-held beliefs. He tossed out a figure of $90 billion as the savings that could result from such a transfer. This sweeping program resulted in substantial controversy, and the rather arbitrary $90 billion figure provided Ford (and newswriters) with a point of attack. Stuart Spencer, Ford's campaign manager at the time, said:

> We had to get Reagan off-balance on that first trip in [to New Hampshire], and I think we succeeded. His trip was a floppo. He didn't take New Hampshire by storm. He was up there three days or so and he staggered around on that ninety-billion-dollar flap. . . . That kind of evened up the game in New Hampshire, and from there on it was a horse race.[13]

Reagan, as office-seeker, surely realized that the $90 billion plan was poor policy. His response was *not* to change his position, even in its specifics. Rather, he simply chose to quit *talking* about the plan and talk about something else. As Witcover relates, on the morning after the New Hampshire primary, Sears, Reagan's campaign manager, and Wirthlin, his pollster, laid plans for the Florida primary, two weeks off:

> "I think we've got to go after Ford on the foreign-policy issue," Sears said. Wirthlin agreed. For one thing, it was a way to get the press' focus off his $90-billion plan, and perhaps Ford could be drawn into making a mistake himself. . . . Republicans, Wirthlin's surveys showed, were not especially concerned about foreign policy; only 12 percent of those asked said they were. But Reagan's hard-line approach offered a more clear-cut contrast with Ford's leadership style than did his handling of any domestic issue.
> Sears went to see Reagan. . . . "We're going to have to start talking about foreign policy."
> Reagan was agreeable.[14]

As will be seen in chapter 7, foreign policy dominated the rest of the Republican nomination campaign.

This example illustrates three points. First, Ford and Reagan were further apart on foreign policy than on domestic issues. Thus, Reagan should have been less willing to compromise on foreign than on domestic policy. Second, Reagan did not attempt to change his position on decentralization. Rather, he tried to change the emphasis of the campaign. As I shall argue in more detail in chapter 7, he—and candidates in general—attempted to affect the relative salience, or importance, of the issues. They attempt to emphasize the issues on which their position appears to align better with the electorates' rather than changing their own position or the position of the electorate as a whole. Third, this example illustrates the tradeoffs involved in the candidate-as-office-seeker and the candidate-as-policy-seeker. At times, the candidate must make the hard choice between yielding a little on policy and lessening the probability of attaining office.

Two goals of candidates have been isolated so far: office seeking and policy seeking. A third goal may be called the *utility of campaigning, per se*, including that of policy advocacy for its own sake. Candidates for a presidential nomination face extensive publicity and scrutiny by the media. While public scrutiny is often uncomfortable if not undesirable (e.g., Senator Eagleton in 1972), this scrutiny provides a candidate with a forum that few people ever achieve. Both costs and benefits may be associated with campaigning itself. The physical costs of campaigning may be tremendous. At the same time, there may be some cost or benefit associated with the advocacy of a particular program. One may be forced to take stances that do not mesh well with one's personal beliefs or, like Reagan, one may be forced not to campaign on particular issues. The mere statement of a position (or lack thereof) may result in some loss. There may be also the pleasure of arguing for what one believes, perhaps changing some citizens' minds, influencing the behavior of other policy makers, or placing some propositions on the public agenda.

To capture this aspect of goals, a series of policy dimensions could be defined. Other relevant dimensions could be added to measure the costs of campaigning, loss of privacy, etc. An "ideal" set of positions for the candidate also can be defined as before, and the set of strategies open to a candidate compared to this ideal. Here, however, the analysis stops. As compared to policy-seeking, there is no comparison with the strategies of other candidates. For each candidate, the loss of advocacy consists in the difference between their actual strategy and their ideal position. This loss is a certain one intrinsic to the campaign itself. With respect to policy advocacy, for example, what is of concern is what the candidate says compared to his ideal, not what he expects government or party policy to be. What other candidates are doing is irrelevant.

Some examples of candidates as policy advocates may help illustrate the point. Eugene McCarthy challenged Lyndon Johnson for the 1968 presidential nomination for one basic reason: he believed that Johnson's policy on the Vietnam War was wrong and that someone had to try to stop Johnson and/or change that policy. Neither McCarthy nor anyone else thought he had a realistic chance to become the nominee until well after his campaign was under way. That McCarthy desired to be president may be true, but to assume that he was purely an office seeker would miss the point of his candidacy entirely. Ellen McCormack's candidacy also illustrates the advocacy of an issue with the goal of affecting public opinion or actual policy. Her campaign was designed solely to promote the "right to life" and to end abortions. She never believed that she would be the Democratic nominee in 1976 or any other year. She simply wanted to advocate her beliefs publicly.

Senator McCarthy and Mrs. McCormack illustrate the positive aspects of a candidate-as-advocate. In general, such candidates focus exclusively on one issue or on a small set of related issues. So narrow a focus usually stems from a belief that current policy and the beliefs of other candidates are very different from one's own opinions. Such a narrow focus also usually means that the strategy is a poor one for attaining a major party's presidential nomination. A president, after all, cannot focus on one issue, but must deal with many issues. To assume that such advocates are office seekers or even policy seekers in the sense defined above is to misunderstand their candidacies.

George Wallace proves that a narrow focus is not necessary to a candidate-as-advocate. Wallace ran for president in four elections. Given the circumstances, his chances of obtaining the Democratic nomination in any of the four elections were small. While he enunciated a clearly related set of concerns, his focus was much broader than McCormack's or McCarthy's initial base. Yet his goals were similar. He hoped to influence public opinion and federal policy makers, including his competitors for the presidency. His oft-stated goal was "to send Washington a message." That he had other goals may be true, but advocacy was predominant.

The final goal of at least some candidates involves viewing the campaign for the presidential nomination as a means to some other end.

The most common example is the candidate who is setting the stage
for a more realistic assault on the presidency four or eight years later.
A presidential candidacy can also serve to increase the chances of being
named as the vice-presidential nominee (e.g., Senators Harris, Baker,
and Percy) or perhaps to aid one's candidacy for another office (as
some suggested underlay Bentsen's motives). In 1976, the best example
might have been Governor Brown. Curtis Sitoner of the *Christian Science Monitor* attempted to assess Brown's goals:

> Politicians . . . view . . . [Brown's candidacy] . . . in a variety of
> ways. Among them:
> • A genuine quest for the White House via convention deadlock
> and compromise.
> • A strong signal that Mr. Brown is available as a vice-presidential
> running mate. . . .
> • An attempt . . . [to make] Mr. Brown a powerful force in forg-
> ing a convention platform in New York City [site of the Democratic
> Convention] and shaping the issues of the campaign.
> • Advance notice that the youthful California Governor is ready
> to step into the front ranks of Democratic leaders nationally . . .
> paving the way for a 1980 candidacy.[15]

Note that this list includes all four types of goals. Sitoner then con-
curred with the majority of "close observers" in suggesting that Brown's
primary motive was to form a Humphrey-Brown ticket and to become
vice-president. He notes that, to Brown, Humphrey was "once an unacceptable 'old guard' Democrat," but that Brown had recently stated
that he "admires" Humphrey and is "reexamining some assumptions."

No one candidate is motivated by all four goals simultaneously, nor
do all candidates weigh all four goals identically. Moreover, these four
goals are not always compatible. To understand the strategies followed
by candidates, it is important to consider all the relevant goals, how the
candidates weigh them, and how they resolve the necessary tradeoffs.
To be accurate in all details is virtually impossible. Nonetheless, under a wide variety of circumstances, most goals are furthered if the
candidate receives more support at the convention. Therefore, the assumption that the candidate's goal is the nomination is a reasonable
first approximation.[16]

3 The Institutional Context and Campaign Resources

Individuals who run for the presidential nomination enter a unique institutional context. No other democracy has nominating procedures at all like those of the United States. Even here, the institutional context of the presidential nomination is vastly different from that of other elective offices. Moreover, the details, and at times the large patterns, of the preconvention campaign change every four years. Two of the purposes of this chapter are to examine some of the key institutional structures affecting candidates in 1976 and to show how these structures have changed. In the first chapter, the broad historical evolution of the nominating process was outlined. Here the specific features of the current context will be discussed.

A central theme of this book is that, to understand the behavior of the candidates and the outcome of the preconvention portion of the campaign for the presidential nomination, one must understand the goals of the candidates and other relevant actors, the choices that each candidate can make, and the possible outcomes of those choices. The institutional context shapes each of these aspects of decision making. That is, the "rules of the game" have tremendous import for how the game is played.

Three aspects of the preconvention institution will be studied: financial regulations, delegate selection, and the role of the mass communications media. These three aspects, while not exhaustive, cover the largest and most important aspects of the preconvention campaign structure. Major features of each of these three will be reviewed, recent changes in each discussed and, finally, the role of each assessed.

Financial Regulations

One of the basic resources a candidate needs, and needs to use wisely, is money. In recent elections, the sheer cost of running a presidential campaign has increased astronomically. The 1968 Republican nomination campaign cost the major candidates $20 million. Nixon spent more than half of that, and Rockefeller spent $8 million without contesting a single primary.[1] The Democrats spent over $25 million in 1968 (McCarthy, $11 million; Kennedy, $9 million; and Humphrey, $4 million without entering any primaries). In 1972, the contested Democratic nomination cost $8 million more than it did in 1968. The cost of the general election campaign has also skyrocketed. In 1968, Nixon spent nearly $25.5 million, more than Eisenhower *and* Stevenson spent in 1952 and 1956 combined. Humphrey spent $11.6 million in 1968 even though he had difficulty raising money. By 1972, the cost of the general election had more than doubled: Nixon spent $51.4 million and McGovern spent $30 million. This sheer weight of expense was an important reason for the enactment of federal reforms in 1971 and 1974, by far the most sweeping measures ever enacted.

The Federal Election Campaign Act of 1971 was the first comprehensive revision of the Federal Corrupt Practices Act of 1925. Reforms were in three areas. The significance of the first, limits to contributions, is that the subject was raised at all. Limits were placed only on the contributions that candidates or their immediate families could make in their behalf. The second limited a candidate's expenditures. Limits were placed on the amount of money that could be spent on advertising through communications media (defined as radio, television, newspapers, magazines, billboards, and automatic telephone equipment). The third concerned public disclosure of contributions and expenditures and methods of enforcement. Regular reports had to be filed, disclosing all individual contributions and expenditures in excess of $100.[2]

The Revenue Act of 1971 provided the basis, via tax checkoffs and incentives, for public financing of presidential election campaigns, beginning with the 1976 election. It provided for the earmarking of $1 of each individual's income tax for a campaign fund. It provided for a tax credit or deduction for contributions to political candidates. The Act also authorized public financing for candidates of both major parties and provided some potential for public financing of candidates of minor or new political parties. Further, major party candidates who chose to accept public financing could spend no more than the amount of public funds to which they were entitled.

The Federal Election Campaign Act was substantially modified by a series of amendments in 1974. First, the Federal Election Commission was created as a full-time bipartisan organization to administer and monitor the financing of federal elections. Second, limits were placed on the amount of money any individual or organization could contribute to candidates for federal office. Individuals could donate no more than $1,000 to any campaign and no more than $25,000 to all federal candidates annually. Organizations were limited to contributions of $5,000 per election. The limits on spending for advertising were replaced with total spending limits. Each candidate was limited to $10 million for the entire nomination campaign. Ceilings were also placed on the amount any candidate could spend in any one state as well as in the District of Columbia and the territories, (for details see the appendix). Candidates were allowed to spend 20% more to raise funds. The major party nominees were allowed to spend no more than $20 million in the general election, and various other limitations were imposed. Thus, as of 1974, a presidential nominee could spend no more than $30 million throughout the year—less than half Nixon spent in 1972. The only increases in such limitations were pegged to inflation. Third, provisions for public financing were extended. Major party nominees were automatically qualified for the full $20 million for the general election campaign. In the preconvention campaign, a candidate could qualify for up to half of the $10 million maximum expenditure allowed by the law. This "matching funds" provision doubled the value of each dollar contributed, except that only the first $250 of an individual's contribution would be matched. Accepting public financing was voluntary, but all the major candidates chose to do so. A presidential candidate could qualify for matching funds by raising $5,000 or more in each of twenty states to prove that he or she was a "serious" candidate. Finally, the disclosure and enforcement provisions of the 1971 Act were strengthened. Most candidates chose to file monthly reports of contributions and expenditures in the 1976 preconvention campaign.

The 1974 Amendments were major reforms, but their practical implications were unclear. In addition, they were controversial. In early 1975, an unusual coalition of conservatives—e.g., Senator James Buckley (R., N.Y.) and the Mississippi Republican Party—and liberals—e.g., former Sen. Eugene McCarthy and the New York Civil Liberties Union—increased this uncertainty by filing suit charging that several aspects of the amendments were unconstitutional. The Supreme Court did not render its decision on *Buckley v. Valeo* until January 30, 1976. Thus, the candidates had to plan their expenditures without knowing whether the amendments would stand or be struck down in whole or part. In fact, they were struck down in part. The Court upheld the limit to contributions (except the candidate's personal contributions), the public financing provisions, and the disclosure procedures. It struck down the spending limitations, but only for candidates not accepting public financing.

On the other hand, the Court declared the Federal Election Commission to have been formed in violation of separation of powers. Until new legislation was enacted, therefore, no public funds could be disbursed. Although a short-run problem, it had serious consequences in 1976. The Commission "went out of business" on March 22 and was not reconstituted until May 17, 1976. During this period, candidates had to rely on their own sources of money. Jackson and Harris stated that this change of rules in mid-campaign was a major reason for their dropping out of the campaign.

The reforms of the 1970s were massive, fundamentally changing the financial context of the campaign for the presidency. One reason that these reforms were enacted is the already mentioned escalation of the cost of elections. Systematic comparisons of the cost of nomination campaigns are difficult to make. For example, one would have to consider how competitive the nomination campaigns were, how many primaries there were, how many of them were competitive, whether or not there was an incumbent president, etc. In the absence of disclosure laws before the middle of the 1972 campaign, records of actual expenditures are almost impossible to find. Herbert Alexander has estimated the cost of the general election campaign for each party from 1860 through 1972.

Figure 3.1 is a vivid portrayal of the increased costs, even considering inflation.

David Adamany and George Agree list other reasons for the recent reforms. First, campaign contributions have come from a narrow spectrum of our society. National surveys have demonstrated that the percentage of people reporting giving *any* money to *any* election campaign varied between 9.0 and 11.6% between 1956 and 1972. In 1976, after the reforms were enacted, 16.2% reported making a contribution. Second, popular support for public financing of campaigns has emerged only in recent years. Adamany and Agree report that in 1964, only 11% of respondents to a national sample of public opinion favored

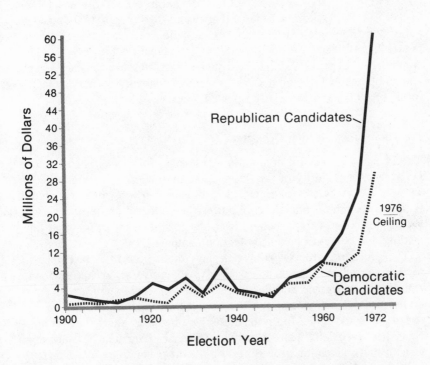

Figure 3.1   Cost of General Election Campaigns for the Presidency, 1900–1976.
Data are taken from Herbert E. Alexander's *Financing Politics* (Washington, D.C.: Congressional Quarterly, 1976), p. 20.

public financing of presidential campaigns; 71% rejected it. By the fall
of 1973, 65% favored tax support of federal campaigns and 24% opposed it. This poll was conducted in the wake of Watergate and related
disclosures. Third, Common Cause and other public interest groups provided the first effective lobby for reforms. Their effectiveness was enhanced by the data gathered about federal campaign contributions and
expenditures in 1972, as reform itself generated impetus for later reforms. Many states had already enacted serious reform measures; six
legislated public financing before 1974. Finally, public opinion was influenced by Watergate and related illegal and unethical acts, many of
which involved campaign contributions and expenditures by Nixon's
reelection organization. For example, his Committee for the Reelection
of the President raised 28% of all its funds from 124 contributors who
gave $50,000 or more before April 7, 1972, the date of the enactment
of the 1971 act. Alexander states that twenty-two corporations pleaded
guilty (or "no contest") to the illegal donation of nearly $1 million to
the 1972 presidential campaign, 89% of which went to Nixon. The
combination of increased cost, existing reform, disclosure, illegal acts,
and public support combined with effective lobbying to make the reforms of 1971, and especially of 1974, possible.[3]

Procedures for Selecting Delegates

The key to a successful nomination campaign, of course, is to capture
the votes of a majority of the delegates to the national nominating convention. One way to make certain that delegates vote for a candidate
is to see that the candidate's supporters are selected as delegates. The
various procedures for selecting delegates constitute the most important
institutional context of the nomination campaign.

The procedures for selecting delegates often bear little resemblance
to those in effect four years earlier. An extensive set of reforms was
enacted in the Democratic Party after the 1968 convention, and it continues today. Nominating procedures were extensively reformulated between 1972 and 1976. Many of these measures also affect the Republican Party, especially their primaries, which are regulated by state law.
Caucus and convention procedures, on the other hand, are internal party
matters. Such procedures may vary widely from party to party as well as
from state to state. Indeed, no two states employ exactly the same procedure. Nonetheless, several distinctions stand out as particularly impor-

tant structural features that candidates must consider to devise effective campaign strategies.

Three characteristics are common to both caucuses and primaries. The most important is the size of the delegation each state is to select. The 3,008 Democratic and 2,259 Republican convention votes were distributed among the various states by formulas that combined the state's population with the party's successes in the state. In 1976, for example, Massachusetts was allocated more delegates by the Democratic Party and fewer by the Republican Party than its population would dictate, because it voted for the Democratic presidential candidate in 1972 and because most major offices were held by Democrats. The difference in the size of the states' delegation is substantial in any event. Wyoming and Alaska, for example, cast but 10 votes each at the Democratic nominating convention, while California cast 280, the most of any unit. The District of Columbia was the smallest Republican unit, with 14 votes, followed by Delaware and Wyoming, which had 17 delegates each. California had the largest Republican delegation, with 167 votes. The size of each delegation, along with pertinent information about procedures for selecting the delegates, can be found in the appendix.

Each state party can allocate its delegation in various ways. Many states select all delegates on a state-wide basis ("at large"). Others select a portion of the delegation at large and apportion the rest among smaller units, usually the congressional districts. Several states reserve a few at large "slots" (seats) for key party personnel. The proportions of the two parties' delegates selected at large, apportioned to substate units, and reserved for appointment are summarized in table 3.1. These procedures affect the amount of organizational effort that a candidate needs to expend in a state. They become particularly important in states that hold primaries, depending upon the form of primary involved.

Actually, one must distinguish between who is selected as a delegate and how this delegate votes at the convention. The latter distinction is our concern. Some delegates appointed in 1976 were bound to vote according to the results of their states' primary elections. Other appointed delegates, those reported in table 3.1, were not bound by the results of the primary. These are free agents, selected *and acting* independently of the major delegate selection procedure in their states.

The final common variable is the length of time a delegate is legally bound to vote for the candidate he or she was selected to support. This becomes important when more than one convention vote is required to

Table 3.1   Level of Selection of Delegates to
                   Presidential Nominating Conventions, 1976

Level	Number of States	Number of Delegates	Percentage of Delegates
Republican Party			
Substate[a]	46	1,232	54.9
Statewide	41	935	41.7
Appointed	7	76	3.4
Democratic Party			
Substate	46	2,315	77.8
Statewide	38	616	20.7
Appointed	5	43	1.5

[a]The substate level is usually the Congressional District.

select the party's nominee. Reagan, for example, had "hidden support" at the Republican convention. That is, some delegates who personally favored him were bound by state or party law to vote for Ford on the first few ballots. As it happened, of course, this restriction (indicated in the appendix) was irrelevant in 1976 because both presidential nominees were selected on the first ballot.

The problem of hidden support is unlikely to arise in the Democratic Party because its rules allow the presidential candidate to approve any delegate selected to support him or her. This provision was enacted as part of the more general reforms in the Democratic Party, the purpose of which was to provide the public with as much control over the nomination as possible. The argument for this rule is that a delegate selected to support a particular candidate should support that candidate. All bets are off, of course, if a candidate releases the delegates, say by withdrawal of a candidacy.

Presidential Primaries

The use of primaries in which voters are asked to express their preference for a party nominee in the voting booth, is a relatively new procedure. The primary itself evolved out of the reforms initiated in the progressive era early in this century.[4] As can be seen from table 3.2, the number of states employing the primary has recently increased, reaching an all-time high of 30 in 1976, when 70% of the Republican and 75% of the Democratic delegates were selected in primary elections.

Primaries differ from one another in many ways. To begin with, for whom do voters in the primary cast their ballots? In 1976, some voters (e.g., in Massachusetts) cast their ballots for a presidential candidate, and that vote was the basis for the allocation of delegates to the various candidates. Voters in Texas and Alabama, on the other hand, voted for individuals seeking to become delegates to the national convention and did not vote at all for presidential contenders. Still other states allowed voters to express a presidential preference and to vote separately for individuals running for delegate. There were also "beauty contest" primaries, (e.g., in Vermont) in which the vote did not affect the selection of delegates at all. Table 3.3 summarizes these procedures in both parties in 1976.

Second, how are the votes counted? The California Republican primary is the last remaining statewide "winner-take-all" primary in which the candidate winning a plurality of the votes wins all of the delegates. The national Democratic Party ruled that delegates to their convention could not be selected via a statewide winner-take-all primary, a rule to take effect by the 1976 Convention. Therefore, the state of California used a different rule for the two parties. The Democratic Party used proportional allocation, which is the other extreme.

The goal of the proportional plan is to allocate delegates to the candidates in proportion to the percentage of the vote they receive. A candidate who receives 45% of the votes wins 45% of the delegates. In a winner-take-all primary, 45% of the vote can yield all or no delegates, but nothing in between.

One complication of proportional allocation is that most states also imposed a "threshold." Candidates who received a smaller percentage

Table 3.2   Growth of Presidential Primaries, 1964–76

Year	Number of States with Primaries[a]	Percentage of Delegates Selected in Primaries	
		Democrats	Republicans
1964	17	50.8	49.9
1968	17	48.7	47.0
1972	23	66.5	58.8
1976	30	75.8	70.2

[a]Includes the District of Columbia.

Table 3.3　　　Procedures for Selecting Delegates in States with Primaries

	Republican Party			Democratic Party		
Procedure	No. of States	No. of Elected Delegates	% of Elected Delegates	No. of States	No. of Elected Delegates	% of Elected Delegates
Beauty contest	2	0	0	1	0	0
Voters express presidential preference only	19	924	61.8	16	1,037	46.2
Voters express presidential preference and vote separately for delegates	3	142	9.5	5	370	16.5
Voters elect delegates who have indicated a presidential preference	0	0	0	5	719	32.0
Voters elect delegates who have not indicated a presidential preference	4	296	19.8	1	33	1.5
Voters elect slots[a]	2	133	8.9	2	85	3.8

1,495 Republican delegates were selected in primaries; 2,244 Democratic delegates.

[a]Slots are the list of delegates under the name of a presidential candidate.

of the vote than this threshold could not receive any delegates. In most primaries, this threshold varied from 0 to 15% of the vote. Rhode Island used a 33⅓% threshold. Reagan, who received 30.8% and 31.7% of the vote in the two congressional districts, was thereby denied any delegates. The purpose of the threshold is to inhibit minor candidacies. In chapter 6, it will be shown that unusually high thresholds radically alter the nature of the primary and the behavior of the candidates. In chapter 8, the recent Democratic Party maneuverings over the use of the threshold as a political tool will be examined.

The Democratic Party debated requiring all primaries to be proportional (a measure finally enacted at the 1976 convention). Eventually, a compromise was reached, for the 1976 campaign, banning state-wide winner-take-all primaries but permitting a district-wide winner-take-all rule (generally referred to as the "Democratic Loophole," although ironically it was a procedure used only in the Republican Party). A similar rule was used in states in which citizens voted directly for delegates. In those states, delegates who received a plurality in a district were elected. For example, a district might select three delegates. The three winners, then, are the three delegate-candidates receiving the most votes. Since one presidential candidate's delegates ordinarily swept a district, this "Plurality" rule worked out virtually the same as the "Loophole." The intention of these compromise rules was to produce outcomes that fell in between the results of the two previous rules. In general, the intention of the compromise was realized. For example, in Florida, Ford received 52.8% of the popular vote. With proportional allocation, he would have won about 53% of the delegates. In a winner-take-all election, he would have won 100% of the delegates. Florida was a "loophole" primary on the Republican side, and Ford won 65% of the delegates.

In general it can be said that more candidates are likely to compete in a primary of the proportional type than in a winner-take-all primary. A candidate expecting to come in third would win some delegates in the former case but could expect to win no delegates in the latter case. The distribution of these rules in states with primaries is reported in table 3.4.

Another question, one I shall not consider at great length, is who the eligible electorate is. There are three possibilities. If a state has no party registration—that is, there is no formal declaration of being a Democrat, Republican, independent, or other party member when registering to vote—then all eligible voters can vote in the primary and are free to choose in which primary to vote. Some states have registration by party, and only those registered as, say, a Democrat can vote in the Democratic primary. Some states with party registration have had crossover primaries in which any registered citizen can vote in any party's primary. When Wisconsin changed its laws, in early 1976, the last of these "crossover" primaries was eliminated. The Democratic Party Rules forbid crossover primaries in states with party registration on the grounds that only the "party faithful" should have a say in selecting the party's nominees. Some observers feel that Reagan benefited from Democratic defectors in several key crossover primaries (e.g., Texas and Indiana)

Table 3.4   Delegate Apportionment Rule in States with Primaries

Level	Winner-Take-All			Democratic Loophole			Plurality within District			Proportional Allocation			Total		
	No. of States	No. of Delegates	% of Delegates	No. of States	No. of Delegates	% of Delegates	No. of States	No. of Delegates	% of Delegates	No. of States	No. of Delegates	% of Delegates	No. of States	No. of Delegates	% of Delegates
Republican Party															
Nonappointed delegates, substate level				7	254		9	517		6	127		22	898	60.1
Nonappointed delegates, statewide-level	1	167		6	111		4	54		9	265		20	597	39.9
Total	1	167	11.1	13	365	24.4	13	571	38.2	15	392	26.2	42	1,495	100.0
Democratic Party															
Nonappointed delegates, substate level							12	957		16	813		28	1,770	78.9
Nonappointed delegates, statewide level	1[a]	1								24	473		24	474	21.1
Total	1	1	0.3				12	957	42.4	40	1,285	57.3	53	2,244	100.0

[a]One delegate seat in Montana was awarded to the winner of a plurality of the statewide vote.

and that Ford benefited in his home state. States without party registration are identified in the appendix.

The last major distinction is one of the simplest but most important. What is the date of the primary? In 1976, the first primary was held on February 24 (in New Hampshire) and the last three primaries were held on June 8 (in California, New Jersey, and Ohio). The thirty state primaries were scattered over fourteen specific dates. This more than three-month period of repeated elections gives the preconvention campaign its unique flavor. To understand the nature of the presidential campaign it is necessary to understand how this protracted period of time, filled with repeated and highly publicized elections, affects the strategies that candidates pursue and influences the outcome of the campaign.

The sequence of the 1976 primaries is shown schematically in figure 3.2 and in more detail in the appendix. As can be seen (from fig. 3.2) the sequence of primaries began fairly slowly. There were five individual primaries (ignoring Vermont's beauty contest), one a week, two primaries two weeks later, and finally Pennsylvania's, three weeks after

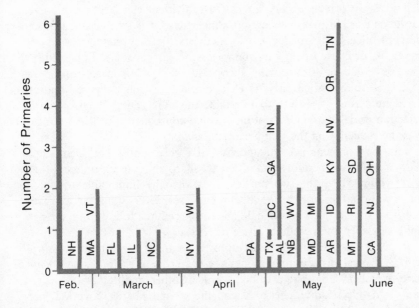

Figure 3.2   Dates of Presidential Primaries, 1976

that. The first eight primaries, then, were spread over two-thirds of the entire period in which primaries were held. These eight were followed by fourteen in the month of May, including six on May 25 alone, and six more during the first eight days of June.

All campaigns are waged over an extended period of time and are, thus, affected by similar temporal forces. The close observation of repeated election returns in the presidential primaries means that changes in the candidates' fortunes should be clearer than in other types of campaigns. At the same time, the mere fact that the dynamics of preconvention campaigns are easier to observe may induce its own effects. Observing the dynamics (and having them analyzed in the media) may alter the nature of the dynamics themselves.

State Caucus or Convention Procedures

States that do not use primaries to select delegates to the national party conventions employ a method usually referred to as the "caucus" or "convention" procedure (I use the terms interchangeably). The basic idea is that interested party members meet (or caucus) to select their delegates. In principle, any interested individual can become involved in the caucus; in practice, few do. Since turnout is small, caucuses can be controlled by a small group of activists, be they supporters of one candidate or cause or be they supporters of party leaders. For example, George McGovern's surprising success in the 1972 Kansas caucus was attributed to this situation. The Democratic Party has proposed and enacted numerous measures to minimize the party élite's control of the selection of delegates. One not unintended consequence of these reforms was the reduction in the number of states that use the caucus system.

The party caucus is regulated by party rules only. The Democratic Party's reforms, therefore, have led to sharp differences in the procedures followed by the two parties. It is virtually impossible to obtain much information about Republican caucuses. Even state party organizations often do not know the details of procedures followed in substate units—or even the results of these caucuses!

In general, state parties that employ the caucus use a multistage system. A typical procedure may consist of as many as four steps. First, party members from one precinct, ward, or other small electoral district caucus to select individuals to attend the second caucus, covering, perhaps, a state legislative district. Those who attend the legislative district caucus select individuals to attend the next caucus, often covering a congressional district. The final step is the statewide caucus. Delegates to the national convention may be selected at the state caucus only or, more commonly, at the congressional district and state caucuses (see table 3.1).

In the Republican Party, the important variables are: (1) the size of the delegation to be selected; (2) how many delegates are selected in statewide and how many in the congressional district caucuses; (3) whether delegates are committed to a candidate and are legally bound to support him (and if so, for how long); and (4) the date(s) of the selection of the delegation.

As I have mentioned, the national Democratic Party has a much stricter set of rules for caucuses. Basically, the first step in the caucus procedure must be open to and publicized among eligible individuals. Those who attend the first caucuses must announce which presidential candidate they support or whether they are uncommitted. Individuals are elected to the next caucus according to the percentage of each presidential candidate's supporters in attendance. For example, the first step in the Iowa caucus consisted of precinct-level meetings on January 19; the first—and highly publicized—formal proceedings of the 1976 campaign. Approximately 45,000 Iowans (10% of the registered Democrats) attended. Of these, roughly 37% were uncommitted, 28% supported Carter, and 13% favored Bayh. Therefore, 37% of the individuals selected to attend the next round of caucuses were uncommitted, 28% were Carter supporters, and so on. This proportional allocation continued until the delegates to the national convention were selected. The purpose of this procedure was to ensure that delegates selected via the caucus represented the preferences of the mass of the Democratic electorate. Such caucuses were intended to be as similar to primaries as possible.

Three factors weaken the analogy between primaries and caucuses. First, the turnout at the initial caucuses is much smaller than even at presidential primaries. Second, the final caucus often ends weeks or even months after the first step. For example, the Iowa state convention was held on May 29, more than four months after their caucuses began. Not only might the list of candidates change, but many other relevant events can alter the voters' preferences. Third, no proportional rule is ideal.[5] In general, proportional rules tend to exaggerate the proportions for the leading candidates at the expense of those receiving the smallest support.

For example, the first stage of the Minnesota caucus consisted almost entirely of Humphrey and uncommitted supporters (51 and 42% respectively). The delegates finally selected, therefore, should have divided along the same lines. In fact, step by step, the percentage of those who favored Humphrey increased—from 51%, to 74% of delegates to the national convention—while those uncommitted declined from 42% to 26%.

Thus, the caucuses in the Democratic Party are affected by the same four variables that affect the Republican caucuses. In addition, the following two may be important: (5) how many steps are in the process; and (6) the date of the first caucuses.

The Media

Presidential nomination campaigns were remarkably different in the last century. Their cost was much less, and therefore there was no need to regulate it. There were no primaries at all. Another development, the rise of the mass media of communications, is of such magnitude that it alone would make preconvention campaigns vastly different.

While all the media report the campaign, two dominate: newspapers and television. Michael Robinson notes that "by 1974 only 12% of the population relied on media other than television or newspapers as a principal source of news."[6] Moreover, both media can be characterized as nationally oriented, albeit often especially responsive to local issues. The most influential newspapers in politics, the *New York Times* and *Washington Post*, are often termed "national" newspapers, as are several others. Most stories about the presidential campaign in more locally oriented papers originate from national sources, such as Associated Press, United Press International, and *Times* or *Post* wire services. Much the same is true of television news. The basic national sources are the three commercial network's nightly news shows, as well as the various "primary night" election return specials, etc. Local news shows (the most popular source of news) also carry network stories about the presidential campaigns, usually stories that also appear on the networks' nightly news. It is not unfair to say that the entire nation receives similar information about the campaigns from the media. Even while the candidates are campaigning for votes in New Hampshire, they are being watched by the entire nation.

The importance of the national media in presidential politics has generated considerable scholarly interest and, indeed, self-analyses by the media themselves. Several generalizations about their role are widely accepted.

First, the candidates are well aware of the importance of the media's role and design their strategies accordingly. Speeches and public events are scheduled with an eye on the deadlines of afternoon newspapers and network news shows. Events are designed to interest the television networks (be highly visual) and national newspapers. In 1976, most candidates provided me with their daily schedules. One candidates' schedule included the following two entries: "Monday, Jan. 5 . . . Medford, Mass.: Rail media event"; and "Friday, Jan. 23 . . . Boston, Mass.: attend media event, Interfaith House."

Second, the media have limited time or space in which to report the campaign. News coverage often consists simply of stating where the candidates are and to whom they are speaking. The nature of day-to-day campaigning forces the candidates to have a set piece, a stock speech that is modified little and repeated at each campaign stop. This speech provides little new material for reporters. Charges and countercharges between candidates are more dramatic and, thus, more reportable. Often, there is little time or space for complex issues. These constraints are especially true of television, where the need for relatively brief and visual stories means that questions of policy receive little attention. Patterson and McClure have calculated that about 15% of network news time was devoted to the presidential preconvention campaign in 1972. Of this figure, about 72% was devoted to what they called "hoopla" (e.g., rallies and motorcades), 8% was devoted to the qualifications of the various contenders, and about 20% addressed the candidates' statements about issues (30% of which dealt with the Vietnam War).[7] The candidates are not unaware of this fact and plan their strategies accordingly, although they often lament the difficulty of obtaining coverage of their carefully formulated issue positions.

Third, the media are interested in the "horse race" aspect of the campaign. Many stories focus on who is ahead, who is behind, who is going to win, and who is going to lose, rather than examining how and why the race is as it is. By this kind of reporting, the media may exaggerate or distort the outcome of a political event. In 1972, for example, Edmund Muskie was initially declared the front runner. Perhaps simply so saying made him so, and possibly even increased his lead. More importantly, by so labeling him, expectations that he would win were built in the minds of the reporters themselves, the candidates, and the electorate. His "failure" in New Hampshire effectively terminated his candidacy, even though he won by a plurality of nearly 10%.

Fourth is the role of the media in declaring winners and losers of primaries. Getting the most votes does not mean that the candidate (Muskie, e.g.) will be seen as—and reported as—the winner. Robinson terms this practice the declaration of "moral winners and losers."[8] The process involves generating expectations. If candidates exceed the expectations, they have a reported victory even if they did not win even a plurality of the votes cast. The power of the media to interpret what winning and losing mean is often seen as a discretionary power that can be misused too easily. Media personnel were not insensitive to such charges, and they attempted to reduce the more imaginative exercise of their power. Winning and losing were interpreted more narrowly in 1976. Reagan received barely 1.2% fewer votes than Ford in New Hampshire. He tried to claim a moral victory, but was unsuccessful. Udall repeatedly came in second in the crowded field. In previous campaigns, his record might have meant the early demise of his candidacy, yet he was considered a "serious" candidate for months in 1976. In general, the media used a plurality as a criterion of winning in 1976.

However, winning and losing is more complicated than that. If winning is everything in a primary, a crowded field can produce odd effects. Jackson came in first in Massachusetts with 22.3% of the vote. Yet calling that a win (as in the headline "Massachusetts: Jackson Deals Himself In") can exaggerate the importance of receiving about one vote in five.[9] The New York Democratic primary, for example, was won by Jackson (he received a substantial plurality) but *he* had claimed that he would win a majority. His falling short of his own expectations was reported, and it hurt his candidacy. Claims by Reagan or his staff that he would defeat Ford in New Hampshire and in Florida did not help his chances when he fell slightly short of victory.

Related to this question of the media is the technique of specifying in advance that certain primaries are crucial to a candidate's fortunes —are "must" wins. For example, Carter had to defeat Wallace in the Florida primary; New York, Massachusetts, and Pennsylvania were key events for Jackson; Udall's hopes for the nomination were pinned on the Wisconsin primary. The priority of these events is determined in part by the candidates and in part by the media. While the candidates appear to be the important "agenda setters" in this sense, once a primary is placed at the top of the agenda, the unfavorable publicity that follows a failure there will hurt the candidate's chances significantly.

I am suggesting that there is a symbiotic relationship between the media and the candidates. While the media and their reportage are crucial to the candidates, the candidates are crucial to the media. The symbiosis is clearest in their day-to-day relations. Candidates and media personnel virtually live together on the campaign circuit. Where one goes, so goes the other. When a reporter is assigned to cover a presidential candidate, the candidate's staff makes many of his daily living arrangements—providing food, drink, accommodations, travel arrangements, etc. Further, the candidate arranges his schedule to suit the needs of the reporters and is more or less at the mercy of how they cover the campaign. Reporters, especially those traveling with a candidate, are at the candidate's mercy as well, for basically they can report little that he or the campaign staff do not tell them. The press briefings and handouts, formal and informal interviews, and public pronouncements are virtually the only basis for writing or broadcasting stories.

In many ways, the goals of the candidates and the media are similar. Both want to see their story in the paper or on television. At the same time, their goals are incompatible. The candidate wants to win the nomination while the reporter wants to cover the news, whatever its content. The two are in a partially cooperative and partially conflictual situation, and there is a fundamental and irradicable tension in their close working arrangements. Both measure personal success by how much they can take advantage of the other. At times, the advantage is mutual. At other times, only one, perhaps neither, can attain the advantage.

The role of the media will be studied directly in several chapters (especially 5, 7, and 8). However, the indirect effect of the media permeates the entire study, as it permeates the entire campaign. At the very least, this indirect effect is felt any time the electorate is directly involved in the campaign. More generally, since presidential candidates, more than any others, are scrutinized in exhaustive detail, they make all their decisions with an eye on the media and on how and whether these decisions will be reported.

The three sets of rules or institutions discussed here: financial regulations, delegate selection procedures, and the media, do not exhaust the list of relevant institutions. However, they are by far the most important. If they are indeed crucial institutional structures, they ought to affect the behavior of the candidates. Some of the most important decisions that candidates must make concern the use of resources; how to get them and how to expend them. If rational candidates do respond to the context of choice, we ought to be able to observe how the deployment of their resources varies with the context in which they operate.

Time

One of the candidates' principal resources is their own time. A personal visit attracts crowds, boosts the morale of campaign workers, and gets the attention of the local and national media. It is a somewhat unusual resource, because each candidate has essentially the same amount to expend. Thus, how it is utilized—where a candidate goes, and when—is the sole question. There are exceptions to this equality of endowment, of course. Frank Church, for instance, felt constrained from entering the race until after the Senate hearings on the CIA that he chaired were completed. Consequently, he began his first campaign swing in the second week of April. As a general rule, the candidate who holds no office has more time for campaigning (in line with the analysis in chapter 2), while the executive, especially the governor, has less.

In figure 3.3, the length of the active candidacy of the various Democratic candidates is plotted against the major party events of 1976. (Ford and Reagan, of course, were in active competition throughout the year.) The early going was difficult for most Democrats. The winnowing-out began before the first primary. Sanford terminated his campaign early in part on financial grounds. Moreover, he was hospitalized in January, a fact that tipped the scales sufficiently to force him to withdraw very early. Bentsen's poor showings in early caucus states (especially Mississippi and Oklahoma) terminated his candidacy. By the end of the fifth primary, five candidates had withdrawn and a sixth, Harris, had ceased to be a major figure.

In general, candidates campaign in person only in states that are currently selecting delegates, that are important to their chances, and in which they expect their presence to make a difference (and to be reported by the media). During the primary season, therefore, candidates campaign in the primary states and not the caucus states. Typically, they campaign in the state just before the primary is held.

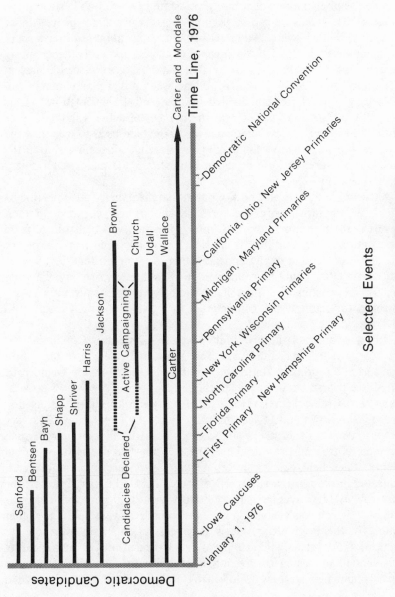

Figure 3.3   Duration of Campaigns of Declared Democratic Candidates, 1976

To measure the candidates utilization of time, their itineraries were gathered, and each day spent in a given state in some public forum was recorded. This measure can be used to assess which states proved to be the crucial battlegrounds. To arrive at the average number of days spent campaigning in a state, the visits by all the candidates of each party were totaled and then divided by the number of active candidates at that time. Thus, the average Republican visits are the total number of visits by Ford and Reagan divided by two, and the calculation for the Democratic candidates varies with the number of active candidates (see figure 3.3). For the Democratic caucuses, the date used to calculate the number of active Democratic candidates was that of the first step in the caucus procedure, because attendance there was the major determinant of the eventual outcome.

All candidates except Frank Church supplied their full daily itineraries. All itineraries were checked against the daily coverage of their travels in the media monitored (Church's itinerary was constructed from these sources). A candidate is considered to have been in the state for one day if he made a public appearance in the state on that day. Therefore, a candidate could be counted as in two states on one day. The reason for this treatment is that, if he campaigned in a state only in the morning, for example, his campaign in that state still would receive full coverage in the local media.

The rank order of the fifty states (plus the District of Columbia) for the two parties is presented in the appendix. It is clear that the candidates go to the primary states and not the caucuses. For the Democrats, only three caucus states appear in the top half of the order; Iowa, Oklahoma, and Connecticut (which used a party-run "primary" as its first stage). Only Iowa and Oklahoma were visited by many candidates very often, and both caucuses began weeks before the first primary. Much the same is true on the Republican side. While five of the most-visited twenty states held caucuses, Republican visits were much more concentrated in the top ten states, all of which held primaries. Further, the only caucus state averaging two or more visit-days per candidate was Missouri, which was visited after the last primaries were held. One other feature of the Republican side is that most of the visits were due to Reagan, Ford often playing the "White House strategy" of appearing presidential and using the resources of office to counteract the more typical campaign strategy followed by Reagan. Ford regularly invited journalists from the relevant state to the White House, guaranteeing extensive local reporting.

Not only were primary states visited more frequently than caucus states, but the particular states visited often provide a good indication of the battlegrounds of the campaign. This feature will be seen again and again as we trace the different resources and will be dealt with more systematically later.

Money: Income

Money is perhaps the key resource for running a vigorous campaign. Without it, candidates find it impossible to get their message across to the electorate (beginning with name recognition and extending to policy positions, qualifications, and the like). Without a sufficient monetary base, the candidate simply cannot compete well.

Financing a campaign is a complex task. One of the first key aides selected by a candidate is a finance chairman, who often has several expert assistants. Raising money requires the expenditure of other resources: time, effort, and money itself. As we shall see in the next chapter, money is a "replenishable resource." That is, the expenditure of money can increase the candidate's ability to raise even more money—if that expenditure leads to some electoral success. Thus, successful candidates are able to raise money relatively easily. Unsuccessful candidates are not able to do so. In fact, the most commonly cited reason in 1976 for a candidate's withdrawal was the inability to raise sufficient funds to conduct an adequate campaign. Terry Sanford said, in his withdrawal speech: "The ordeal of running a political campaign from a non-political position is tougher than I anticipated. The difficulty of getting attention is like swimming upstream, and raising campaign funds has been more like swimming the Atlantic."[10] Even the more successful and well-heeled Jackson campaign ended on these grounds. As Witcover says, "The will to continue was there, but not the resources." Jackson had hoped that his matching funds could be released from a reconstituted Federal Election Commission, but it was not to be. "It was money, Jackson told [Witcover] later, 'There wasn't any question but that money was the overwhelming direct causal connection.' "[11]

Raising money then, is a prerequisite for success. The obvious questions are who was successful at it and where did their money come from.

Table 3.5 reproduces the reports issued by the Federal Election Commission.

The two Republicans were very successful at raising money. Each gathered over $14 million, $3 million more than the most successful Democrat. Indeed, the two of them raised over 70% of what the thirteen Democrats were able to gather. While Ford and Reagan raised essentially the same amount of money, the sources of their support were different. Ford raised much more money from large individual contributors ($4.5 million from those who gave $500 or more, while Reagan raised $1.6 million) and also received much greater support from nonpartisan, political committees. For his part, Reagan raised over $6 million from the smallest contributors (those giving less than $100), nearly twice what Ford raised. Ford's financial support was more typical of a Re-

Table 3.5 Financial Contributions and Expenditures of Candidates in the Preconvention Campaign, 1976

Candidate	Adjusted Receipts ($\times$ 1,000)[a]	Percentage of Receipts from:		Adjusted Expenditures ($\times$ 1,000)[b]
		Individual Contributions	Federal Matching Funds	
Democrats				
Bayh	$ 1,233	58.4	38.1	$ 1,169
Bentsen	1,605	59.1	31.8	2,250
Brown	1,784	65.0	32.6	1,747
Carter	11,560	68.1	30.0	11,388
Church	1,506	59.8	41.3	1,500
Harris	1,473	55.4	43.0	1,407
Jackson	5,342	59.9	37.1	6,214
McCormack	526	53.3	46.4	524
Sanford	571	55.6	43.1[c]	583
Shapp	894	41.1	33.4[c]	830
Shriver	824	49.0	34.6	640
Udall	4,568	57.3	41.6	4,532
Wallace	7,728	57.6	42.6	7,899
Republicans				
Ford	14,031	66.3	33.2	13,575
Reagan	14,224	64.6	35.8	12,611

SOURCE: FEC Disclosure Series, No. 7, May 1977, pp. 15–17.

[a]Besides adjustments, total receipts include contributions from nonpolitical committees, cash on hand as of 1 January 1975, and other sources. [b]Includes fund raising and legal and accounting expenditures exempt from spending limitations. [c]Repayments by Sanford and Shapp not included in these figures.

publican regular, and Reagan's reliance on the small contributor was more like that of an "outsider" or ideological challenger to the party establishment.

The same variation can be seen in the Democratic Party. Carter, Jackson, Bayh, and Bentsen relied heavily on the largest possible contributions from individuals and nonpartisan committees. These three received only 39.0%, 38.4%, 36.1%, and 28.4%, respectively, from those giving less than $100. At the opposite extreme were Harris, McCormack, Udall, and Wallace, who relied much more heavily on small contributions. These four received 84.8%, 80.1%, 72.7%, and 89.2%, respectively, from those giving less than $100 apiece. The candidacies of Jackson, Bayh, and Bentsen may be thought of as party regular or establishment-supported campaigns, while the Harris, McCormack, Wallace and, to an extent, Udall campaigns were supported more heavily by issue-concerned or ideologically outsider groups. In both parties, then, an insider-outsider distinction is clearly demonstrated by the sources of financial support.

Carter is an anomaly. He began his campaign as an outsider, yet he was able to draw more heavily from large individual contributors and political action committees than other such candidates. The explanation lies in the fact that his financial contributions were concentrated most heavily in May and particularly in June (see chapter 5 for details) and that, by the end of the preconvention campaign, his policy appeals had become much more typical of Democratic party regulars (see chapter 7). Not only did he move towards a more insider type of campaign, but the party and its supporters moved toward him as he became all but assured of the nomination in early June.

In table 3.5 we can see the effect of the new federal matching funds on the 1976 campaign. The federal dollars went disproportionately to the smaller campaign treasuries—and often to the least successful campaigns. Carter, Brown, Ford, Reagan, and Jackson (in that order) depended least on matching funds. McCormack, Sanford, Harris, Wallace, Udall, and Church (in that order) relied on the federal government for over 40% of their income.

Money: Expenditures

The purpose of raising money, of course, is to spend it in ways designed to aid one's candidacy. Table 3.5 shows that the Democratic candidates

were able to spend their money. Both Republicans ended up with surpluses, but those surpluses can be attributed to the mandated spending limits. They also included funds raised after the primary season. The
general picture, then, is one of fairly efficient translation of funds raised
into funds expended.

Of more interest is *where* candidates spent their money. The average
expenditure by active candidate per state was computed. The state-by-
state breakdown is found in the appendix. As before, the Republican
candidates concentrated their efforts more than the Democrats, but they
also simply spent more.

Money, like time, was spent largely in the states that held primaries.
This finding reflects in part the fact that most large states (presumably,
therefore, the most expensive states in which to campaign) held primaries. Caucuses were held primarily in the smaller states. For the
Democrats, only Connecticut, with its hybrid system, ranked in the top
20, while Iowa, Oklahoma, and Colorado were also above the median.
For the Republicans, the Missouri, Colorado, and Iowa caucuses were
ranked between 18 and 23 in terms of expenditures.

The candidate's expenditures, like their visits, reflect the crucial
events of the campaign. There are exceptions, however. California was
high on the lists of both parties, and Wisconsin ranked high on the Republican list, but these primaries were not crucial events. The reason
for this lies in the nature of candidate strategy. The candidates can make
the primary or caucus important or unimportant, as they see fit. Just
what "as they see fit" means will be discussed in subsequent chapters.
Still, the expenditure of resources does not in itself make a primary
crucial.

The similarity between visits and expenditures can be seen by cor-
relating the rank orders of states by visits and expenditures. These cor-
relations are very high in both parties (Spearman's rho = .69 for Republicans and .89 for Democrats). Thus, candidates and their money
tended to go together. As a consequence, it is possible to compute an
average rank for each state that provides a fairly accurate statement of
the key primaries or caucuses in each party.

The top twenty are listed in table 3.6. The composite index is closely
related to its two components in each party. The Spearman's rhos between the composite index and spending and visitation rank orders are
.92 and .90 for the Republican Party and .97 and .97 for the Democratic Party. The similarity between parties is seen by the rho of .61
for the two composite rankings.

Table 3.6   Composite Rankings of States by Candidate
Resource Allocation and Media Attention

Composite Ranking of Visits and Expenditures by Candidates		Composite Ranking of Coverage in *New York Times* and *Washington Post*
Democrats	Republicans	
Mass. ⎫	Calif.	Ohio
N.Y. ⎭	Fla.	N.Y.
Fla.	Ill. ⎫	Pa. ⎫
Pa.	Tex. ⎭	Fla. ⎭
Ohio	N.C.	Calif.
N.H.	N.H.	N.J.
Calif.	Ind. ⎫	N.H.
Md. ⎫	Wis. ⎭	Tex. ⎫
Wis. ⎭	Mich.	Wis. ⎭
Mich.	Ohio	Mass.
N.J.	Ga.	Mich.
Ill.	Nebr. ⎫	Nebr.
Oreg. ⎫	Oreg. ⎭	Ill. ⎫
Tex. ⎭	Tenn.	Ind. ⎭
R.I. ⎫	*Mo.* ⎫	*Colo.*
Iowa ⎭	Ala. ⎭	W.Va.
Nebr. ⎫	Ky.	N.C. ⎫
N.C. ⎪	*Colo.* ⎫	*Miss.* ⎭
Okla. ⎪	Nev. ⎭	Md.
Ga. ⎭	*Minn.*	*Iowa*

Braces denote ties in the composite rankings. The italicized states are caucus states; the rest held primaries.

The dominance of primary over caucus states is clear. So too is the importance of an early primary and of a large state delegation. If the goal of the candidate is to win delegates, these conclusions are not surprising. There are significant exceptions to these general rules. For example, several small states appear on the lists for each party, but not all early primaries do (e.g., Vermont and Massachusetts). Nor do such large states as New York and Pennsylvania appear on the Republican list. The logic of both the general rules and their exceptions will be demonstrated in chapter 6.

The Media as Resource

The general view of informed observers is that the media exert substantial influence on the campaign in general and on the future of the candidates in particular. The argument advanced earlier is that influence is a two-way street; the candidates can also influence the news coverage of the campaign. Two major areas of this influence will be analyzed in this book: the setting of the policy agenda (in chapter 7) and the setting of the agenda of major events.

That the media follow the candidates from one state to the next is not surprising. However, this provides the candidate with an important degree of control over the situation. Candidates choose to compete in state primaries and caucuses where they can best further their chance for the nomination. They can also make other events seem relatively inconsequential. Reagan avoided New York and Pennsylvania purposefully, for example. From the point of view of coverage of the Republican race, those two primaries became nonevents.

This relationship becomes clearer when the media's coverage of the various events is examined. To do so, a file of three newspapers was collected (from January 1, 1976 on). All stories relevant to the campaigns were collected and coded in several fashions: what candidates were discussed, what issues were examined, and what state events were covered. The last category is relevant here, and this category will be analyzed by using two of the files—the major political and nationally oriented newspapers, the *New York Times* and *Washington Post*. One difficulty in analyzing these stories is that many stories discussed both parties, reporting Ford's reaction to a major Carter address and so on. Therefore, each story was coded without regard to party. A story was considered relevant to a state if: (1) it was about the state primary or caucus, or (2) the major thrust of the story was about the candidates (or, very rarely, issues), but the story could not be properly understood without knowing where the candidates were campaigning. Stories about the Mississippi Republican contest late in the campaign illustrate this last possibility. Reagan and Ford made major efforts in that state in June and July to win the support of an essentially uncommitted delegation. Their maneuverings were coded as a story about Mississippi. However, when Ford delivered his standard campaign speech in, say, New Hampshire, it was not coded as relevant to any state. A simple count of the number of stories about each state was then made. The total number of stories was divided by the number of then-active candidates to measure the average number of stories per active candidate. Removing the coverage of local states (e.g., New York for the *Times*), rank orders of the average volume of coverage were combined to form a composite index for both papers. The top twenty states in terms of media coverage, are listed in table 3.6 for comparative purposes (and the detailed results are in the appendix).

The third column of table 3.6 shows the close correspondence between the efforts of candidates and the attention of at least one medium (albeit probably the most sensitive for our purposes). More generally, the ranking of states in terms of news coverage is closely related to the ranking of states in terms of the candidate's expenditures (Spearman's rho for the two rank orders is .71 for the Republicans, .80 for the Democrats). Thus, we can conclude that the media follow the candidates as they seek the nomination. As noted, not only is this an important calculation for the candidates, but media attention is itself an important resource that candidates seek to attain and nurture. We can expect that, whenever candidates can control the media, they will attempt to do so and use them to serve their interests in any way possible.

4

The Citizens' Participation and Choices in the Nomination Campaigns

Two of the key elements of the preconvention campaign have been discussed to this point: the candidates themselves, and their backgrounds and goals, and the complex institutional context of nomination campaigns. One of the major purposes of many of the recent reforms of the nominating institutions has been to involve the citizen much more directly in the selection of major party nominees. As a result of these reforms, candidates now must take the public into account much more directly as they formulate their nomination strategies.

My purpose in this chapter is to analyze the decisions facing the citizen: Should I participate in my state's primary or caucus, and if I do, whom should I support? After analyzing the logic of this choice problem, the rates of participation in the 1976 nomination campaigns will be investigated and the results of this participation considered. The candidate is the central focus of this book. The final concern, therefore, will be to consider how the candidate might evaluate the consequences of this participation.

The Logic of the Citizens' Choice

A great deal of attention has been paid to the logic of the citizen's choice in elections of all sorts, but especially in general election campaigns. Political scientists are in general agreement about the variables that underlie this logic, although there is considerable controversy about the interpretation of these variables, their relative importance in determining the citizens behavior, and how these variables might (or might not) have changed. There is general agreement that the citizens' evaluations of "parties, issues, and candidates" are the basic determinants of voting behavior. There is less agreement about just what these three terms mean, their relative importance in determining the voter's behavior, and how these patterns have changed.[1] There has also been general agreement about the variables that explain turnout but, empirically, the various models are much less successful.

Citizens faced with the choice of voting or abstaining in primaries confront much the same logical problem as those deciding whether or not to attend caucuses. Indeed, these two decisions about participation rest on the same logic as decisions about general elections. To be sure, the contexts differ, and these differences account for the much lower participation in caucuses than in primaries, and the generally lower turnout for primaries than for general elections. The choice problem, however, is much the same. Citizens turn out when the benefits outweigh the costs. The contexts help to determine relative costs and benefits.

My purpose, in this section, is to lay out the determinants of the cost and benefit and to examine their relationship to actual participation in 1976. As will be seen, there is one fundamental structural difference between preconvention participation and participation in the general election. The first setting is designed to help select the alternatives in the second setting. Citizens, therefore, should be expected to consider the effect on the general election when they decide about participating in primaries and caucuses. One goal of intraparty elections is to select a candidate likely to do well in the interparty campaign in the fall. Thus, electability should play a role in determining which candidate to support in the primary or caucus.

Citizens must make two decisions: to turn out or not and, if they participate, whom to support. While these are two separate decisions, they are not independent. One way of conceptualizing the problem is to imagine the potential participant asking the following two questions. First, Whom should I support? Second, Are my reasons for supporting that candidate sufficient to make it worth my time and effort to participate?

The Calculus of Participation

As in our modeling of the candidate's decision about whether or not to run, I begin constructing a model of the citizen's participation with a consideration of the potential outcome, develop some method of specifying how the citizen evaluates these outcomes, compare the alternative behavior or choices available to the citizen, and assume that the citizen will participate if the benefits outweigh the costs.

The alternatives available to Democrats in 1976 were quite simple. A Democrat could support one and only one candidate by voting for him or her in the primary (or by participating in the first stage of the caucus), or the Democrat could abstain. The situation was different for Republicans in caucuses states, because they generally had to attend the first stage of the caucus with the goal of being selected to attend later stages or selecting like-minded Republicans to do so. Only at the last stages of Republican caucuses were preferences for candidates explicitly stated and translated into delegate allocations. Unfortunately, the less nationally structured Republican caucus procedures meant that data about turnout for local Republican caucuses were not gathered even by the state party organizations. Therefore, in what follows we must ignore these contests.

The evaluation of the outcomes differs from primary to caucus. In primaries, the only outcome is the vote and delegate results for candidates. In caucuses, the participants have that goal in mind, to be sure, but there may be others. The occasion of a caucus presents the party organization with a convenient opportunity for taking care of local and state party affairs in general. For some, that is a benefit. For others, it is a large expenditure of time spent in meetings, to say nothing of the tedium. Regular party activists—a small percentage of party members—receive the benefits of participating in party business. In addition, they have a relatively high probability of being selected to attend subsequent stages in the procedure, up to and including the national party convention itself. Consequently, those aspiring to become delegates to the national or state party convention make up a substantial bloc of those attending the local caucuses.

In either case, a major reason for participation is to help affect the fortunes of a presidential candidate. It is for this reason that the question of whom to support must be answered before the question of whether or not to participate can be answered.

The Costs of Participation

In general, it is thought that the costs of participating in general elections are high, in relation to the benefits. The costs of participating in the general election include obtaining information, processing it, and deciding which candidate is preferable. To these decision-making costs must be added the more narrowly physical costs of becoming registered and going to the polls. The total cost is offered as an explanation of why participation rates are as low as they are in the United States.[2]

The comparable costs of participation in nomination campaigns are even higher. The physical costs are at least as great in primaries and often much greater in caucuses. The decision-making costs are substantially higher in nomination than in general election campaigns. First, information is scarcer in February than in November, and hence more costly to acquire. Second, the intraparty nature of nomination campaigns makes obtaining sufficient information even more costly. Partisanship can be a useful cost-reduction mechanism in general elections. There is no such easily conveyed, simplifying device in intraparty struggles. Third, multicandidate campaigns are more complex and confusing than two-candidate races.

Even in two-man nomination campaigns, however, there is the complicating factor that one is seeking to nominate a party representative to stand in the general election, rather than choosing a president directly. The additional complication requires the expenditure of still more decision-making costs.

Fourth, as we saw in chapter 3, most primaries are complicated electoral mechanisms. Many include an election of delegates that is separate from the expression of presidential preference. In Texas and Alabama, voters were required to vote for delegates about whose presidential preference nothing was specified on the ballot. Caucus procedures are always complicated, so much so that a means-ends relationship between behavior and outcome is often obscure.

Finally, since the nomination campaign unfolds over a long period of time, it is by no means clear that events held early in the campaign will be evaluated the same by the citizen as those held towards the end. All of these costs point towards the conclusion that we should *expect* turnout to be lower for caucuses than primaries and lower for primaries than general elections.

Whom to Support

The benefits of the citizen's participation are the votes and delegates received by the candidates. In a two-candidate general election, the decision about whom to support is straightforward: support the candidate one prefers or support no one. As we shall see shortly, voting for one of two candidates in a nomination campaign need not be so straightforward, because one might be influenced by the chances of the two candidates in the fall campaign. Regardless of the electoral context, however, choosing among three or more candidates is qualitatively different. A rational citizen might choose to vote for someone other than the most preferred candidate.

The rational citizen is assumed to maximize *expected* utility. In a multicandidate contest, citizens must consider two factors; their preferences over the candidates and the chance each candidate has to win the nomination and election. New York and Pennsylvania Democrats, for example, chose among Carter, Jackson, and Udall in 1976. Some might have preferred Udall most, then Carter, and finally Jackson. In the New York primary, all three were still viable candidates, and so those who most preferred Udall might have chosen to vote for him (he came in second to Jackson). By the time of the Pennsylvania primary, however, Udall had lost to Carter in the Wisconsin primary. Pennsylvania Democrats, otherwise similar to those in New York, might have reasoned that Udall was no longer a viable candidate. Therefore, it would be better to support Carter in order to avoid the nomination of the least preferred alternative, Jackson. Voting for Carter might have yielded higher *expected* benefits than voting for the more preferred Udall.

Before turning to the criterion of electability, let us consider the basis on which preferences for candidates are formed. Massive volumes of empirical and theoretical studies have isolated two basic elements that are relevant to nomination campaigns; the candidate as an individual, and the candidate as a policy maker. The individual qualities of the candidate include experience, executive ability, trustworthiness, and integrity. One indirect function of the nomination campaign is to reveal how well a candidate can form and lead a large organization (e.g., a national campaign staff) and how a candidate responds to challenges, reporters' inquiries and scrutiny, and unforeseen events.

The citizen's preferences for particular policies varies substantially from individual to individual. Some have vague opinions about some issues, well-formed opinions about others. Some, of course, are "liberal,"

some "conservative," and others "moderate." Some are very concerned
about one issue, some about another. While no two individuals have
exactly the same preferences or degrees of concern over issues, all can
compare their preferences to the positions advocated by a candidate.
Such a comparison yields a policy-related evaluation of each candidate.

Citizens, then, combine their evaluation of the personal qualities of
the candidate with their evaluation of the candidate's positions on policies of concern. The citizen's preference for a candidate is based, then,
on a comparison of the benefit that citizen expects to derive from the
selection of each candidate.

This description of how citizens evaluate candidates ignores party, a
factor of great relevance in determining the behavior of voters in general elections. Party does enter into the preconvention decision, but in
an indirect fashion. The party member has to consider that whoever is
nominated must face the other party's nominee in the fall. Democrats
usually prefer the Democratic nominee, whoever that might be, to any
Republican nominee, and Republicans often prefer the Republican to
the Democrat. The decision about whom to support for the nomination
should involve a consideration of how each candidate is expected to do
in the general election against the other party's nominee. I call this the
electability criterion.

Suppose there is one issue in a campaign with two Democrats and
one Republican. Suppose they and a Democratic voter take positions on
the issue as shown in figure 4.1. The voter has the choice of voting in
the primary for candidate A or for the more distant candidate B. If the
voter decides on policy terms exclusively, he might choose to vote for
the closer Democrat. Suppose, however, that candidate B has a much
better chance of defeating the Republican in the fall. Should the voter
support A and run a larger risk of seeing the Republican elected presi-

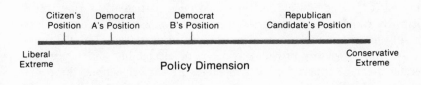

Figure 4.1   Hypothetical Tradeoff between Policy and Electability

dent, whose policy would be very different from the voter's? Or should the voter give a little on policy to help support a more electable nominee and, thus, stand a better chance of avoiding the worst possibility—the election of the Republican?

There is no straightforward answer to the question. The best choice of action depends on:

1. A comparative assessment of the policies espoused by the two Democrats.

2. How their positions compare with the position of the other party's candidate(s).

3. How intensely the voter feels about the policy.

4. A comparative assessment of how likely each Democrat is to defeat each Republican in the general election.

In general, there is a tradeoff between policy and electability that many citizens must face in preconvention campaigns. Candidate's strategies are designed to play up this tradeoff (see chapter 7 for examples). The best decision for the citizen depends upon the specific features of the situation. However, as a candidate begins to appear more electable during the preconvention campaign, more party members should be willing to support that candidate. One method by which a candidate appears more electable in the fall is by winning elections in the preconvention campaign. Winning primaries provides prima facie evidence that the candidate will be able to generate votes in the fall, and this evidence should help convince the party's members that, even if they must give a little on policy, they should support the candidate's nomination. Moreover, by failing to support this advantaged candidate, they risk a divided party, potentially hurting whoever wins the nomination.

John Kennedy's campaign for the 1960 Democratic nomination illustrates the importance of electability. As I noted in chapter 1, the two key events in his successful campaign were his defeats of Hubert Humphrey in the Wisconsin and West Virginia primaries. The first was considered a strong Humphrey state, and the second was considered one in which Kennedy's Catholicism would be a particularly serious problem. By winning both primaries, Kennedy demonstrated sufficient electability to overcome the potential liabilities of youth and Catholicism.

A primary victory provides evidence of electability and hence generates greater support for the candidate. At the same time, the defeat of rivals for the nomination can only diminish their apparent "elect-

ability quotient," a point not lost on Carter, for example. Thus dynamic
forces are generated over the campaign and are two-edged, helping the
victors and simultaneously hurting the losers. In the next chapter, this
momentum will be examined from the candidate's perspective. It must
be remembered there that momentum has a logical bearing on the citizen's choice.

Turnout

Once citizens have determined which candidate to support, they still
must decide whether or not it is worthwhile to actually support the
candidate. The relatively high costs of determining which candidate to
support and of voting in primaries or attending caucuses have been
discussed. These costs are a barrier to participation. In addition, the
citizen must compare the candidates to see if there are sufficient grounds
for bearing these costs.

Two basic forms of abstention have been identified in the literature
on rational choice.[3] One is "indifference." Suppose there are two candidates for the nomination. If, after taking all factors discussed above
into account, the difference in expected benefits from the support of one
candidate over the other is less than the costs involved, the citizen will
fail to participate because he or she is relatively indifferent. Such might
have been true of some Wisconsin Democrats in 1976, for example
those who preferred Udall on policy grounds but thought Carter more
electable.

A second type of abstention is called "alienation." Suppose, even
though the best alternative may be substantially better for the citizen,
this best candidate may be considered too poor to be worth supporting.
A liberal Republican might have reached that decision in 1976. While
Ford would have been noticeably better than Reagan, he still may have
been far too conservative to be an attractive candidate. In other words,
a citizen is said to abstain from alienation if the lesser of two evils is
too evil.

Alienation, so defined, might explain the phenomenon of crossover
voting. In such primaries, Republicans can choose to vote in the Democratic primary and vice versa. Some thought that Wallace's surprising
success in some 1972 primaries (e.g., Michigan) could be traced to
Republicans who found his political philosophy especially attractive.
There has also been speculation that Reagan's 1976 successes in cross-

over primary states (e.g., Texas and Indiana) was attributable in part
to the support of erstwhile Wallace Democrats who preferred him to
an unacceptable member of their own party.

Herbert Weisberg has defined "abstention from satisfaction," a reversal of "alienation."[4] In this case, even the worst alternative might be
so good that the citizen stays at home to leave it to others to decide
which of the desirable candidates receives the nomination.

There is empirical evidence for all three sorts of abstention in general
elections. The two important points are that all types of abstention depend upon the particular candidates who present themselves to the primary or caucus electorate and that all forms of abstention depend upon
a comparison of expected benefits and costs. Ordinarily, these costs are
high in preconvention campaigns, but they may vary from state to state.
Therefore, we should be able to find variations in turnout among the
states as a function of costs.

Turnout in 1976

The Caucuses

Data about turnout at the first stage of state caucuses are difficult to
obtain. For Republican caucuses in 1976, they were simply unavailable.
Austin Ranney has estimated the turnout for 1976 Democratic caucuses,
using data from the *Congressional Quarterly*. He examined the proportion of all voting-age residents in the state who attended the caucuses
and found that, in 21 states, attendance at the first stages of the typical
Democratic caucus was only 1.9% of the total voting-age population.

Such a low turnout figure is misleading, however, since it would be
reasonable to expect that only Democratic Party identifiers would attend.
Unfortunately, there is no state-by-state breakdown of party identifiers.
(It should be noted that party identification and party registration are not
equivalent.) Ranney does report that the state with the largest attendance
at caucuses was Connecticut, with 4.8%. That figure represents 19%
of the voters who were registered Democrats. Oklahoma, which ranked
fourth, with 3.3% attending, was estimated to have a record turnout of
6% of the Democratic Party members.

Whatever the details, then, it is clear that participation in caucuses
is remarkably low, much lower than in the typical primary. Some of the
reasons for this low participation are traceable to the high costs discussed above.

Even given these low turnouts, there are variations that are consistent
with the effects of costs and potential benefits. The Connecticut and
Louisiana Democratic parties conducted a primary-like vote as the first
step in their caucus procedures. These two states had the two largest
turnouts, each exceeding 100,000 (third was Oklahoma, with 65,000),
and the two largest percentages, 4.8% and 4.7%, respectively.[5]

The candidates campaigned most heavily in Connecticut and the early
caucuses in Iowa, Oklahoma, and Mississippi. These caucuses were also
the ones in which the contenders spent the most money organizing get-
out-to-the-caucus campaigns. As would be expected, these four states
ranked in the top six in percentage of attendance.

Carter alone campaigned in Maine, the other caucus held prior to the
first primary, and expressed considerable surprise that everyone else ignored the opportunity. His campaign manager, Hamilton Jordan, said:
"We couldn't believe we would not be challenged in Maine. All we did
was have three hundred people in Portland on a Sunday. I was amazed
other people were skipping so much."[6] As a result, only 6,500 people
attended Maine's Democratic caucus, less than 1% of the voting-age
population, and Carter handily won a victory that was described as a
"windfall."

The Primaries

Turnout is much higher in primaries than caucuses. Ranney estimates
that 18.6% of the voting-age population voted on just the Democratic
side in closed-primary states.[7] Since this comparison is the best direct
one available, it indicates that turnout was ten times larger in primaries
than the average of 1.9% in caucus states.

Primary turnout in twenty-eight states and both parties averaged 28%
of the voting-age population.[8] In the 26 states with statewide registration figures, about 43% of the *registered* voters voted in a primary
(peaking at 74% in California). Moreover, in the 13 closed-primary
states, the percentage of registered voters in each party who turned out
was virtually identical and a bit over 50%. Thus, a substantial proportion of the population participated in the presidential primaries in 1976.
However, turnout in primaries was about 24% less than in the general
election campaign. Thus, primaries fall somewhere in between caucuses
and presidential elections in terms of participation. Ranney also estimates that turnout was down about 4% from comparable primaries in
1972 (even though there was essentially no Republican nomination

campaign in 1972), and that turnout declined about 11% between 1948
and 1968.

A number of factors that affect the costs and benefits of participation
should affect turnout rates. For example, voting directly for one's preferred candidate and having that vote binding on delegates at the national convention should be associated with high turnout. It is. Those
states with a binding preference poll had an average turnout of 44.9%
among registered voters; those with nonbinding preference polls averaged 41.0%; and those with no method of expressing presidential preference averaged 37.0%. In Vermont, the only "beauty contest" primary
(i.e., one unrelated to delegate selection) in both parties, only 27.1%
of the registered voters turned out.

The amount of attention the candidates pay to the state ought to be
related to turnout. As we saw in chapter 3, there was a very close correspondence between the time candidates spent in the state, the money
they spent, and the amount of attention paid to the state contest by the
media. The states actively contested were the ones crucial to the fortunes of the candidate's nomination campaigns. Moreover, the invest-
ment of substantial resources by the candidates should be expected to
stimulate turnout by: (1) increasing interest in the campaign generally;
(2) increasing the salience of the choice; (3) increasing the amount of
information available and decreasing the cost of obtaining information;
and (4) organizing local get-out-the-vote and related campaigns. The
first two points should increase the expected benefit of participation, the
last two should reduce the cost. Ranney tested the relationship between
campaign spending and turnout in primaries and found "that campaign
spending is one of the factors most strongly associated with turnout"
(Spearman's rho of .42).[9]

The Outcomes

The citizen's purpose in participating in a primary or caucus is the same
that motivates candidates to expend scarce resources in a state: to increase a candidate's chance of obtaining the nomination. In this section,
I present a brief overview of the results of major primaries and caucuses
in each party. The specific results of each state's primary or caucus are
in the appendix.[10] Later, it will be seen that the results correspond closely
to variations in the acquisition and expenditure of resources. The focus
in this section is the consequences of the voters' choices on the fortunes

of the candidates. The candidates are the objects of the citizens' choice, and yet they are also actors who act and react to some summation of the citizens' participation decision. A crucial question, therefore, is how the candidates evaluate the results of the citizens' choices.

The Democratic Campaign

The Democratic campaign can be divided into three periods: (1) the winnowing-out phase; (2) the dominance of Carter over the survivors remaining in the initial field; and (3) the late challenges.

The Winnowing-Out Phase. Eleven Democrats actively contested the early primaries and caucuses. Eight candidates were eliminated as serious contestants between the Iowa caucus in January and the end of March (including the North Carolina primary but excluding New York and Wisconsin). The first major question, then, was whether a candidate survived or not.

Sanford withdrew in January, in part for reasons of health, without actually testing his strength in a primary or caucus. Such a test appeared irrelevant. Bentsen withdrew in early February after suffering setbacks in the early caucuses in Iowa, Oklahoma, and especially Mississippi. Bayh withdrew after a series of surprisingly weak showings, especially in Massachusetts. Shapp withdrew after failing to make any inroads in the New Hampshire, Massachusetts and Florida primaries (receiving 2.5% of the vote in Florida, for example). The next casualty was Shriver, who withdrew after his last-ditch effort in Illinois yielded him third place (of four candidates) with only 16.3% of the vote. Harris, after showing surprising if not overwhelming strength in the early caucuses, was rendered ineffective by a series of weak showings in the early primaries. He remained active until after the New York and Wisconsin primaries, but was not a serious candidate that long. Wallace remained an active candidate throughout the primary season. His quest for a significant role ended, however, after he was defeated by Carter in Florida and North Carolina. He made a major, last-minute effort in Massachusetts, seeking the vote of antibusing advocates and the working class in general in Boston. While his 16.7% was good enough for third place there, he apparently diluted his efforts in the key Florida primary the following week. There, Carter was able to emerge as *the* southern candidate, ending Wallace's long reign as a Democratic spoiler. McCormack never made any show of strength and was not able to become an effective voice for pro-life advocates. Thus, eight campaigns ended early in the winter and spring of 1976. All foundered at the voting booths or conventions. Yet, as we shall see, all were terminated because of a more complex interaction between resources (both broad and narrow) and revealed electoral weakness.

Who, then, survived? Carter survived because of a string of major successes: pluralities in the New Hampshire, Florida, Illinois, and North Carolina primaries (as well as the Vermont beauty contest), and strong showings in early caucuses (Iowa, Oklahoma, and Maine, all held prior to the first primary). As such, he inherited the title of front runner. However, Jackson and Udall also survived this period. Jackson won a plurality victory (with only 22.3% of the vote) in Massachusetts, defeating Carter in Jackson's first major contest. His only other serious campaign was a last-minute effort in Florida. Udall survived less by winning than by avoiding losing. By strong second-place finishes in the first two primaries (his only serious campaigns in this period), Udall emerged as the lone liberal candidate with any electoral credentials. Further, he had announced that the Wisconsin primary was his crucial battleground, so a first-place showing was not essential until then. This strategy was paralleled by Jackson, who set New York as his goal.

The winnowing-out phase, then, consisted of two major stories, the demise of most campaigns and the emergence of Carter as the "first among equals" of the three survivors. Carter attained that status by campaigning vigorously and essentially everywhere in this first phase of the campaign, by defeating rivals, especially Wallace, in key state events, and by developing an impressive series of plurality victories.

Carter's Dominance over the Survivors. In the month of April, Carter solidified his front-runner status by defeating his remaining rivals on their chosen battlegrounds. Udall's campaign ended, for all intents and purposes, in Wisconsin. Wisconsin was a two-man race that Carter narrowly won. However, that narrow victory appeared unusually consequential. Two national networks had declared Udall the victor on primary night, and morning newspapers headlined his apparent success. Carter eventually overtook Udall late in the night, and the reaction of the media made his 1% margin more telling. Udall was to continue his campaign with more very narrow losses to Carter. By that point, however, his role was more that of a spoiler than as a candidate in his own right. The argument against him was, "If a liberal Democrat cannot win in Massachusetts or Wisconsin, where can he win?"

Jackson claimed that he expected to win a majority of the delegates in the New York primary. His victory over Udall and Carter by a plurality was thereby tarnished. This setback was followed by an outright defeat in Pennsylvania, and he formally withdrew shortly thereafter. His chances in these two states were complicated by Humphrey's campaign of availability for the nomination. Humphrey was the first choice of key groups in these states, and his mere availability was sufficient to dampen the enthusiasm of union leaders and others for Jackson. Union leaders in Pennsylvania, for example, argued that a vote for Jackson was a vote for Humphrey, a tactic that neither, especially Jackson, encouraged. Humphrey's noncandidate candidacy ended two days before Jackson's formal withdrawal, when Humphrey refused to become an active candidate in New Jersey or anywhere else. Thus, Carter was the sole active campaigner as May began.

The Late Challenges. Church and Brown began active campaigns in May. Church defeated Carter in Nebraska on May 11, and later in Idaho, Oregon, and Montana. Brown upset Carter in Maryland on May 18, later in Nevada and California, and made a surprisingly strong showing in Oregon as a write-in candidate. Finally, he won an outright victory in New Jersey as part of an uncommitted slate of delegates who announced their support of both Humphrey and Brown. These late challenges were too little, too late. Carter was able to balance these defeats with victories elsewhere (Michigan, Arkansas, Kentucky, Tennessee, South Dakota, and Ohio, among others). And his lead, in terms of delegates and resources, was substantial enough to withstand a series of defeats. His victory in Ohio on June 8 (even matched with defeats in California and New Jersey) was the final breakthrough, after which most other candidates (e.g., Udall and Wallace), and many party leaders (e.g., Mayor Daley of Chicago) conceded him the nomination he finally won on the first ballot at the Democratic National Convention.

The Republican Campaign

Throughout 1976, the Republican campaign was a close, tightly fought struggle between Ford and Reagan. The campaign was conducted almost exclusively in the primary states until the last primaries were over. From that point on, the campaign entered an end-game phase in which both candidates competed for the remaining uncommitted delegates on a personal, candidate-to-delegate, basis. The primary season can be divided into three parts: (1) the Ford victory phase; (2) the Reagan victory phase; and (3) a final phase of mixed results.

The Ford Victory Phase. All the first primaries were won by Ford. Reagan competed actively in New Hampshire, Florida, and Illinois, conceding Massachusetts (and Vermont) to the president. All three contested primaries were close, but Ford gained slightly in each (from a majority of 50.6% in New Hampshire to one of 58.9% in Illinois). By this point, Reagan's resources began to be depleted, and some Republican leaders were calling for his withdrawal on the grounds of party unity. However, Reagan defeated Ford narrowly in North Carolina, quieting these calls and surprising himself, Ford, and pundits alike.

Reagan's next campaign was to be in Wisconsin. After hearing of his North Carolina success and noting that he had virtually run out of money, Reagan withdrew from Wisconsin and made a national television address (an expensive move, unprecedented in a preconvention campaign), combining policy statements with an appeal for funds. This move forfeited substantial resources, was not looked on with favor by his Wisconsin organization, and cost him any chance, however slight, of a victory there. He well might have picked up some delegates in a narrow loss, rather than the zero he actually scored. Further, he failed to contest a primary for a month, focusing his efforts on the Texas primary of May 1. Thus, this period ends in a transition brought about by a highly irregular strategic ploy.

The Reagan Victory Phase. By failing to contest Wisconsin, New York, and Pennsylvania, Reagan forfeited large blocs of delegates to Ford, but he removed the media spotlight from these likely defeats. On May 1, he thoroughly dominated Ford in Texas, winning all the delegates and two votes to every one for Ford. Three days later, Reagan defeated the president in Alabama, Georgia, and Indiana (an especially telling victory). One week later, Reagan defeated Ford in Nebraska. Even though Ford won in West Virginia that day, the Nebraska primary was the scene of the most vigorous campaign—and the media's attention. By the middle of May, Reagan's comeback was complete.

The Mixed Results Phase. Ford won a decisive victory on May 18 in
his home state. That this outcome was seen as a major triumph indicates the difficult times into which the president's campaign had fallen.
The six primaries of May 25 were split three each. The next week, Reagan won one primary (and one beauty contest) and Ford won the other.
The final primaries were also split, Reagan winning all delegates from
his home state, and Ford winning the other two primaries. However,
only Ohio was perceived as the direct battlefield that day, so Ford's
victory there was crucial.

The result of these primaries was that Ford had a slight delegate edge,
but neither candidate had a clear path to victory. The fight was moved
to the caucus states (e.g., Missouri and Colorado), to states (e.g., Mississippi) where there were large blocs of uncommitted delegates, and in
fact to wherever there was a single delegate to be won. In this end game,
the see-saw nature of the last set of primaries continued. Reagan made
gains in early and mid-June, but these were more than offset by Ford
in July. Thus, Ford's slight edge in delegates was retained as the convention neared, and Reagan needed to try a new strategic move—virtually anything he or his staff could conceive of would do.

On July 27, Reagan announced that Richard Schweiker, a liberal senator from Pennsylvania, was to be his choice for vice-president. Historically, presidential nomination hopefuls do not announce their choice
of running mates (if, indeed, they even know their choice themselves).
The exact reasons for this move remain unclear. Among other things,
Reagan probably hoped to pick up support from erstwhile Ford delegates, especially in New York and Pennsylvania (who were formally
uncommitted and thus able to be wooed from Ford's camp). He appears
to have been trying to attract more liberal support, hoping that his impeccable personal credentials as a conservative would hold conservative
delegates in his camp. Ultimately, the move was unsuccessful, apparently
swinging few if any delegates his way and hurting his chances in Mississippi's delegation. However, the move led to a further ploy at the convention. His supporters introduced resolution 16C, to be voted on as
part of the party rules. The resolution required every presidential candidate to announce a running mate prior to the vote at the convention.
The unsuccessful convention vote on 16C proved to be the show of
strength that demonstrated that Ford in fact had the support necessary
to win the nomination the next day.

A Measure of Competitive Standing

The preconvention campaign is a combination of state-by-state elections and one national campaign. The citizen deciding about participation should consider the chances of the candidates in his home state but, perhaps even more important, the candidate's chance for the national party's nomination. As the electability criterion indicates, the citizen might consider the chances of the candidates in the general election. In short, citizens must consider the full national campaign as well as the campaign in their own state. For the candidate, the situation is quite the same. From week to week, attention is focused on specific primaries and caucuses, yet each one fits into the national campaign as well. The candidate has to keep track of both the individual primary or caucus and the campaign as a whole.

To keep track of the flow of events, a candidate, citizen, or campaign observer could mentally record each event, vote-by-vote and delegate-by-delegate, or attempt to get the general flavor of the campaign, as we did in the last sections. However, a more general view of the nomination campaign is possible. The media commentators, for example, like to talk about front runners, who is ahead and who is behind. To provide this general view of the overall success and failure of the candidates, to sum up the results of the citizens' choice, as it were, I shall propose a measure of competitive standing. This measure will serve to summarize the results of the citizens' participation in the various events of the campaign.

What features should any measure of competitive standing possess? First, it should tell us the number of delegates a candidate has won. It should also keep track of the delegates the opponents have won. An obvious measure is simply the number of delegates a candidate has, less the number won by the opponents. A third desirable feature is to keep track of the remaining possibilities. For example, Ford had 15 more delegates than Reagan after the New Hampshire primary (an 18-to-3 lead). While this small lead was unimportant so early in the campaign, it would have been sufficient at the convention itself. What matters, then, is the pool of delegates available to be won (uncommitted delegates, delegates yet to be selected, etc.). If we divide this 15-delegate edge by the pool of available delegates, the ratio captures the desired information. Thus, after the 21 delegates in New Hampshire were awarded to the two Republicans, there were 2,245 delegates yet to be won. The 15-vote lead for Ford was a small proportion of the pool, certainly much smaller than if Ford had a 15-vote lead with 30 delegates yet to be selected.[11]

The competitive standing measure (or CS) as defined above has several other desirable features. First, it is always largest for the leading candidate, next largest for the second-place candidate, etc. Second, it equals 1 only when a candidate is guaranteed at least 50% of the vote at the convention. If the leading candidate does not have a sure tie, the measure is less than 1 (and often negative). It exceeds 1 if, and only if, the candidate is certain to win a first-ballot nomination. Third, it expresses the relative uncertainly of the outcome of the campaign. Finally, if calculated over time, it expresses the ebb and flow of a candidate's fortunes. Indeed, it is not too farfetched to assume that rational candidates seek to maximize their CS value.

Figures 4.2 and 4.3 display the CS values in the primaries for Carter and Ford. In a two-candidate contest, the CS for one candidate is just the opposite of the other. Thus, Reagan's CS is the negative of Ford's in figure 4.2. It should be noted, in figure 4.2, that the uncommitted delegates in New York and Pennsylvania are attributed to the two candidates as these delegates actually voted at the convention. Tallies that had Reagan winning more delegates than Ford in the primaries ignored these delegates and were less reflective of the true competitive standing of the two candidates. (Reagan won a few more delegates than Ford in the caucuses.)

The three phases of both campaigns can be seen clearly. For example, Ford's early lead and the inertia it generated are apparent. Just as apparent are the setbacks Ford suffered in the second phase of the campaign, and the fact that, although he held a slight edge in the primaries throughout, he approached a first-ballot victory very slowly. That is, Reagan had an excellent chance of success beyond the primary season. Similarly, Carter's survival in the first phase, rise to dominance in the second phase, and relative invulnerability to the late challengers in the last phase are apparent. The Democratic case is more chaotic, of course, because candidates' withdrawals moved heretofore committed delegates back to the uncommitted category. Yet the general trend of Carter's success remains clear.

Figure 4.4 illustrates these trends even more clearly, as it records the difference between Carter's CS and that of his next closest opponent each week. The first-among-equals description of Carter in the win-

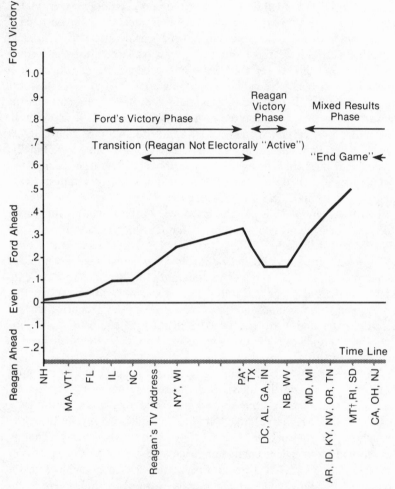

* Nominally uncommitted delegates awarded to candidates in proportion to their vote at the convention.
† Delegates from "beauty contest" primaries not included.

Figure 4.2   **Ford's Competitive Standing (CS), Delegates Selected in Primaries.** Nominally uncommitted delegates were awarded to candidates in proportion to their vote at the convention. Delegates from beauty contest primaries are not included. Reagan's CS = (−1) (Ford's CS); CS of both is undefined after last primaries (pool = 0).

nowing-out phase is evident. So, too, is his rise to dominance by the
end of April. The successes of the late challengers in slowing, but not
stopping, Carter are quite visible, giving substance to their description
as too little, too late. In sum, the measure of competitive standing clearly

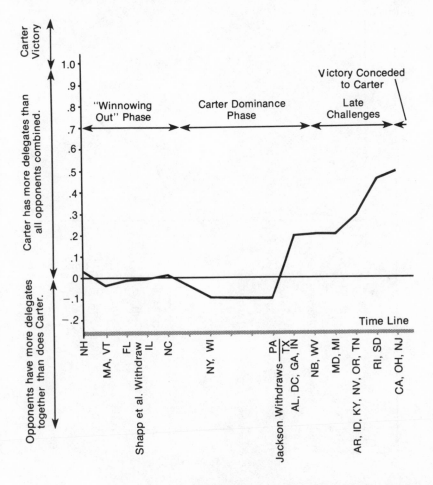

Figure 4.3   **Carter's Competitive Standing (CS), Delegates Selected in Primaries.**
              The CS of all other candidates was much lower. CS of "Everyone
              but Carter" = (−1) (Carter's CS). CS is undefined after June 8
              and the last primaries. Jackson's delegates are considered released
              after his informal withdrawal between the Pennsylvania and Texas
              primaries.

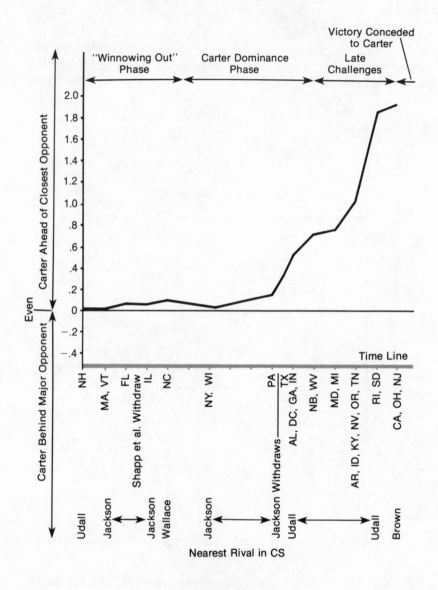

Figure 4.4   Carter's Competitive Standing (CS) Minus That of His Nearest Rival, Delegates Selected in Primaries. The CS of Carter and Brown, his nearest rival, is undefined after June 8 and the last primaries.

documents the results of the decisions of the citizens, as well as demonstrating the extent to which the outcomes of individual primaries and caucuses are intertwined.

Perhaps most important, the figures presented above illustrate the importance of the fact that a nomination campaign is played out over a period of time and that there is a dynamic, or time-related, pattern to the outcome of each campaign. Journalists employed the word momentum often in 1976, as they have in many elections. In the next chapter, I examine the dynamics of the preconvention campaign to see if there is momentum and if the dynamic elements shed light on the candidates' central questions—who wins, who loses, and why?

5

Some Dynamics of Campaigns

Pundits and political scientists alike explain general electoral victories in such terms as issues, the qualifications and images of the candidates, and partisan affiliations. Yet analysts of presidential primaries often place a much heavier emphasis on the dynamic features of campaigns, i.e., how the fortunes of candidates shift over time.

Momentum

Roger Mudd, in describing the Democratic Florida primary on the CBS primary night coverage, said that "momentum was the word of the week." "Word of the year" would have been more accurate. In fact, momentum and related dynamic concepts, although they are well applied to preconvention campaigns, are important (if often difficult to observe) aspects of all campaigns.

Hubert Humphrey's campaign in the 1968 general election is a classic example of the impact of dynamic elements on the fortunes of candidates. Theodore White wrote the following description of these events:

> September, for all Democrats, had been a month to be forgotten. From the day of their convention down to October 24th, their destitute National

Committee had been unable to find the money to schedule even a single advertising spot on national radio or television for their candidate. . . . On September 27th, Humphrey received a forthcoming Gallup poll reporting Nixon fifteen points ahead of the Vice-President, by 43/28. And George Wallace, with 21, ran only seven points behind Humphrey himself! . . . that night, September 30th, from Salt Lake City, Hubert Humphrey was to appear nationwide on television for the first time since his acceptance speech, . . . The famous Salt Lake City speech will go down in history as no great document of diplomacy. It was flawed . . . But as a document in Humphrey's recapture of initiative, it was critical. . . . Within forty-eight hours, more solid response began to come. . . . And the appeal [for money appended to the speech] was to bring in two and a half times as much as the $100,000 the broadcast had cost. By October 10th, the first $1,000,000 had been contributed to the Humphrey campaign, and gradually the oscillation of money/public-opinion-polls impact began to reverse itself. . . . By mid-October the turn in Humphrey's fortunes was publicly apparent, as first the Harris poll reported that Humphrey had closed to within five points of Nixon (40/35).[1]

Is there something to this supposed dynamic, one manifestation of which is called momentum? If any candidate had it in the 1976 campaign, it was Carter. He started as a little-known former governor of a southern state and by the end of the primary season he was the certain victor. The probability of his winning the nomination, therefore, increased during the first six months of 1976. But was there something more to it than that? Consider figure 5.1. In that figure are plotted the difference between his competitive standing (CS) and that of his closest competitor at each week of the campaign (as in figure 4.4), the financial contributions he received each month, his Gallup Poll standing at the time of each survey, and the proportion of *New York Times* stories about the active Democratic candidates each week that was about Jimmy Carter. All of these measures started low, began to rise early in the campaign, and continued to rise virtually unchecked until Carter had won the nomination. If there is ever to be an observable dynamic we might call momentum, Carter had it in 1976.

The measures used require a little explanation. The contributions do not include matching funds, funds raised from sales, or those raised through collections (e.g., sales of bumper stickers, tickets to rock concerts, and fund-raising dinners). The Gallup Poll question used reads

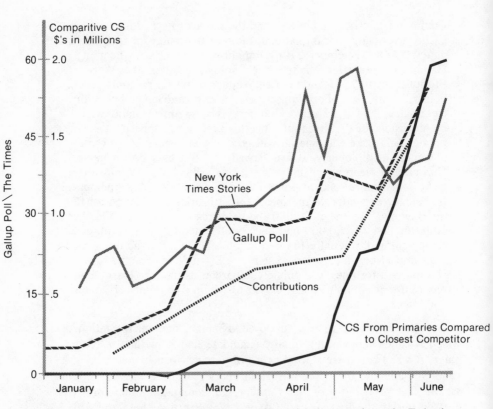

Comparitive CS
$'s in Millions

Gallup Poll \ The Times

60 — 2.0

45 — 1.5

30 — 1.0

New York
Times Stories

Gallup Poll

15 — .5

Contributions

0

CS From Primaries Compared
to Closest Competitor

January | February | March | April | May | June

Figure 5.1   **Jimmy Carter's Momentum.** Financial data are from the Federal
Election Commission's Form 3, line 15D (monthly matching funds
subtracted). Gallup poll information is from the *Gallup Opinion
Index* (Princeton, N.J.: The Gallup Poll), Report 127, February
1976, p. 21; and Report 133, August 1976, pp. 6–7, 12.

as follows: "Here is a list of people who have been mentioned as possible Presidential candidates for the Democratic Party in 1976. Which one would you like to see nominated as the Democratic candidate for President in 1976?" The corresponding question used for Republican contenders listed only Gerald Ford and Ronald Reagan. CS and the method used to analyze the stories in the *New York Times* were explained earlier.

My purpose, in this chapter, is to model some of the dynamic elements of preconvention campaigns and to use this model to examine the fortunes of the candidates in 1976. The mathematical model itself is presented elsewhere.[2] This effort will provide first answers to such questions as why Carter was able to achieve a first-ballot nomination, why others failed, and why the Ford-Reagan campaign took its shape as a closely fought battle throughout the period, while the Democratic race did not.

Basic Dynamics of the Campaign

Any explanation of the dynamics of preconvention campaigns must consist of a number of basic variables as well as their sometimes fairly complex relationships. Here, I identify three general classes of variables and some reasonably simple interactions between them.

The Probability of Winning the Nomination

The idea of momentum and related evaluations of a candidate's fortunes rests on some notion of probability. The central question is, How likely is this candidate to win the nomination? Candidates may be said to have momentum if their chances are improving. This idea is at the heart of any dynamic process in campaigns, and must represent the bottom line to any office-seeking candidates when they ask, "Are things going well? Am I doing better?"

The probability of winning the nomination is not observable directly. The measure of competitive standing (CS) developed in the last chapter is related to it. In the final analysis, winning the nomination is achieved by obtaining the support of a majority of national convention delegates. Along the way, how one candidate is faring in comparison to others and in comparison to remaining opportunities should capture this probability. However, there is more to it than CS.

Success in Primaries and Caucuses

While the candidates are campaigning more or less continually, the campaign moves in fits and starts. Delegates tend to be won in blocs as individual primaries and caucuses culminate. Moreover, the aura of success is generated by events that the media cover. Thus, changes in candidates' fortunes must be tied to the timing and results of specific events, and particularly to the contended primaries that generate most of the delegates and the greatest media attention.

If a candidate's fortunes are tied to success in such primaries, what does success mean? Henry Jackson suffered a setback in the New York primary even though he won more votes and delegates by far than either of his active competitors. In 1968, Eugene McCarthy "defeated" President Johnson in the Democratic primary in New Hampshire, even though Johnson received 49.6% of the vote to McCarthy's 41.9%. In the same primary four years later, Edmund Muskie won 46.4% of the vote but "lost" to George McGovern's 37.1%. How can we explain these interpretations?

The three examples occurred early in the respective campaigns, when there was still a very large pool of available delegates. Further, all three "losers" (Jackson, Johnson, and Muskie) fell short of expectations, while the "winners" exceeded expectations. The question then, becomes one of understanding how expectations are generated. Unfortunately, a rigorous and unproblematic explanation of the formation of expectations is impossible, owing in no small measure to the ill-formed and imprecise nature of the expectations themselves. However, the Jackson example illustrates a major source of expectations, at least among candidates that have any plausible chance at the nomination.

Jackson, like most candidates, developed a plan for winning the nomination. His plan was to reformulate part of the New Deal coalition. The cornerstones of his candidacy were the large, northern, industrial states, with their large proportions of blue-collar workers, ethnic groups, and other traditional Democratic loyalists. To this large bloc of hoped for delegates, Jackson planned to add others, a few from the urbanized, heavily Jewish cities of Florida, for example.

Carter, too, made explicit plans. He hoped to do well enough in early events to look like a serious candidate, to defeat Wallace in southern primaries to cement his hold on southern delegates, and then to combine

this regional base with delegates gathered from other areas. The implication is that candidates plan on a state-by-state basis just where they
can hope to gather a sufficient number of delegates to win the nomination. The expectations about a candidate, then, are based in large part
on what that candidate needs in that state to win the nomination.

Actually, Jackson concentrated most on New York and Pennsylvania.
Massachusetts was added to his core list when it moved the date of its
primary to March 2. (The idea had been to have a regional primary
in New England consisting of Massachusetts, New Hampshire, and Vermont. The New Hampshire legislative, however, moved its primary date
a week ahead so it could hold the first primary). Jackson did not expect
to compete seriously in Illinois, where the nominating procedures were
complex, where Chicago's Mayor Daley was attempting to control an
uncommitted delegate slate headed by Senator Stevenson, and where
Governor Walker was attempting to hold a countering uncommitted
delegate slate. The result was that Jackson, like Udall, left a gap of
one month from the Massachusetts primary to his next major contest.

Combined with these expectations must be an outright first-place victory in a contested primary. At minimum, this victory should occur in
the first primary in the candidate's central core of hoped-for support.
Thus, the April 6 primaries were crucial to both Udall and Jackson.
Udall's narrow loss to Carter in his crucial Wisconsin campaign, which
set back his candidacy, illustrates the importance of a victory. Jackson's
disappointing victory in New York illustrates the interaction of winning
a plurality victory and meeting expectations. One can assume that had
Carter not won in Florida, his campaign would have faltered, possibly
irretrievably. (For more on these points, see the next chapter.)

Donald Matthews has written about this process, arguing that the
media play key roles in creating expectations and also in publicizing
whether the candidates lived up to those expectations. Matthews also
notes several sources the media can and, at times, apparently do use in
creating expectations: past history, polls, results in neighboring states,
and campaign effort.[3] It seems evident that this process of expectation
formation is one aspect of the symbiotic relationship between candidates
and media. It also seems evident that expectations, rough and arbitrary
as they may seem, are based to some extent on the interpretation of
objective and factual evidence (e.g., past history and polls). What is
required is, first, that expectations be formed (and be formed prior

to the primary election or caucus meeting itself) and, second, that there be some "rough consensus," to use Matthews's term, about the expectations.

However formed, exceeding these expectations generates momentum by increasing the candidate's chances for the nomination. Meeting expectations yields no change in the candidate's likelihood of becoming the nominee, but falling short of expectations decreases that likelihood.

One aspect of the dynamics of the preconvention campaign is, thus, the effect on the probability of winning the nomination of the comparison between actual and expected results in contested primaries and other delegate selection procedures. There is a second major aspect of the dynamics, one that involves resources.

Resources

The acquisition and utilization of resources are important elements of the preconvention campaign, as they are in all campaigns. As the Humphrey example illustrated, there is a cyclical phenomenon at work. A small likelihood of success makes raising sufficient money difficult. Failure to raise money in turn makes it difficult or impossible to increase the chance of victory. As we have seen, most of the candidates in the Democratic preconvention campaign withdrew, blaming their defeat in large part on the lack of resources. Carter's history was the exact opposite. His success apparently generated ever-increasing flows of money and other resources. Increased resources in turn improved his chances in later primaries and caucuses and eventually culminated in victory.

"Resources" should be defined here in the most general sense, including four distinct types. First, some resources are more or less unvarying throughout the campaign. For example, Reagan's impeccable credentials as a conservative candidate provided him with a core of committed campaign workers. His effectiveness as a campaigner may also be considered a constant asset.

A second category of resources may vary during the campaign, but in fixed ways known or knowable to all candidates a priori. Reagan's conservatism gave him an advantage over Ford in strongly conservative states. When such a state's primary or caucus came due, he could cash in on his ideological resource. It is less than coincidental that Reagan's string of victories came in the North Carolina, Texas, Alabama, and Georgia primaries and that it ended when the primaries in less conservative states, such as Michigan, were held. Presumably, these assets were knowable by any reasonably informed candidate or observer.

Still other resources or portions thereof may fluctuate, but in ways that are unrelated to campaign events themselves. For example, the ending of federal matching funds in March, and their reinitiation two months later, seriously affected the resources of many candidates, yet was clearly an unforseeable event and external to the campaign itself.

The final type of resource is the most important for this discussion. Some—and some of the most important—resources fluctuate, as the campaign unfolds, in ways that seem directly related to the campaign itself. It is this last class of resources that enters directly into the dynamics of campaigns. Money, media attention, and national popularity are crucial resources, ones that appear to be attained by successful showings in highly publicized and contested primaries. Gallup Poll standings may be interpreted both as a resource and as a measure of success. This point serves to emphasize the close relationship between resources and success. Money, media attention, and popularity are not the only important ones that vary during the course of the campaign, but they are the ones that can be measured systematically.

The central concepts for modeling the dynamics of preconvention campaigns may be summarized as:

1. The probability of winning the nomination.

2. The comparison between actual and expected performance by a candidate, at least in contested and publicized primaries.

3. Actual delegates won, measured by the competitive standing of a candidate.

4. Resources generated and expended, especially those whose rates of acquisition can and presumably do vary with campaign events.

The Model of the Dynamics of the Campaign

Candidates begin the campaign with some sort of resource base, a base that varies both in quantity and type. These resources are cashed in or drawn from to affect the candidate's chances in primaries or caucuses. Everything else being equal, the more resources candidates can draw upon, the better they will do in a primary or caucus. Similarly, the more resources the candidates can bring to bear on a primary or caucus, the worse their opponents will do. Thus, having and expending greater resources will have a positive effect on one's own fortunes and a negative effect on one's opponent's fortunes. Two assumptions of this model are that if candidates can increase their resources, they will and that if candidates have more resources, they will expend them.

The second crucial assumption is that exceeding expectations leads to greater rates of incoming resources. In general, donors give more money to a successful than to an unsuccessful candidate. Other resources undoubtedly increase with success as well. Finally, as a candidate succeeds in primaries and caucuses—relative to expectations and the success of other candidates—his chance of winning the nomination increases. The candidate has momentum.

Unsuccessful candidates face just the opposite, rather bleak, circumstances. Their resources begin to dry up and they cannot compete as effectively in subsequent events. In turn, their potential resources shrink even further. Consequently, their chance of winning the nomination diminishes, for many to a point where, at last, they must withdraw from competition.

The media play central roles in this process. The mechanism that generates many of the variable resources is the report of campaign events. Financial contributions that increase with success are made by individuals who learn of the successes of candidates, as well as about the candidates themselves, primarily through the media. This point is especially true now because recent financial reforms have required much greater emphasis on mass-based fund-raising. Further, the amount of coverage candidates receive in the media is itself a resource.

Mere coverage is particularly important in the early stages of the campaign. At the beginning of the 1976 Democratic campaign, many active candidates were little known by the public. In October 1975, the Gallup organization handed respondents a card with the names of fourteen potential Democratic nominees on it. The question was, "which of these people have you heard something about?" Table 5.1 indicates that most of the actual candidates began the campaign with less than 50% of the public recognizing their names. Even fewer respondents knew any more about the candidates than their name.

As table 5.1 makes obvious, initially high levels of public recognition do not lead to early success. Yet voters must know something about a candidate to support him. The average citizen could learn of a candidate like Carter only through the media. Further, the media help specify and communicate the expectations about each candidate, report whether

Table 5.1   Public Recognition of Names of Potential
Democratic Candidates, October 1975

Name	Percentage of Recognition
Kennedy	96
Wallace	93
Humphrey	91
McGovern	89
Muskie	84
Shriver	76
Jackson	64
Bayh	50
Udall	47
Shapp	31
Carter	29
Bentsen	24
Harris	22
Sanford	21

SOURCE: *Gallup Opinion Index: Campaign '76* (Princeton, N.J.: The Gallup Poll, 1975), p. 98.

or not the candidate exceeded expectations in a given primary, state whether the candidate's probability of winning the nomination is increasing, decreasing, or remaining stable, and in general help interpret the preconvention campaign.

Figure 5.2 is a schematic diagram summarizing the dynamic relationships among the ingredients of the model of a two-candidate campaign such as Ford's and Reagan's. The multicandidate case is essentially the same. One point that deserves special emphasis is that the actions of each candidate affect the fortunes of all the candidates in the contest. For example, if one candidate decides to expend greater resources in a primary, that decision should increase not only his vote in that primary (all else being equal), but should decrease the votes obtained by all other candidates. Similarly, if one candidate does unexpectedly well in a primary or caucus, that strong showing cuts into the results of others. If one candidate's chance for the nomination increases, the chances of other candidates must be affected negatively. In the simplest case, where there are only two candidates, one candidate's success necessarily comes at the expense of the opponent. In multicandidate campaigns, the situation is more complicated. For example, Carter's early success hurt other candidates, but it appears that Udall's chances remained fairly constant

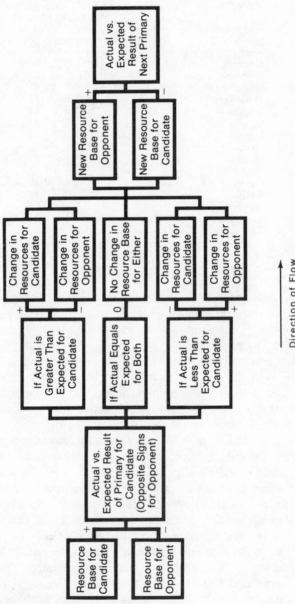

Figure 5.2   Schematic Diagram of the Dynamics of a Two-Candidate Campaign

Direction of Flow

during this period. Later, as Carter continued to sweep towards victory, Brown's campaign also appeared to have momentum. Nonetheless, the campaign of each candidate is inexorably intertwined with that of all opponents.

The Instability of the Campaign

One of the most important questions to which this model is addressed is stability. "Stability," in this context, means that the acquisition of resources, delegates, and votes, and thus the probability of winning the nomination, remain virtually constant. In a stable race, for example, the initial front runner will remain the leading candidate throughout. Only in the unstable campaign is there sufficient permeability to allow the outsider or long shot to emerge as nominee. The Republican campaign would have been stable if the chances of Ford or Reagan receiving the nomination were the same at the end of the period as at its beginning. The Democratic campaign was marked by substantial instability. Thus, one important question is, Under what conditions will a campaign be stable and when will it be unstable?

The following propositions are logical consequences of the formalized model.[4]

Proposition 1. In either the two or multicandidate campaign, the acquisition of resources cannot be stable, and can appear stable only under unusual circumstances (to be discussed below).

Proposition 2. If there are only two candidates in the campaign and if one candidate's resources are increasing, the other's must be decreasing to the same extent.

Proposition 3. In general, the more candidates there are in the race, the less stable it is. Therefore, the 1976 and 1972 Democratic campaigns should have been less stable than the 1976 Republican race.

The idea that stability is apparent only in unusual circumstances (proposition 1) is important. Resources in a campaign will remain stable, for example, if both candidates obtain their expected vote in the primaries. They can, in a two-candidate race, but it becomes impossible in a multicandidate race. For example, in 1976 both Republican candidates had a very good chance at the nomination initially, and the early primaries were very close. However, this apparent stability is knife-edged. Any substantial deviation will upset it, and stability, once upset, is very difficult to reestablish. If Ford had had one or more dramatic victories, instead of very narrow ones, the apparent stability would have been lost, possibly irretrievably. That is, there may be an equilibrium, but it is an unstable one.

The two important conclusions so far are the general instability of all campaigns and its exaggeration as the number of candidates in the race increases. In general, the instability of the multicandidate contest is revealed by the elimination of most candidates, usually fairly early in the campaign (as shown earlier, in fig. 3.3). The winnowing process which was evident in the 1972 and 1976 Democratic campaigns is characteristic of multicandidate campaigns.

A common argument about the rules and procedures that encourage the proliferation of active candidates is that the convention will open with no candidate having enough committed delegates to win. The Democratic National Convention, for example, was previewed as follows in *Newsweek*:

At the moment, it seems unlikely that any candidate will arrive at Madison Square Garden with the 1,505 delegates needed for the nomination. Thus, a spate of high-stakes bargaining is expected among the leading contenders, and Democratic National Chairman Robert Strauss himself is predicting no final resolution before the second or third ballot . . . to help cook up a compromise . . . Strauss is planning to set up a "negotiating committee" that represents all elements in the party.[5]

The fear of some, and the hope of others, is that the convention will be deadlocked. I shall return to this point later, but the implication of proposition 3 and of the consequent winnowing process is that deadlocked conventions become less likely, regardless of the number of opponents.

The first three propositions involve the ability to gather resources and how it changes. We can look at votes, delegates, and expected versus actual results at the polls in much the same way. Doing so yields parallel propositions:

Proposition 4. In either the two or multicandidate campaign, the ability to win votes and hence delegates cannot be stable, and can appear stable only under unusual circumstances. Thus, a candidate who exceeds (or fails to meet) expectations at one event is more likely to exceed (or fail to meet) expectations at other events, and to do so by an increasing amount.

Proposition 5. If there are only two candidates in the campaign, and one exceeds expectations and continues to do so, the other must fail to meet expectations and continue to do so.

Proposition 6. In general, the more candidates there are in the race, the less stable it is.

Proposition 7. There is a decreasing probability that candidates who fail to meet expectations will win the nomination. There is an increasing probability that candidates who exceed expectations will win the nomination—they have momentum.

Proposition 8. Resources and delegates move in tandem. That is, if resource-gathering ability is increasing, so too is the ability to win delegates.

Propositions 4–8 extend the notion of instability. For example, as resources decrease, so too does one's fate at the polls, and hence one's chances at the nomination. Thus, there is Theodore White's cyclical phenomenon in this model, one aspect feeding on the other. Moreover, the possibility of a deadlocked convention is weakened. The greater the number of active candidates at the outset, the greater the instability. The more candidates there are, the greater the role of the dynamics of the primary and caucus system in reducing the number of candidates. Those who fear that deadlocked convention will occur argue that the point of opening up the nomination process was to make the bulk of party members in the electorate influential in choosing the party's standard bearer and to remove the nomination from smoke-filled rooms inhabited by party leaders only. But the real fear is that opening up the process too much will have the ironic effect of tending to close it up again through indecisiveness. The instability of the preconvention campaign, an instability that is greater the more candidates there are, implies that a large number of candidates will not alone produce deadlocked conventions. On the contrary, the larger the number of active candidates, the greater the tendency to narrow the field during the preconvention campaign. The dynamics simply force large numbers of candidates out of the field. This tendency does not eliminate the possibility of a deadlocked convention, but it does reduce its probability.

In 1976, Hubert Humphrey presented himself as a candidate who would not conduct an active campaign, but would be an alternative should the preconvention campaign prove indecisive. This strategy was not unique. Adlai Stevenson, in 1960, and Richard Nixon, in 1964, used a similar strategy. In none of those elections did a crowded field yield a deadlocked convention; rather, a dominant candidate emerged from the preconvention campaign. Carter's emergence as front runner meant that Humphrey had to make an agonizing personal decision following the Pennsylvania primary. It was clear to all that if he were to have any chance at the nomination, he would have to enter the New Jersey primary and campaign actively there (and, likely, elsewhere). He chose not to do so, and his hopes for the 1976 nomination ended. As we have seen, this emergence of a front runner should not be surprising at all. The opposite case should be considered the more unusual. While, for a variety of personal reasons, Humphrey, Nixon, and Stevenson could not or would not make an active bid for the nomination, they should have (and well may have) recognized that their chances were poor, at best.

Recent Reforms

Two conclusions can be drawn about the impact of the recent reforms on the preconvention campaign. First, the reformulation of delegate selection procedures has strengthened the dynamic forces. The central question is the influence of party leaders versus the influence of the public at large. The reforms have shifted the balance heavily toward the side of the public. When party leaders hold the power, they can be relatively uninterested in the rise and fall of a candidate's popularity, publicity, financial support, and even public preference as expressed in primaries and caucuses, *if* they choose to be. The reforms have created a system in which the bulk of the delegates is selected directly by the electorate; thus, one that can be influenced by the dynamics outlined here. The growing use and reporting of public expressions of opinion, notably in regular Gallup and other public opinion polls, have led to a direct and undeniable quantitative measurement of the candidates' changing popularity. The various media have conducted much more immediate, extensive, and direct coverage of preconvention campaigns, bringing the nomination campaign home to the public. Finally, the financial reforms have created a system in which financial support must be drawn, much more than before, from broad segments of the public. All these changes have led to a nominating system in which the dynamic aspects play a larger and more important role.

The financial reforms were designed in part to minimize the influence of money in politics. One sense in which the phrase "money in politics" is used is to indicate the influence of a very few, very large contributors on presidential politics. This influence has been curtailed. However, in a second sense, the problem has not been attacked directly. Candidates must still rely primarily on contributions to finance their campaigns. To the extent that campaign money is central, the fortunes of candidates rest on their ability to generate funds, an ability that shifts with the candidates' electoral successes. The matching funds provisions do not reduce the importance of money in politics. If anything, these provisions exaggerate it by doubling the impact of each dollar given (at least, within the limits described in chapter 3). Thus, a candidate with momentum generates not just more money, but nearly twice as much money as could be generated without matching funds. *Complete* federal funding, of course, would eliminate this important role that money still plays in politics.

Strategy

Candidates are not unaware of the importance of dynamics. Questions of timing, of building to a peak at the right time, and of gaining momentum often color the candidates' discussions of their strategies. Candidates are not only cognizant of these dynamics, they attempt to capitalize on them in creating or modifying their strategies.

One interpretation of campaign dynamics is that they are facets of the institutional context of preconvention campaigns. Candidates who ignore or are ignorant of them run the same risk as those who ignore the rules and laws governing financial regulations or the selection of delegates; they are likely to select poor strategies.

The dynamics of the campaign, thus, are not mechanistic. Rather, they are manipulable, and they are manipulable by rational, goal-seeking candidates.

Carter's strategy, for example, was designed to capture momentum by successes in early caucuses and primaries. The Massachusetts primary became central to Jackson's plans only after its date was set early in the campaign. Until then, Jackson thought of the New York primary as his first showdown. All the candidates' budgets are based on the assumption that more money will be available for later events if they are successful in earlier ones. Few seriously project income far into the future, and virtually no candidate fails to spend nearly all funds on hand when key events arise. Candidates enter small and early primaries, such as New Hampshire, not to capture the few delegates available there but on the hopes of obtaining large spillovers for later events. Candidates also refuse to enter primaries if they decide that a negative spillover is likely. In short, the dynamics of the campaign are integral to the candidates' decisions. Candidates attempt to set, to alter, and to capitalize on the dynamics of the campaign.

In chapter 4, it was argued that the electability of a potential nominee ought to be reflected in voting behavior. That is, success in one primary should increase success in a later primary, as more and more participants resolve the various tradeoffs in favor of a candidate who has demonstrated strength in the voting booth. At the same time, the citizen is able to gather more information about the personality and policies of a candidate from past performance and the greater news coverage attendant upon success in an earlier primary. With more (and more favorable) information available about a successful candidate, potential participants become more likely to support that candidate. This last point is particularly crucial to the candidate who begins as a relative unknown. Alternatively, the candidate who does poorly, especially one who does so unexpectedly, is likely to receive less positive treatment by the media. Further, the lack of success is usually attributable to a poor campaign or to the demonstration of some weakness. Thus there is likely to be a more negative evaluation of the unsuccessful candidate by the average citizen, as the candidate appears less and less electable.

Uncertainty

There is one more important ingredient in this model—uncertainty and unforeseen events. This uncertainty looms large early in the campaign, when candidates are first testing themselves and their strategies. Later, when some voter reaction has developed and, in multicandidate contests, when the field has narrowed, the uncertainty lessens. Voters in early primaries and caucuses must make decisions with less information about candidates, their qualifications, their positions, and their track record in earlier events.

This great uncertainty affects the dynamics of the campaign. At the first event, for example, no candidate has momentum. Generally, too, the first few primaries are as crowded with active competitors as any events will be that year. The difference between first place and second, third, even fourth may swing on but a few thousand votes. Carter edged out Udall by fewer than 4,600 votes in New Hampshire; Ford defeated Reagan in New Hampshire by fewer than 1,600 votes.

Had McGovern received the votes given to inactive candidates in the 1972 New Hampshire primary, he would have outpolled Muskie. Had Muskie picked up those votes (and it is likely that he would have received most of them), his first-place "defeat" would have been large enough to have been perceived as a victory, and his campaign would not have been untracked there. All these possibilities were well within the range of uncertainty attendant upon the first few primaries. Had they eventuated, the Democratic campaign would have been quite different than it was.

The point, of course, is that even miniscule variations in early events would have changed the dynamics of most of the recent nomination campaigns. The smallest changes in strategy could have led to very different results. A more efficient get-out-the-vote campaign by Udall's organization in New Hampshire in 1976, for example, might have given him an early win and momentum. It certainly would have slowed, if not stopped, Carter's.

Evidence about the Propositions

What sort of evidence can be marshaled to document these propositions concerning the dynamics of the campaign, and what can this evidence tell us about the 1976 campaigns? One sort of evidence is the candidates' own views of the dynamics of their preconvention campaigns. A second type of evidence is based on a more systematic examination of available data.

Quotations used throughout this book reflect the actors' belief that there is something to momentum and related dynamics. Three further quotations, two from Republicans and the other from a Democrat, solidify this view.

Reagan's pollster, Richard Wirthlin, in discussing Reagan's general preconvention campaign strategy, noted the importance of the first primary:

> Some have said that the Reagan strategy appeared erratic. I think it was really two-tiered, rather than erratic. The first tier was heavily based upon developing momentum out of New Hampshire. I was skeptical of that initially, because I had read all of the classic academic papers which say that the bandwagon effect doesn't exist.

But then we did some very careful analysis of the impact of the New Hampshire primary on past elections, particularly on the Democratic side, and found that we could expect either a gain or loss of about fifteen to eighteen percentage points in the primaries following. I turned from being a skeptic to being a strong supporter of the momentum hypothesis.[6]

John Sears, Reagan's campaign director, followed these comments with a statement illustrating the uncertainty attendant upon and the exogenous factors which can have a material effect on the dynamics, particularly in early events such as New Hampshire:

One more thing: I've always believed that weather doesn't have much to do with anything, but I can recall getting off the plane on primary day and noticing that it was some ungodly temperature for that time of year in New Hampshire—like forty degrees—and the sun was out. And I found out that evening that more people than expected had voted that day. Even though the race itself was very close, we felt that, with our superior organization, we could deliver the votes that were there for us. Usually, if your organization in a primary is better than the other fellow's, that's worth a point or two. What actually happened in New Hampshire, though, was that a lot of people voted on their own, without benefit of organizational help. We thought approximately 100,000 people would vote; actually about 110,000 people voted. I strongly suspect that the extra 10,000 people, who had indicated in the polls earlier that they had little interest in actually voting, mostly voted for the incumbent.[7]

Udall expressed a poignant view of momentum:

We had thirty primaries, presumably all of them equal. After three of those primaries, I'm convinced it was all over. The die was cast. . . . If there was ever a state in America where I was entitled to relax and feel confident, it was Wisconsin. . . . Well, I take a poll two weeks before the primary and [Carter's] ahead of me, two to one, and he has never been in the state except for a few quick visits. That was purely and solely and only the product of that narrow win in New Hampshire and that startling win in Florida.

It's like a football game, in which you say to the first team that makes a first down with ten yards, "Hereafter your team has a special rule. Your first downs are five yards. And if you make three of those you get a two-yard first down. And we're going to let your first touchdown count twenty-one points. Now the rest of you bastards play catch-up under the regular rules."[8]

The Republican Campaign

Let us review the propositions relevant to a two-candidate campaign, listed earlier in this chapter. Resources (proposition 1), and the ability to win votes and, have delegates by exceeding expectations (proposition 4) are unstable except under unusual circumstances. As one candidate's ability to acquire resources increases, the other's decreases (proposition 2). There is a very close correspondence between variation in the acquisition of resources and the success or failure of the candidate's campaign (proposition 8). Does the available evidence about the Republican campaign of 1976 support these propositions?

The last chapter contained an overview of the outcome of several primaries, and the following two points were made about the Republican contest. First, neither candidate was able to make a significant advance comparable to Carter's in 1976 or McGovern's in 1972. There were more modulated variations that fell into three periods: a Ford victory phase (from the New Hampshire primary to a time prior to the Texas primary on May 1); a Reagan victory phase (from May 1 to the Maryland and Michigan primaries two weeks later); and a final phase of mixed results. In figure 4.2, these changes were graphed in terms of the CS measure. At the end of the Ford victory phase, the president had a 316 delegate edge over Reagan. In less than one week, this edge fell to 99 delegates. At the end of the Reagan victory phase, Ford's edge climbed to 169 delegates, and he maintained that level throughout the mixed results phase.

If proposition 8 (that resources and delegates move in tandem) is correct, then resources should have changed in the same way. While there was no clear break in resource acquisition, as will be found on the Democratic side, there was a systematic, if dampened, set of phases.

The data relevant to these propositions are drawn from three sources. The first are Gallup Poll reports of Republican identifiers' preferences for Ford or Reagan as nominee. The standings of the two candidates in the various polls conducted between January and August are reported in figure 5.3. Two other resources are money contributed by individuals to each candidate (reported monthly and reproduced in the appendix) and media coverage (see the appendix for the proportion of stories about the two candidates each week in the *New York Times* and *Washington Post*).

Even cursory examination of these three sorts of data over the course of the campaign demonstrates the plausibility of proposition 1. That

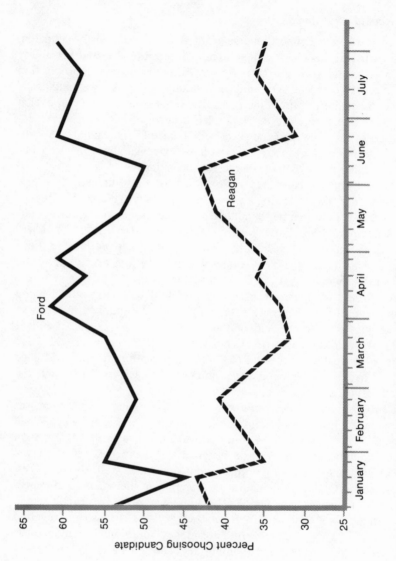

Figure 5.3   **Gallup Poll Standing of Ford and Reagan**

proposition proposes that there should be variation in resource acquisition over time. Even though neither Republican was able to break significantly from a close, competitive campaign, each resource shows ebbs and flows. The more important question is whether or not these ebbs and flows align with each other and with electoral success.

Evaluation of the relative attention paid to the two candidates in newspapers presents two problems. First, many news stories covered both candidates. The most common type of story, for example, concerned where candidates were campaigning and what their prospects were in the next primary. This symmetrical coverage, however, measures the competitiveness of the campaign and is therefore consistent with proposition 8. Second, news stories are sensitive to short-term fluctuations. Since the media cover current events, their attention shifts to what is apparently most newsworthy at the time. For example, the Pennsylvania primary was a "Democratic primary" only, so attention was focused on Carter, Jackson, and Udall there. But covering what is newsworthy is what makes media attention a variable resource. For example, the shift toward coverage of Reagan in early April (especially in the *Times*) measures reportage of his TV address, whereas his edge in July (especially in the *Post*) captures his selection of Senator Schweiker as running mate. And that is just what Reagan planned. The coverage of his TV address had the desired effect of attracting attention, allowing him to refocus his campaign effectively in the hope of recapturing electoral initiative in the Texas and subsequent primaries.

Given the above, variation in candidate coverage was perforce modulated. Even so, there are signs of the three campaign periods. The Ford victory phase is perceptible in the *Times*, the Reagan victory phase in the *Post*, and the mixed results phase is reflected in even coverage in both papers. In short, there was *some* instability, in line with proposition 1, and this instability corresponded to the changes in the outcome of primaries, which is consistent with proposition 8. Interestingly, both papers covered Ford more heavily after the primaries, at a time very close to the point at which Philip Straffin argues that a Ford bandwagon began.[9]

Financial contributions fluctuated widely. Unfortunately, they were reported monthly, so that only four observations, corresponding to February through May, are directly relevant to the major portion of the delegate selection phase. June figures are irrelevant in part because both candidates, especially Ford, had already raised close to the maximum amount allowed to be spent by law. Even during this short period, each candidate raised nearly $1.5 million more in his most successful month than in his least. To be sure, there was a systematic trend of increased financial contributions (the combined contributions to Ford and Reagan increased by $320,000 per month from February to May; the correlation with time was .49). Nonetheless, there were wide fluctuations. The candidate able to raise more money changed virtually each month. In March, Ford raised some $1.37 million more than Reagan, but Reagan raised $741,000 more than Ford in April and the two raised equal amounts in May. Ford's financial strength in March corresponds with his victory phase. Reagan's gain in April is more than accounted for by the contributions garnered by his televised address (more than $1 million). The May figures, which reflected Reagan's victory string and the subsequent period of mixed results, is at least not inconsistent with proposition 8. At the very gross level of available financial data, both propositions 1 and 8 are reasonably well supported by the monetary figures.

The Gallup Poll measured support among partisans more frequently, but somewhat erratically. These data present strong evidence for the propositions about resources. Between the Gallup Poll that preceded the first primary and the last Gallup Poll, taken two weeks after the last primaries, there are nine relevant measures of Republican opinion. Ford never trailed Reagan in these polls, but his lead varied from as few as 7 to as many as 30 percentage points. This range was large enough to have allowed Ford to make varying claims about his popular support. Interestingly, support for each candidate increased slightly because of a movement away from responses that could be group as "others" and "unsure." Ford's popularity increased by one-third point per poll, Reagan's by about one-fifth.

Proposition 8 implies that the candidates' standings in the polls are related to the outcome of primaries. The evidence for this proposition is strong. The close outcome in New Hampshire was reflected in the post-primary poll; Ford and Reagan supporters were divided as equally as in any intraprimary poll. Ford's victory phase was reflected in an ever-widening gap. Reagan's nadir came just before his televised address which, at best, produced a slight increase in his popularity. Ford, in the meantime, continued to gain until his peak of support, about 60%, was reached. After the Texas primary, Reagan made substantial gains; Ford's support waned. This convergence continued until the poll taken two weeks after the last primaries. Again, this sharp change corresponds closely to Straffin's identification of a Ford bandwagon. Reagan was unable to make significant gains until after his first major, clearcut victory in Texas, just as McGovern's popularity in 1972 did not increase until his first outright victory.

Most of the polls were taken soon after selected primaries, presumably to measure the consequences of the primary on partisan support of candidates. One crucial aspect of the model of the dynamics of campaigns is that there is a close correspondence between actual votes and public-opinion polls. If the change in Ford's support, as measured by the Gallup Poll, is correlated with the change in his CS between primaries, we indeed find a close correspondence ($r = .92$). The acquisition of delegates, that is, is very closely related to popularity.

Since the three resources were measured at such disparate and irregular times, it is difficult to provide systematic evidence of the proposition that the flows of resources move in tandem. Yet my discussion suggests that the flow of each resource aligns at least roughly with the outcomes. Broadly, the various resources ebb and flow systematically.

Proposition 2, which refers to two-candidate campaigns, is that changes favorable to one candidate come at the expense of the opponent. Given the data, it is difficult to test this proposition. By definition, the news stories about Ford are those not about Reagan. Thus the proposition is upheld perfectly, but artificially. Much the same is true of the Gallup Poll reports about support, except insofar as respondents chose some other Republican or withheld judgment entirely. The correlation between the change in Ford's popularity and the change in Reagan's during the nine polls is $-.83$. Only the very few and highly time-aggregated financial contributions offer a direct test. The correlation between contributions to Ford and Reagan supports the proposition moderately well ($r = -.31$). At the very least, there is some positive and no negative evidence for proposition 2.

The evidence for all eight propositions is, I believe, quite clear. The model predicts instability, but I have argued that there was modulated instability throughout the campaign. The pattern is thus not inconsistent with the model, particularly when juxtaposed with the efforts of the candidates to regulate these forces (see the following discussion, particularly about Reagan's strategic moves). However, the pattern is also not inconsistent with the concept of oscillation about a point of equilibrium. That is, these data do not allow one to distinguish these two predictions. Formally, however, the model of the dynamics of the campaign cannot result in oscillatory behavior about an equilibrium.[10] It is not clear what sort of data could be gathered to distinguish between "apparent stability," in part governed by the candidate's behavior, and oscillation about a stable equilibrium.

The Democratic Campaign

The same propositions, excepting 2 and 5, apply to a multicandidate campaign. Propositions 3 and 6 should hold; in particular, resources and delegates should be even more unstable than in a two-candidate contest. Within the unstable multi-candidate model, however, it is possible for one or more campaigns to seem stable.

The outcome of the Democratic primaries was also divided into three phases: the winnowing phase (through North Carolina), the emergence of Carter as the dominant candidate (until the Nebraska primary), and the late-challengers. According to proposition 8, these same phases should be discernible in the flow of resources. Gallup Poll preferences of Democratic identifiers are reported in figures 5.4 and 5.5. Financial and media data are reported in the appendix.

The fortunes of the various candidates must be summarized in quite different forms. Some, notably Carter and Brown (upon commencing his active candidacy), are best described as having increasing resources. The resources of others, especially Wallace, dwindled. The resources of Jackson, Udall, and others were either stable or nonmonotonic.

Such a characterization is of course to say that proposition 8 is supported. In effect, the campaign periods amount to an overlaying of these various changes in candidate status. Carter, for example, had a more or less continuous drive toward the nomination. Wallace's campaign typified those "winnowed out" in the first few primaries, except that he, unlike Bayh or Shriver for example, did not formally withdraw (perhaps because he started with an unusually large base of resources). Jackson's success in Massachusetts is reflected by a growth in resources, and that enabled him to survive this first period, only to be vanquished in the second. Udall was able to survive the first winnowing phase but did not achieve any primary victory. Thus, he was able to keep a low but rather constant rate of resource acquisition and maintain a string of credible second place finishes. Carter's continuous increase was virtually unchecked by the two late entrants, but Brown like Carter fashioned a victory string—and a more or less continuous increase in resources.

Church also was not defeated outright, and his pattern of resource flows paralleled Udall's.

Carter's standings in the Gallup Poll (fig. 5.4), while somewhat irregular, are roughly linear. From one poll to the next, his standing increased an average of 3.7 points (r = .88). Brown's popularity, even if somewhat inflated at the start, increased by 1.5 points per poll (r = .70). Measured from the first poll after he began his national campaign, Brown's standing actually increased 2.5 points per poll (r = .95) (fig. 5.5).

Similarly, the coverage of Carter's campaign in the two national papers surveyed increased by nearly two stories per week: a correlation of .84 in the *New York Times* and .76 in the *Washington Post*. Brown also made rather clear and rapid inroads into this medium until the end of the primary season.

Contributions to all Democrats, except Carter, were much less than to either Republican, and Carter's reached their height only at the very end. Nonetheless, exactly two Democrats gathered as much as $0.5 million dollars in any one primary month; Carter, in April to June and Brown, in May and June. In general, financial contributions to both these candidates rose.

Although both Carter's and Brown's campaigns gained in intensity, the gains were not continuous throughout the campaign. Carter, for example, was not able to gather relatively large sums of money until May. The media coverage he received was also not relatively large until after the first primaries in April. Carter's popularity, which rose quickly following his early wins, then leveled off in April. Only after Jackson had withdrawn and Humphrey had failed to campaign actively did Carter popularity begin to exceed Humphrey's (fig. 5.4). At that point, Carter's standing in the polls of Democrats moved toward and then beyond 50%.

George Wallace began his 1976 campaign with very large sums of money contributed in 1975 and earlier. He was also the favorite for the nomination in the Gallup Poll of active Democrats (fig. 5.5). His coverage by the media was as extensive as any of his rivals. He was unable to sustain his resources at these levels for long, however. He lost an average of more than a point in each succeeding Gallup Poll, and this decline was almost linear (r = −.89). After his defeat in Florida, Wallace lost more than 2% in coverage by the *New York Times* each week

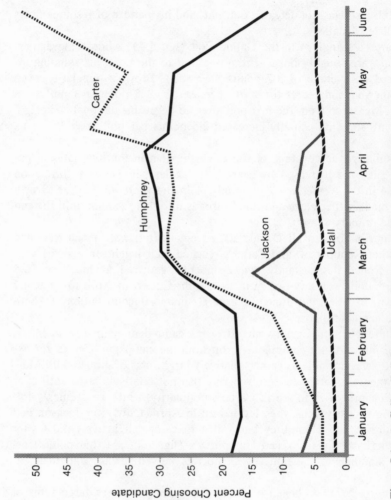

Figure 5.4   Gallup Poll Standing of Carter, Humphrey, Jackson, and Udall

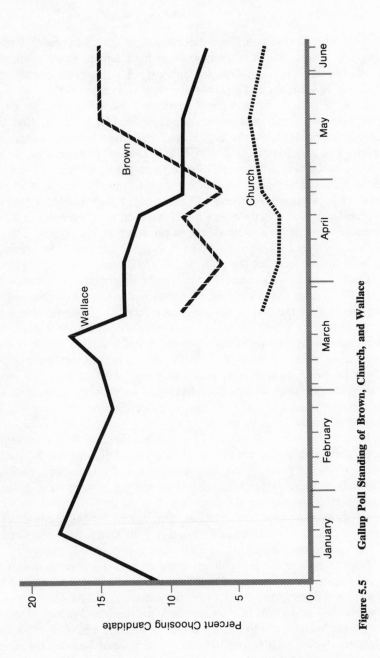

Figure 5.5   Gallup Poll Standing of Brown, Church, and Wallace

(r = —.91). In the course of the campaign, the coverage of Wallace dropped almost one story each week in both papers (r = —.70, *New York Times*; r = —.67, *Washington Post*). His financial contributions declined as well, about $300,000 per month (r = —.76).

It is, of course, more difficult to discuss the effect of time on the candidates who were winnowed out. It is notable, however, that such candidates as Bayh, Harris, and Shriver began the primary season with levels of popularity, media attention, and rates of contributions not dissimilar to Carter's. Bayh and Shriver, for example, were favored by more Democrats for the nomination than Carter. All three, who were soon to be winnowed out, trailed Carter but slightly in media attention before (and even shortly after) the New Hampshire primary, and their financial contributions were of the same order of magnitude. The differences between Carter's candidacy and these others can be attributed only to his successes at the polls and their failures.

Udall and Church's resources can best be described as constant—and low. To be sure, Church received a substantial amount of attention from the media near the end of the campaign. Basically, however, these two candidates were unable to achieve any breakthrough in resources. Neither increased his popular standing by as much as five points. Udall's popularity increased linearly (r = .78), but only .025 percent per poll. Their financial contributions failed to exceed $0.5 million per month during the primary season. Like Bayh and the others, both were able to meet or exceed Carter's resources before his first few victories, but could not budge from these low levels.

Jackson's resources were curvilinear rather than linear. Contributions, popularity, and media attention rose to a peak following his Massachusetts victory but generally declined thereafter. Indeed, his New York and Pennsylvania campaigns were visible in news reportage only. Even in those states, considering the fewer numbers of active candidates to be covered, his reportage in and around the time of the Massachusetts primary exceeded any subsequent period. Of all Democrats, his fortunes alone can be described best as a rise and fall.

With respect to the propositions themselves, then, it is clear that the propositions of instability are supported very well. If there is a tendency toward any limits, they have to be the extremes. While Carter rose to dominate all opponents in resources and in delegates, Wallace, Jackson, and those winnowed-out earlier found both their resources and their prospects fading well before the end of the primary season. Udall and, to a lesser extent, Church provided examples of tranquility—but stability at very low levels. Only Brown's campaign was exceptional, paralleling Carter's campaign two months earlier. Making swift gains in a short period of time, he refused to concede the nomination to Carter until weeks after the primary season had ended, a refusal consistent with the concept of momentum offered here.

The preceding discussion demonstrates, I hope, the plausibility of the relationship between the flow of resources and success in acquiring delegates stated in proposition 8. The failures of most Democrats illustrates the proposition, as does the success of Carter and Brown. Jackson's only major success is quite clearly reflected in his resources. Even more striking is the failure of his plurality in New York (a substantially larger plurality than in Massachusetts) to show up in the resource figures. Instead, his failure to meet self-proclaimed expectations is visible in decreased resources; a point precisely consistent with the model of campaign dynamics. Perhaps the only anomaly is presented by Church, whose several victories led to increases in media attention only—but even there, well after his first victory.

It is more difficult to establish that changes in a Democratic candidate's CS affected, say, his Gallup Poll standing. Even so, the correlation for Carter's campaign was substantial ($r = .44$).

In sum, there is very little evidence that contradicts the propositions and a great deal of supportive data. Both parties' campaigns are not well described by stability of resources or delegates, nor do the variations appear to converge toward some stable equilibrium. The variations in electoral fortunes, however, seem to be closely related to the flow of resources. Moreover, while neither campaign can be described as stable, the Democratic campaign, with its larger field of candidates, was substantially less stable than the Republican.

Momentum and Bandwagons

Wirthlin, in his comments about the role of New Hampshire in generating campaign momentum, noted that he was familiar with "classic academic papers which say that the bandwagon effect doesn't exist." Actually, there is an academic literature that claims that bandwagons can indeed exist under the appropriate conditions.[11] The question is, Are bandwagons and momentum identical or related?

The answers are, quite simply, that the two phenomena are different and that there is no logical connection between them. *Momentum*, as used here, refers to increases in a candidate's chance of winning the nomination. The connection between momentum and resources, as measured here, involves the candidate's strategy and the public's response to it. Much of the academic literature dealing with what I call bandwagon effects is an examination of the decisions of the party élite in general and the delegates to the national convention in particular. Thus, the essential actors are not the candidates. A second major distinction is that the typical bandwagon, once it begins to roll, *inevitably* leads to the victory of the candidate fortunate enough to benefit from it.

While there is a sense of inevitability in momentum, it is not an irreversible phenomenon. A candidate can gain momentum and lose it, just as Ford gained in his early victory phase and slowed down later. Moreover, when there are more than two candidates, it is possible for two or even more of them to gain momentum simultaneously. Both Carter's and Brown's campaigns gained momentum toward the end. Therefore, momentum does not guarantee victory, whereas a bandwagon does. The existence of a bandwagon, therefore, may be discernible only retrospectively (and the same may be true about distinguishing momentum that leads to a bandwagon). However, formal models of bandwagons contain predictions of points at which bandwagons take off. In these cases, bandwagons can be predicted.[12]

The authors of the literature about bandwagons usually assume that delegates and party leaders are independent actors who can affect the nomination materially in convention balloting or in the proverbial smoke-filled rooms. A central argument made throughout this book is that this assumption has become increasingly implausible. Except in unusual circumstances, recent nominations have been decided prior to the party conventions, and the recent reforms have reinforced this trend. The uncommitted delegates and those committed to a candidate who has since withdrawn form the bulk of delegates who can act independently, at least until after the first few ballots at the convention. It is only when a nomination is close that there are sufficient numbers of free delegates to generate the classic bandwagon.

The 1976 Republican campaign was close enough that the relatively few uncommitted delegates and those selected in very late caucuses could become decisive and initiate a bandwagon. Philip Straffin has modeled the bandwagon situation, derived a "bandwagon curve," and applied it to this campaign. The bandwagon curve is based on the number of delegates committed to one candidate, to the other, and as yet uncommitted, much like the CS developed here. Once one candidate has a sufficient

edge and the bandwagon curve is crossed, he should win the nomination as the uncommitted delegates flock to his standard. Straffin found
that "the path entered the bandwagon region for Ford in week 22—
more precisely, on July 17, when the Connecticut delegation gave Ford
35 votes." He marshaled evidence in support of this claim. Two pieces
of evidence here buttress his claim. First, Ford's Gallup Poll standing
increased rapidly, and Reagan's decreased just as markedly, very near
July 17 (actually preceding it by a week or so). Second, both national
newspapers turned their attention to Ford at precisely that time, attention later offset only by Reagan's last minute gamble of selecting
Schweiker as his running mate, a move Straffin attributed to Reagan's
awareness of the bandwagon effect.[13]

While precise calculations of the complex Democratic campaign are
impossible to make, it is clear that Carter's edge must have exceeded
the bandwagon curve at or near June, the month of his Ohio triumph.
At any rate, Democratic party leaders and most of his remaining opponents swung over to Carter publicly very shortly thereafter. That is, Carter benefited from a bandwagon at that time. Before the collapse of his
opposition, Carter did not have the committed support of a majority of
the convention delegates. However, the bandwagon did not make a winner out of a likely loser. Rather, it merely served to affirm the obvious.
Carter had in fact won the nomination before the bandwagon rolled.

Collat, Kelley, and Rogowski have provided a rather different model
of "bandwagons" than Straffin's.[14] Their findings are not dissimilar,
however. They, too, find "bandwagon-like" effects in contended conventions and in polls of delegates prior to the conventions. They find
as well that primary voters' preferences for candidates are susceptible
to bandwagon-like forces that have been termed "momentum" here,
although they are weaker forces than those among delegates as independent actors in conventions. However, they were not able to find
bandwagons, per se, in primary elections. Thus, their broader definitions, models, and data supplement well the arguments made here.

Polls and Primaries in Previous Campaigns

Sufficient data for full analysis of resources and electoral success in
previous nomination campaigns are unobtainable. However, Gallup has
been asking similar questions about the preferences of self-identified
partisans since 1936. The purpose of this section is to demonstrate that

the patterns of support in 1976 were not unique. Rather, polls and primaries have been related throughout our recent electoral history, and something very much like the dynamics of the 1976 campaign can be found in other years.

James Beniger has studied the relationship between Gallup preferences and primary election returns over the period from 1936 to 1972. He asked three questions. First, Do the outcomes of primaries yield immediate changes in the poll standings? The answer is yes, they do lead to immediate changes. On average, winning a plurality in any primary yielded an increase of 3.36 points for Democratic and 0.93 points for Republican candidates in the immediately subsequent poll. Other candidates fell by about 0.50 points. This change is most pronounced after winning a plurality in the earliest primaries. The New Hampshire primary, always the first, yielded a net gain of 8.38 points for the winner and a loss of 1.00 for all others. (This relationship holds even though in 1968 and 1972 the Democratic plurality victor was perceived as the loser.) The Wisconsin primary, always early and usually the second, yielded the next largest average gain for the winner (5.60 points) and was the second most harmful primary to all other candidates (a loss of 3.38 points). Thus, winning helps a candidate's standing, and winning early helps a lot.

Beniger's second question involved the relationship between the number of primary victories and the extent of the increase in support in immediately subsequent polls. He found a strong, positive relationship. The larger the percentage of victories a candidate has in primaries he contested up to a given date, the larger the increase in national popularity in the next poll.

Beniger's last question was addressed to whether a high standing in the poll prior to the first primary is related to the percentage of victories in primaries entered. Thus, he was asking about a reciprocal relationship between polls and primaries, one that is at the heart of the dynamics of campaigns modeled here. In our terms, he asked if candidates with larger resources, at least of this one type, can translate them into correspondingly large electoral successes. His answer was a resounding yes; he found a very powerful relationship between initial popularity and success in the voting booth.

Beniger also found an historical trend that supports the arguments made here. He postulated a "general model of nomination campaigns." That is, "the conventions almost always nominate the candidate with the greatest support among party voters" at the outset of the campaign. "This," he wrote, "is a model in which state primary elections, held in the closing months of the campaign, might be expected to play relatively little part." He concluded, however, "that the general model—accurate for earlier campaigns—may be breaking down." In particular, he found that most of the exceptions to his general model occurred in the most recent election years.[15]

The 1976 Democratic campaign is another notable exception, and the rationale for this breakdown (i.e., the change in the institutional structure of preconvention campaigns) has been argued throughout this book.

These historical averages, then, support the model developed here. A more detailed look at the 1972 Democratic campaign further supports these propositions. Figure 5.6 is a graph of the changes in fortunes of the principal candidates. Edmund Muskie started as the acknowledged frontrunner and led all comers in the Gallup Polls taken prior to the first primary in 1972. Thereafter, his national following fell even more rapidly than Wallace's in 1976. The reason for this decline can be traced to his electoral fortunes even more clearly than Wallace's four years later.[16] Muskie's "disappointing" victory in New Hampshire, followed by a very poor fourth-place finish in Florida a week later, generated the very opposite of momentum; a downslide from which he was unable to recover.

Humphrey's standings in 1972 were similar to Jackson's or Udall's in 1976 (cf. fig. 5.4). His high initial support in the polls remained essentially constant (like Udall's), rising a few points to a peak following his victories in Pennsylvania and Ohio (like Jackson's following his Massachusetts victory). Then it declined to its original level after his defeats in such May primaries as Nebraska, Maryland, Michigan, and Oregon, and especially after his loss to McGovern in California. Humphrey won or did well in many primaries in 1972 (in fact, he received a few more votes than McGovern overall), but he was unable to put together the necessary victory string. Thus, his relatively high standings in the polls was maintained, but momentum was not attained.

A comparison of figs. 5.4 and 5.6 also shows that McGovern's fortunes paralleled Carter's four years later. McGovern's surprising showing in New Hampshire hurt Muskie, but did not help McGovern much. The Wisconsin primary, on the other hand, demonstrates the importance of a clearcut victory. Following his plurality victory in Wisconsin, McGovern quickly rose in the polls (like Reagan after the Texas primary).

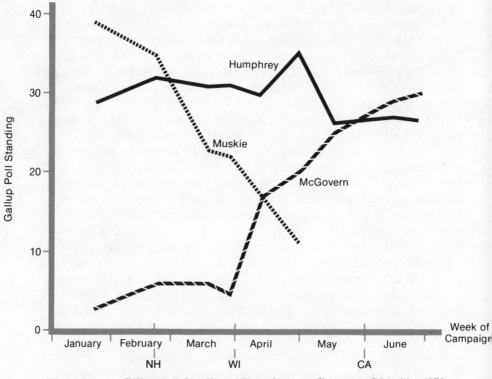

Figure 5.6   **Gallup Poll Standing of Humphrey, McGovern, and Muskie, 1972.**
Data were adapted from the *Gallup Opinion Index* (Princeton,
N.J.: The Gallup Poll), Report 125, pp. 41–48.

He augmented his first win with subsequent ones in Nebraska, Oregon, California, and elsewhere. This series of electoral successes led to (and presumably benefited from) the sort of dramatic increase in popularity matched only by Carter in 1976. McGovern was the first choice of only 3% of the Democrats in January and of only 5% at the end of March. By the end of the 1972 primary season, he was the most preferred Democratic candidate.

These data establish that the dynamics of the 1976 campaign were not exceptional. Rather, such dynamics are common to all nomination campaigns. Further, the parallels between the two Democratic campaigns of the 1970s are strong. Several of the more refined conclusions reached by studying the 1976 campaign are also reinforced: the instability of preconvention campaigns; the possibility of a stable campaign for one candidate amidst a generally unstable campaign; the importance of an outright victory, preferably early; the importance of subsequent victories in augmenting that first one; the importance of avoiding a failure to meet expectations, especially in key and early states; and the apparent inevitability of momentum or its negative once there has been a significant turn in the candidate's fortunes.

Momentum and Campaign Strategy

Momentum does not lead inexorably to victory, as a bandwagon does. However, the dynamics of a campaign, as modeled here, do have a sense of inevitability. Preconvention campaigns are unstable, and stability can be realized only under special conditions. Once the competitive balance is substantially tipped, candidates with momentum have an increasing probability of attaining the nomination, while candidates whose chances begin to decline substantially will see them continue to decline until they are forced to retire from active competition. Inevitably, then, it is very important to achieve a major breakthrough in an early caucus or, even better, an early primary. The importance attached to the New Hampshire primary is not misplaced. The first contested primary plays a major role in shaping the preconvention campaign.

Two factors can upset this apparent inevitability. The first consists of the uncertain, unknown, and exogenous elements that appear to play a large role in determining specific outcomes, especially of early events. This randomness that is particularly prominent early in the campaign, combined with the importance of these same early events, imbues the system with an unfortunate arbitrariness. The answers to such questions as Why Carter? Why Ford and not Reagan? rest in part on arbitrariness. Reagan *could* have won in New Hampshire if only the weather had been worse, if only Governor Thompson had not uttered some of the statements he did, if only . . . The 1,600 vote difference could easily have swung on these or many other such small, possibly irrelevant, details, and a narrow win by Reagan would have changed the shape of the campaign substantially, possibly even altering the outcome.

While many such small incidents can change close outcomes and affect the candidates' fortunes materially, there is another much more substantial factor that can affect the dynamics of a campaign. Candidates are not oblivious of dynamic forces. They are rational actors who would like to win the nomination. To this end, they design their strategies to affect the dynamics and maximize their chances of winning. Reagan's pulling out of Wisconsin, his appearance on national television, and his concentration on the Texas primary demonstrate just the sort of extraordinary move necessary to change the direction of a campaign from slightly unfavorable to slightly favorable. The choice of a campaign strategy consists of a vast number of elements, including how much money to spend, where, in what manner; what themes to stress; and what problems to emphasize and what solutions to advocate. Since the dynamics of a campaign are influenced by obtaining major successes in at least some primaries and by avoiding serious setbacks, the candidate's choice of which primaries and caucuses to contest becomes a fundamental strategic consideration.

If the choice of states in which to compete is crucial to the campaign and its dynamics, how do rational candidates make these choices? This question is the subject of the next chapter.

6

Where Candidates Compete

The dynamic forces studied in the last chapter present each candidate with a problem and an opportunity. The opportunity is to master the dynamic forces and so win the nomination. The problem is how to do it in a competitive environment: one means of doing so is to select the appropriate primaries and caucuses to contest. In this chapter, the nature of this important decision will be studied. By defeating Hubert Humphrey in Wisconsin and West Virginia, for example, John Kennedy demonstrated his ability to win votes. This choice was a gamble, of course: had he failed in either state, he could not have achieved his goals. Had Humphrey not challenged him, Kennedy's victories would have been meaningless. The selection of which state contests to enter is very important given the nature of campaign dynamics. Even though candidates must win as many delegates as possible in primaries, they cannot compete in every state because a visibly poor showing could lead to the negative dynamic that forced most Democratic candidates out of the race in 1976.

This chapter is intertwined not only with the last chapter, but also with the next. The decision about what primaries to contest is only one of a set of related decisions a candidate must make. Candidates cannot simply campaign in this state or that, they must run some *type* of campaign. In particular, they must appeal to the electorate in part on public policy grounds. A major element of the candidate's decision is how well he expects a given state's electorate to respond to his campaign. Reagan did not compete in New York but he did in Texas, because he felt that his conservative image would not benefit him in New York but would serve him well among the more conservative Texans. The choice of which primaries to contest and what policies to advocate are intimately related to each other as well as to the dynamics of campaigns.

The media play a major role in the candidates' selection of which primaries to contest, as they did in the model of campaign dynamics. The media's coverage is what makes a primary consequential and what makes the candidate perceived as active or inactive in that primary. Ford, for example, expended many resources in California in 1976. Yet, even after these expenditures, he claimed to have abandoned the state's delegation to Reagan. Since the media *treated* him as an inactive competitor in California, his loss to Reagan on June 8 was expected and did not damage his campaign. That is, he was able to make the California primary a nonevent. This type of strategy makes it possible for candidates to appear to contest some primaries and not others, provides them with flexibility, and makes it possible for them to manipulate which events enter into the dynamic process described in the last chapter.

In the next sections of this chapter, I shall examine the strategy problem facing Ford and Reagan in some detail. A model is developed, propositions derived, and these are tested. In subsequent sections, I shall turn to the multicandidate Democratic contest.

The Problem of Strategy

The choice of which primaries to contest is one aspect of the general problem of strategy. Each primary offers a somewhat different opportunity to each candidate. But the outcome of the chosen strategy depends not just on what one candidate does, but also on what the opponents do. Ford's successful attempt to be perceived as a noncandidate in the California primary conceded that delegation to Reagan. Because of this, Reagan's active and successful campaign there was not rewarded in terms of campaign dynamics. Ford's strategy made it impossible for Reagan to control the meaning of the California results. The mathematical approach known as game theory has been developed to study decision

making in circumstances where the outcome, and consequently the behavior of each player, depends on all the players in the game.

The Two-Candidate Primary Game

The first assumption of this game is that each of the two candidates can
choose between competing actively and not competing actively. This
dichotomy between action and inaction is particularly useful when there
is but one primary on a given day. The alternative to competing in that
primary is not to compete at all on that date. When several primaries
occur on the same date, a greater range of activity becomes possible.

The second assumption is that both candidates can make this choice
after the immediately preceding primary or primaries. Therefore, the
sequencing of primaries enables the candidates to formulate or revise
their plans for each primary as it occurs.

There are, however, some qualifications. In some states, candidates
must file a petition to have their names, a slate of delegates, or both
placed on the ballot. In other states, such as Oregon, the state government or state party itself places whatever names it chooses on the ballot.
Only under exceptional circumstances will candidates attempt write-in
campaigns (e.g., Brown entered too late to do otherwise in Maryland
and Oregon). Failure to meet such early deadlines may prohibit a candidate from entering the primary. In the District of Columbia, Reagan's
failure to file resulted in the Republican primary being called off, and
Ford being declared the winner by default. On the other hand, failure
to contest a primary may be infeasible or unwise (e.g., either Wallace or
Carter in Florida, most candidates in their home states). The essential
distinction is whether or not a candidate is perceived (by the media, for
example) to be active.

The outcome of the primary is contingent upon the choices of both
candidates. When there are only two candidates, there are only four possible "strategy pairs" or pairs of choices made, one by each candidate:
  1. Both Ford and Reagan contest the primary.
  2. Ford competes, but Reagan does not.
  3. Reagan competes, but Ford does not.
  4. Neither candidate competes actively.
Each of these pairs of decisions leads to different outcomes, and, of
course, both candidates evaluate these outcomes differently.

Suppose, for example, that only one candidate competes. It costs this candidate something to mount the campaign—money, time, effort, and organizational resources that might have been employed elsewhere. In 1976, at least, the candidate was rewarded well for these expenditures. In those primaries in which only one candidate competed actively, that candidate won almost all the delegates. Ford won 91.6% and Reagan won 95.5% of the delegates from states in which they alone competed. The inactive candidate, then, spent few resources, but he received no return. While the victorious candidate won the delegation, he was denied the spillover that comes from defeating an active rival. That is, unless both candidates were active competitors, the dynamic forces (whether for good or ill) did not apply.

When both candidates contest a primary, each expends the costs necessary to conduct an active campaign in that state. The calculation of benefits has two aspects. First, I assume that the two candidates can estimate the outcome likely to occur from this contested primary. The candidates expend substantial resources to make that estimate: hiring polling outfits, sounding out local leaders, obtaining a feel from the grass roots, and so on. On the basis of this information, candidates (and the media) make some estimate of the likely vote. The likely allocation of delegates can then be determined, depending on the type of the primary. Suppose, for example, that Ford estimated he would receive 45% of the votes cast for him and Reagan. In a winner-take-all primary, that means zero delegates. With proportional allocation, Ford would expect about 45% of the delegates. Of course, even in a winner-take-all primary, Ford's estimate of the vote would be uncertain; with so narrow a margin, he might foresee some probability of defeating Reagan. At any rate, one of the major benefits of contesting a primary is the number of delegates a candidate expects to win. This calculation can be measured in terms of its effect on the two candidates' competitive status (CS), which was developed in chapter 4.

The second "benefit" of competing against an active opponent is the spillover. A candidate who exceeds expectations obtains a positive gain (see chapter 5). The opponent's spillover, however, is a negative benefit to him. If both candidates meet their expectations, their competitive status is unaffected.

The combination of these three components—the cost of conducting the campaign, the expected delegates, and the expected effect on the dynamics of the campaign—provides the raw material for each candidate's evaluation of the outcome when they both enter into active competition.

The fourth possibility is that neither candidate competes actively in the primary. While the media will not concentrate on that primary, turning their attention to more newsworthy events, the campaign still goes on, and the media follow it elsewhere. The voters in that state must make their decision anyway. I assume, therefore, that citizens make up their minds and vote for the candidates much the way they would if both candidates were working their state. One important difference, however, is the *level* of turnout. As we saw in chapter 4, turnout is related to the effort made by the two candidates (e.g., monetary expenditure increases turnout). Variations in turnout ordinarily affect candidates' support differentially. Nonetheless, if *both* candidates stimulate turnout, the differences will be more symmetric than if only *one* does. The formal analysis assumes only that the candidate expects nearly all delegates if he alone contests the primary, few if he alone is inactive, and something in between in the other two cases.

The possibility that neither candidate campaigns in a given state has three implications. First, neither candidate expends much in that state. Second, neither stands to gain or lose momentum because the action has moved elsewhere. Third, each candidate will receive some proportion of the delegates; hence their competitive standing will be affected. That is, they can calculate some likely division of the vote and, depending on the type of primary, some likely distribution of delegates.

If the two candidates make such calculations, it follows that each would prefer to reap the greatest expected benefit at the least cost. The elements of these calculations are summarized in table 6.1. The essence

Table 6.1   Four Possible Outcomes of a Two-Candidate Primary Contest: Republican Party, 1976

Paired Strategy	Out-come	Expected Benefit	Expected Cost
1. Ford and Reagan compete actively	0_1	Expected change in CS; change in momentum	Fixed cost of competing
2. Only Ford competes	0_2	Ford's CS increases because he wins all delegates	For Ford, fixed cost of competing; zero expenditure for Reagan
3. Only Reagan competes	0_3	Reagan's CS increases because he wins all delegates	For Reagan, fixed cost of competing; zero for Ford
4. Neither competes	0_4	Expected change in CS	Zero

of the strategic problem, however, is that neither candidate can guarantee the best outcome. Rather, the outcome is a consequence of *both* candidates' choices, and their preferences conflict. The nature of this strategic problem is shown in table 6.2.

Game theory can be applied to each state primary in turn. The reasoning is described in detail in numerous texts, and I have demonstrated its application in this context elsewhere.[1] From this analysis, hypotheses about where Ford and Reagan were likely to compete can be produced. Before stating these, however, there is one important complication that must be addressed.

More Than One Primary on the Same Day

So far, I have considered each primary as a new game. When a primary is the only one on a given date, this treatment is plausible. When there are two or more primaries on one day, the complexion of the game changes: the set of available strategies expands to four, eight, or more. On April 6th, 1976, for example, Ford and Reagan could have chosen to compete in New York and Wisconsin, to compete only in Wisconsin, to compete only in New York, or to compete in neither primary. The game then had sixteen possible strategy pairs and outcomes. However, the basic concepts discussed so far do not need much modification. The sixteen outcomes can be evaluated in the same way, with but three exceptions.

First, while the cost of competing in two primaries is greater than competing in one, the cost may be even greater if they were on separate

Table 6.2 Typical Representation of a Two-Candidate Primary Game

		Reagan Chooses	
		To Compete Actively	Not to Compete Actively
Ford Chooses	To Compete Actively	0_1 a_f, a_r	0_3 c_f, c_r
	Not to Compete Actively	0_2 b_f, b_r	0_4 d_f, d_r

a_f = Expected benefits − cost to Ford if 0_1 occurs; a_r = same term for Reagan, etc.

days. For example, candidates have a finite amount of time. While expending it is costly, they are going to expend it whether they compete in one or in two primaries. This point leads to the second exception.

To run two or more campaigns simultaneously requires that the candidates spread some of their finite resources. Instead of spending five or six days in one state in the last week of the campaign, they must divide their time between two or more states. How well candidates do in New York if they are actively competing there depends in part on whether or not they are also actively campaigning in Wisconsin. The most reasonable assumption is that they will do better in New York if they are *not* actively competing in Wisconsin, all else being equal.

Third, momentum is affected only by the results in states where both candidates are active competitors. If both candidates are active in two or more states, all the results will affect the resource dynamics.

Some Propositions

It is now possible to consider in which states the two candidates are more or less likely to compete. The detailed propositions are derived formally and are reported elsewhere.[2] The general thrust of these propositions can be summarized more briefly.

The key variables are: (1) the size of the delegation to be selected (small or large); (2) whether there is one or more than one primary on a given date; (3) if a primary is small, whether it falls early in the campaign or late in a very close campaign; (4) whether a primary is likely to be close or competitive or whether it is expected to be a pro-Ford or pro-Reagan state; and (5) whether the allocation of the delegates is proportional or governed by other rules.

The propositions, then, are:

Proposition 1. In general, candidates are more likely to compete in a primary than not. This proposition reaffirms the arguments about the changed nature of the preconvention campaign. Earlier, candidates could afford to compete in only one or two primaries to prove their electability (or even avoid all primaries). The current institutional context, as modeled here, makes active competition necessary to win the nomination.

Proposition 2. A close or competitive primary is more likely to be contested by both candidates than a noncompetitive one.

Proposition 3. An uncompetitive primary is more likely to be contested by the candidate likely to win it. For example, California was a pro-Reagan state. Thus, Reagan was more likely to compete in it than Ford, everything else being equal. However, both would be likely to contest a primary such as Florida's, because it was expected to be a very close one.

Proposition 4. If the primary is not proportional and not competitive, it is even less likely to be contested by the opponent (thus exaggerating the effect of proposition 3). That is, if the primary is a winner-take-all or uses the Democratic Loophole or plurality-winner-within-district procedures it is not proportional. (Another proposition advanced by me elsewhere is that a proportional primary that has an extraordinarily large threshold acts like a nonproportional primary.[3] Rhode Island, with a 33⅓% threshold, can be treated as a nonproportional primary, and will be so treated subsequently.)

Proposition 5. The larger the delegation to be selected, the more likely the primary is to be contested by both candidates.

Proposition 6. However, if the candidate has a very poor chance in the primary and if it uses a nonproportional rule, the candidate is very unlikely to compete in it regardless of the size of the delegation at stake.

Proposition 7. A small primary is more likely to be contested if it occurs very early in the campaign or if it occurs very late in a close campaign.

Proposition 8. If there are two or more primaries on the same date, each candidate is more likely to compete in both than in one and more likely to compete in at least one primary than in none. (There is a finite limit to the number of primaries a candidate can compete in actively at once. Apparently, this limit is two or three, especially if the states are large.)

The preceding propositions apply when there are several primaries on one day. I have already said, when there is only one primary on a day, the candidate may contest it or not compete anywhere that day. When two or more primaries are held simultaneously, the choices are greater. For example, there may be four primaries on one day, and all four may be good selections for a candidate. The candidate may choose to contest two of them. The same candidate might have wished to compete in all four, had they been on separate days, but could not handle four active campaigns simultaneously. Thus, to evaluate the accuracy of the proposition, we shall have to examine the full set of choices the Republican candidates faced.

Why Ford and Reagan Competed Where They Did

To test the propositions in the Ford-Reagan campaign, I defined the variables as follows. The delegations selected in the primaries were divided into small and large primaries. The median, 45 delegates, was the cutting point. New Hampshire and Massachusetts, however, being small but early campaigns, were considered large, in accordance with proposition 7. South Dakota and Rhode Island were small but late primaries. According to proposition 7, they might have been considered large. They fell on the next to last day of the primaries, but more than 20% of all delegates to be chosen via primaries were selected the next week. They are classified as small in tables 6.3 and 6.4, but this question will be raised again. (The number of primaries on a day and the type of rule they employ are tabulated in the appendix.)

The expected vote in a state, used to determine whether a primary was designated as competitive, pro-Ford, or pro-Reagan in tables 6.3 and 6.4, is difficult to measure. Typically, region is used to measure likely competitiveness.[4] This classification, as defined by the *Congressional Quarterly*, appears useful. For example, Ford won 90% of all delegates chosen in caucuses in eastern states, 50% in the midwestern and border states, 6% in southern states, and 14% in western states.

In the primaries, Reagan won virtually no delegates in the East and over 80% of those in the South and West. Thus, eastern primaries are considered pro-Ford, southern and western ones pro-Reagan, and those in the midwestern and border states close or competitive. New Hampshire and Florida are the two exceptions. Extensive and widely reported polls conducted in these early primary states indicated that the results were expected to be very close.

The division of primaries by size, type, and likely competitiveness leads to twelve categories of states. The distribution of the twenty-seven relevant primaries is shown in table 6.3, the definitions used in the table are those already developed in the text. That is:

1. A primary was considered large if it selects at least 45 delegates or if it is small but early.

2. Included among the nonproportional primaries is the large threshold primary in Rhode Island.

3. Competitive primaries include all midwestern and border-state primaries, plus those in New Hampshire and Florida. The pro-Ford primaries are all the other eastern primaries. The pro-Reagan primaries
are all the remaining southern and western primaries.

Of the thirty primaries, two (Montana and Vermont) held beauty
contest primaries only. Not selecting delegates, these were considered
irrelevant. (It should be noted that the candidates themselves did not
compete in either one, which is consistent with the model.) The D.C.
primary, since it was not held, was also ignored. However, since it was
likely to be a very bad primary for Reagan, his failure to file a delegate
slate there is consistent with the model.

The final variable in table 6.4 is whether or not Ford and Reagan
actively contested each primary. Some situations are obvious. Both candidates actively contested in the New Hampshire primary, and Reagan
equally clearly did not campaign in New York. Some primaries were
less clear. Objective indicators (e.g., money spent in state) can be mis-

Table 6.3   Distribution of Republican Primaries by Independent
Variables, 1976

Political Situation	Large		Small		
	Proportional	Non-proportional	Proportional	Non-proportional	Number
Competitive	(1) 1	(4) 6	(7) 4	(10) 3	14
Pro-Ford	(2) 1	(5) 3	(8) 0	(11) 1	5
Pro-Reagan	(3) 1	(6) 3	(9) 3	(12) 1	8
Total	3	12	7	5	27

NOTE: See explanations in text.

Table 6.4   Values of Republican Primaries on Key Variables, 1976

State Holding Primary	Size	Type	Political Situation	Cell in Table 6.3	Activity Ford	Activity Reagan
NH	Large	non-PR	Competitive	4	Yes	Yes
MA	Large	PR	Pro-Ford	2	No	No
FL	Large	non-PR	Competitive	4	Yes	Yes
IL	Large	non-PR	Competitive	4	Yes	Yes
NC	Large	PR	Pro-Reagan	3	Yes	Yes
(NY	Large	non-PR	Pro-Ford	5	Yes?	No
(WI	Large	non-PR	Competitive	4	Yes	No
PA	Large	non-PR	Pro-Ford	5	No	No
TX	Large	non-PR	Pro-Reagan	6	Yes	Yes
(AL	Small	non-PR	Pro-Reagan	12	No	Yes
{GA	Large	non-PR	Pro-Reagan	6	Yes	Yes
(IN	Large	non-PR	Competitive	4	Yes	Yes
(NB	Small	non-PR	Competitive	10	Yes	Yes
{WV	Small	non-PR	Competitive	10	No	No
(MD	Small	non-PR	Competitive	10	No	No
(MI	Large	PR	Competitive	1	Yes	Yes
AR	Small	PR	Pro-Reagan	9	No	No
(ID	Small	PR	Pro-Reagan	9	No	Yes
)KY	Small	PR	Competitive	7	Yes	Yes
)NV	Small	PR	Pro-Reagan	9	No	Yes
(OR	Small	PR	Competitive	7	Yes	Yes
'TN	Small	PR	Competitive	7	Yes	Yes
(RI	Small	non-PR	Pro-Ford	11	No	No
(SD	Small	PR	Competitive	7	No	No
(CA	Large	non-PR	Pro-Reagan	6	No	Yes
)NJ	Large	non-PR	Pro-Ford	5	Yes	No
(OH	Large	non-PR	Competitive	4	Yes	Yes

PR = proportional allocation; non-PR = nonproportional allocation. Braces enclose states with primaries on the same day.

leading. Reagan's pull-out of Wisconsin is one notable example, and Ford's expenditures without being an active competitor in California is another. The candidates simply were not treated by the media as active competitors in those primaries. A careful reading of contemporary accounts suggests that, while a subjective decision, it was possible to assess this variable on a state-by-state basis for both candidates.[5] This was done, and the state-by-state results are shown in table 6.4. The braces in the table associate primaries held on the same day.

The activity of both candidates in the following primaries was considered self-evident: New Hampshire, Florida, Illinois, North Carolina, Texas, Indiana, Nebraska, Michigan, and Ohio (Ohio will be discussed again). Reagan clearly was not active in Massachusetts, New York, and Pennsylvania, while Ford relied on state party and Ford committees to carry on his campaign there. His efforts were so slight that only New York was entered as "yes?" in table 6.4. Reagan expended substantial effort and resources in Georgia and Alabama, but less than in Indiana. Ford expended much less in Alabama than in Georgia, hence the coding in table 6.4. The efforts expended in West Virginia and Maryland by both candidates, as well as the media coverage of these two states, was much less than the other primary on each date. Kentucky, Oregon, and Tennessee received the bulk of media attention on May 25. However, according to the *Congressional Quarterly* and other sources, Reagan prepared major organizational efforts in Idaho and Nevada (as Ford did in New York). Therefore, Reagan is attributed active campaigns in those states. While these calls are somewhat questionable, whether or not Reagan *was* active in these states does not affect the success of the model materially. Finally, the two primaries of June 1 are prime examples of non-campaigns.

Let us now look at the seven primaries that were held on unique dates. Table 6.4 shows that there were three large competitive, non-proportional primaries (cell 4 in table 6.3) and one each of the type represented by cells 2, 3, 5, and 6. The propositions stated above imply that both candidates should have been most likely to compete actively in the three large and competitive primaries. After that, Ford should be considered more likely to compete in Pennsylvania (cell 5) than in Massachusetts (cell 2), followed by North Carolina (cell 3), and finally by Texas (cell 6). After the cell 4 type primaries, the order of likelihood should have been exactly reversed for Reagan.

These hypotheses and the actual events are compared in tables 6.5 and 6.6.

It can be seen, in table 6.5, that both candidates did in fact compete in those primaries where active competition was predicted, and that they indeed did not compete when it was less likely. Thus, the results are consistent with this hypothesis. It also should be noted that both candidates were more likely to be active in these seven primaries than not, as stated in proposition 1.

The predictions about each candidate are compared with their behavior in table 6.6. There it can be seen that Reagan's behavior conformed to predictions exactly. It was predicted that he would be especially likely to avoid challenging Ford in Massachusetts and Penn-

Table 6.5   Test of the Propositions about Primaries
Held on a Unique Date: Both Candidates
Compete or at Least One Fails to Compete

	Actual		
Predicted	Both Competed	At Least One Did Not	Cell in Table 6.3
Both Competed	3	0	4
At Least One Did Not	2	2	2, 3, 5, 6

sylvania, and he did. All other primaries were better opportunities for
him, and he took them. Ford's behavior was less consistent with the
hypotheses. He was predicted to have been less likely to compete in
North Carolina and Texas than in Pennsylvania and Massachusetts, yet
his behavior was just the reverse.

Why was Ford's behavior different than that predicted? Several factors were involved. Consider, first, the two states that Ford bypassed.
The assumption is that candidates reveal their choice of behavior simultaneously. This assumption is often a reasonble approximation. At
times, of course, it is simply wrong. In both Massachusetts and Pennsylvania, Reagan tipped his hand early, enabling Ford to do very well in
both primaries, with little effort, knowing that Reagan would not challenge him. For example, Reagan did not enter his name on the presidential preference ballot in Pennsylvania, and his supporters competed
for only a very few delegate positions. Witcover, in his lengthy book on

Table 6.6   Another Test of the Propositions about Primaries Held on a
Unique Date: Which Candidate Competes

	Cell in Table 6.3	Ford		Cell in Table 6.3	Reagan	
		Competed	Did-Not		Competed	Did Not
Most Likely To Compete	4	3	0	4	3	0
	5	1	0	6	1	0
	2	0	1	3	1	0
	3	1	0	2	0	1
Least Likely To Compete	6	1	0	5	0	1

the 1976 campaign, refers to the Massachusetts Republican primary
with only this footnote "President Ford won the Massachusetts and Vermont primaries handily the next Tuesday, March 2, without active competition from Reagan."[6] Further, Ford had the active support of the
Republican leadership in both states. Ford received nearly twice as
many votes and delegates in Massachusetts as Reagan, and over 90%
of the delegates in Pennsylvania (and 95% of the preference vote),
without mounting an active campaign.

The rest of the hypothesis was that Ford was unlikely to challenge
Reagan in Texas and North Carolina. In both states, Ford entered and
lost. *New York Times* reporter James Naughton said, about the North
Carolina result, that "They [Reagan and his staff] were dumbfounded.
They didn't know how to handle it."[7] Later, he said:

In North Carolina both sides seemed surprised by the outcome, and
some changes seemed to occur thereafter. Reagan went on television
and began campaigning more aggressively; the president took on his
second campaign chairman [Rogers C. B. Morton] and began spending more time using the White House.[8]

In response to Naughton's question, "What happened?" Ford's pollster, Robert Teeter, responded:

North Carolina changed it [Ford's initial strategy] immensely. . . .
At one point we thought we had a substantial lead in North Carolina,
and decided not to incur the cost of doing another poll closer to the
election, or of sending the president in during the last week or so of
the campaign. There is no guarantee that either move would have
changed the result, of course, but I think the decisions were based
on political inexperience.[9]

Now, Texas. We have already seen that the Texas primary was a
turning point in Reagan's campaign. Clearly, Ford could fare no worse
had he not campaigned there since he lost all the delegates to Reagan.
In short, while there might have been errors in prediction, it may have
behooved Ford to have failed to challenge Reagan in these states. If
so, his behavior, like Reagan's, would have been consistent with the
hypotheses.

For the cases of several primaries held on the same date, proposition
8 states that both candidates are more likely to compete in two than
only one, and in one rather than none. In general, the two candidates
supported this prediction. The exceptions follow. Reagan did not com-

pete in either of the two primaries on April 6th (one, however, was Wisconsin) and he did not compete in either on June 1st. Ford also failed to contest in either South Dakota or Rhode Island on June 1st. Otherwise, each was active somewhere on all multiple primary dates. Further, on every date on which there were three or more primaries, both candidates competed in at least two.

Which of the several primaries held simultaneously were contested by each candidate requires a case-by-case analysis. The propositions set forth in this chapter lead us to expect both Ford and Reagan to have contested primaries that fell in cells 1, 4, 7, and 10 of table 6.3, in that order. After that, Ford is more likely to compete in a primary of the type falling in cell 2 of table 6.3, followed by cells 5, 8, 11, and then the rest. The comparable order of likelihood for Reagan is cells 3, 6, 9, and 12, the rest being even less likely.

The first case is April 6, the date of both the Wisconsin and New York primaries. The Wisconsin primary has been discussed already. According to Peter Kay, one of Ford's aides, "Wisconsin was [Reagan's] major mistake of the whole year . . . we were damned lucky and it put us on the tracks after North Carolina."[10] About New York, a bad state for Reagan, his campaign manager John Sears said:

> Had we won in New Hampshire and thus created a momentum, we might have entered a few other primaries. But we did not feel that we were necessarily losing anything by not entering New York and Pennsylvania. We felt we probably, by means of the bargaining process, could derive as many delegates as we might have elected by spending a lot of money. I think in New York's case that proved to be true, though I'm less sure about Pennsylvania.[11]

The state was a more attractive possibility for Ford. Ford's actual campaign there is marked "yes?" in table 6.4 because it consisted of an organizational drive by Nelson Rockefeller and State Republican Chairman Richard Rosenbaum to elect an uncommitted slate of delegates that would support Ford over Reagan. This sort of campaign is just the type a candidate should conduct if the opponent is unlikely to compete in the primary.

Indiana was the most actively contested of the three primaries held on May 4. Both candidates ran reasonably active campaigns in Georgia, while Ford's level of activity was much lower in Alabama. Thus, the predictions about the candidates' behavior in these states are borne out by their actual behavior.

Nebraska and West Virginia should have been identical primaries in terms of our propositions. Yet both candidates focused on Nebraska to the exclusion of West Virginia. Why was this so? Quite simply, the cost of competing in West Virginia was substantially greater. The West Virginia primary ballot listed the names of citizens desiring to become delegates but did not indicate which presidential aspirant they supported. The cost of communicating this information to a frequently inattentive public and the possibility of confusion were unusually great. It is not at all implausible that Ford and Reagan decided to compete in Nebraska instead for these reasons.

The Michigan and Maryland primaries, held the next week, illustrate the importance of size and type of primary. Both were considered competitive, but Michigan selected substantially more delegates through proportional allocation. In fact, Michigan was the only primary most likely to be contested by both candidates. Michigan was Ford's home. One might argue, therefore, that it should have been considered pro-Ford. However, as noted previously, commentators (and apparently Reagan and Ford as well) did not consider it Ford's safe home ground. At the time, in large part because of the Reagan victory string, Reagan was believed to have a very real chance in Michigan. This belief was supported further by the argument that people who supported Wallace in 1972 (he won a majority there) would cross over to the Republican side to support the conservative candidate. (Newspaper accounts after the fact suggested that Ford, not Reagan, benefited from the crossover vote.) Maryland, on the other hand, was at the bottom end of the most-likely-to-be-contested range. Thus, the primaries of May 18th fit expectations well.

Three of the six primaries on May 25th were small, competitive, and used the proportional allocation rule. The other three differed only in that they were considered pro-Reagan. It was predicted that the three close primaries were more likely to be contested by both candidates, and all three were. Ford was unlikely to compete in Arkansas, Idaho, and Nevada, and he did not. Reagan campaigned in Nevada (primarily through state party leaders, notably Senator Laxalt, the head of his national campaign). He also campaigned in Idaho (to a lesser degree and by relying on state leaders, some early personal visits, and only a little money). Apparently he did not compete in Arkansas. His behavior is consistent with the propositions.

South Dakota and Rhode Island were uncontested. According to proposition 7, we would expect Ford to have competed in Rhode Island, and both candidates to have been active in South Dakota. However, since both primaries were small, the likelihood of active competition was reduced. The 39 delegates up for grabs on June 1st were barely 10% of the number to be selected seven days later. Quite reasonably, the candidates may have chosen to concentrate on the three large primaries to follow.

June 8th was the date of the California, Ohio, and New Jersey primaries. Each state was to select a large bloc of delegates, under varying conditions. The prediction was that Reagan was least likely to compete in New Jersey (since it was a pro-Ford state) and Ford in California (since it was a pro-Reagan state). These expectations were realized exactly. *Congressional Quarterly* reported, about New Jersey:

> The Republican situation is simpler. There are two competing slates, both at-large and in the districts, but only one active candidate. Reagan, pessimistic about his chances in a state where the party is controlled by moderates, decided not to make an effort here. A group of his supporters formed a slate pledged to the "former California governor," without mentioning his name on the ballot. But Reagan is providing these people no money and is not planning appearances in the state. So the slate is not expected to win many delegate contests [nor did it].[12]

Ford's maneuvering in California was not only consistent with the hypothesis but also illustrates the nature of strategy that is at the heart of game theory. Witcover's description is:

> Ford could clinch the nomination by winning in California, . . . but that looked less and less likely; Reagan needed California simply to remain in contention, and he campaigned long and hard there . . . which suited Ford fine. When it became clear that Reagan was nearly unbeatable in his home state—he was 10 percentage points ahead in early May in the prestigious Mervin Field Poll— *Ford campaigned in California only enough to keep Reagan occupied there.* He concentrated on New Jersey . . . and Ohio. . . . Reagan had managed back in April to file slates in fifteen of Ohio's twenty-five congressional districts plus a statewide slate, but he had done little groundwork, much to the chagrin of Ohio conservatives. "Our strategy was to keep Reagan pinned to California to keep him the

hell out of Ohio," [Ford campaign manager Stuart] Spencer said, "and we were pretty successful."[13]

Ironically, Reagan's initial efforts in Ohio were intended to keep Ford out of California. Only later did Reagan change his tactics, outspending Ford in Ohio. The *Congressional Quarterly* has reported that Reagan

> . . . initially viewed his appearance on the [Ohio] ballot as a diversion that would tie down some of Ford's time and resources, thus enhancing his own chances in California. But confident of his prospects in his home state, Reagan launched a late drive in Ohio that featured a barnstorming tour around the state in the weekend before the primary . . . augmented . . . with television commercials.[14]

To summarize, the hypotheses tested here were well supported generally. Moreover, the exceptions fall into several categories: (1) those that are acknowledged in the model but not generally measured (e.g., the cost of campaigning in West Virginia); (2) those that may be considered "errors" in actual candidate's behavior (e.g., Ford's competing in Texas and North Carolina); (3) those due to unusual decisions (e.g., Reagan's withdrawal from Wisconsin); and (4) those few remaining instances of erroneous predictions.

Multicandidate Campaigns

While the choice of primaries contended by Ford and Reagan support the predictions of the model, the model is limited to two-candidate campaigns. The generality of the model is thereby greatly reduced, since so few nomination campaigns have been two-candidate races. It is important, therefore, to extend the analysis from the two-person to the more general game. Three generalizations will be explored, if less rigorously. The first is a direct extension of the reasoning underlying the two-candidate model. The second is a consideration of the possibility of coordinated strategy choices (or a game theoretic "coalition"). The third is an investigation of competition over policies, which will lead to the more general consideration of policy competition in the next chapter.

A Direct Extension of the Two-Candidate Model

An immediate proposition is that a candidate who hopes to win via the primary route will have to compete often. (This proposition is similar to propositions 1 and 8 about the two-candidate contest. However, the propositions advanced in this section do not rest on formal derivations, like those about the two-candidate race and those stated in other chapters.)

For example, the strategy of John Kennedy in 1960, in which he contested only two primaries vigorously, is unlikely in today's preconvention campaign. Carter illustrated the new strategy well, and his claim that he won at least one primary on every date that primaries were held was effective. Udall, one of Carter's few long-lasting opponents in 1976, used this strategy, having competed actively in New Hampshire, Massachusetts, Wisconsin, New York, Pennsylvania, Michigan, Connecticut, South Dakota, Ohio, and elsewhere. Connecticut used a caucus procedure. However, the first step in the caucus was a party-run vote that resembled a primary. Udall and Carter called Connecticut a primary for this reason (although they did not so call a similar procedure in Louisiana). Udall hoped to win his first primary there. Failing to do so, he allowed Carter's narrow win to count as Carter's only primary victory on May 11th, enabling Carter to claim a victory on every primary date.

A second proposition is that competition for competition's sake is to be avoided. Rather, the states in which to compete should be chosen carefully. The key in a multicandidate contest appears to be to pick a state in which one expects to do well. As I have already observed, Jackson, Carter, Udall, and Wallace selected one or two primaries as crucial.

Although candidates can withstand losses, even exceptionally poor showings, in states outside of their central core (e.g., Carter in Massachusetts, Jackson in Florida), a setback in this small number of core primaries is likely to be fatal. The selection of these states is made basically in terms of the state's electorate and the likely competition, rather than because of the specific features of the primary (e.g., size or voting method). They are also based on where candidates believe they stand the best chance of winning. When there are many candidates, the parallel to the earlier propositions 2 and 3 would be "candidates are more likely to compete in a state, the better they expect to do in the state." Multicandidate contests are very different from two-candidate affairs in this regard. In two-candidate contests, candidates are most likely to compete when votes are expected to be divided 50–50. Thus, Ford could ignore a sure state. Jackson and the other Democratic competitors would be expected to search for that sure state.

The importance of Florida to Wallace (and to Carter, for that matter) was not purely a matter of choice. While candidates have some lattitude in developing their campaigns, they are constrained by reality. Carter's selection of Florida as the showdown primary with Wallace arose as much out of necessity as out of free choice—it was the first southern primary and this, his only natural constituency, was claimed equally by Wallace. As usual, the candidates' choices were constrained by the institutional structure and by the other players in the nomination game.

A third proposition is that winning a primary early is better than winning one late (although, clearly, winning late is better than not winning at all). Therefore, in targeting a key set of states, at least one should come early in the campaign. The characterization of Brown's and Church's campaigns as "too little, too late" illustrates the importance of this point. The earlier a primary is, the more likely it is to be contested and to be contested by more candidates. Therefore, winning an early primary generally guarantees defeating an active rival. This proposition, of course, parallels that for the two-candidate case. The relationship between campaign dynamics and the last two propositions should also be clear. Winning is good, the more one wins the better, and winning early is better still. There is nothing special about New Hampshire, other than it being the earliest primary, but that simple fact is very important. However, candidates have foregone competition there without wrecking their campaigns. Jackson's choice of Massachusetts instead of New Hampshire illustrates this point well.

The rules for active competition against many competitors, then, are to win somewhere, to win as early as possible, to win as often as possible, but most assuredly, to select certain primaries as showcases or must-win primaries—and to win those. The more candidates actively seeking the nomination, the less concern about the type or even the size of the primary. However, more delegates are better than fewer. This point becomes especially true as the campaign unfolds. It follows, of course, that if there are several primaries on a day, winning the largest will generate greater attention, all else being equal.

The importance of a close, competitive primary is less than in the two-candidate contest. When there are only two candidates, both are likely to contest close primaries. Winning where one's only opponent does not compete is not terribly useful. When there is a large number of candidates, one is rarely the only contestant in any primary.

Coalitions

When, as in the Democratic Party in 1976, the campaign begins with no clear front-runner, the candidates tend to try to advance themselves without regard to others. The question is usually, How can I win? and, less directly, How can I win, given what my opponent is going to do? However, if a front-runner emerges, the question changes to How can I slow or stop the front-runner, maintain credibility, build momentum, and eventually win? For example, both Udall and Jackson would have been better off if Carter were slowed in Florida. There might have been an incentive for them to choose strategies that would benefit both at Carter's expense. This formulation of the problem suggests that there might be incentives for coordinated action.

For a variety of reasons, coalitions, as usually defined, are not directly useful. Coalitions arise when two or more players coordinate their actions (i.e., make choices as a unified "team") because they can do better in the coalition than as individual players. In nomination politics, the goal is to win the presidential nomination. Since the nomination can go to but one person, it cannot be true that each member of a coalition can do better than playing alone. Ultimately, only one candidate can win. Thus, all such coalitions are doomed to fail at some point. However, there may be situations where coalitions can form for a short time, even if they dissolve in the longer term. The most common situation occurs when there is one leading candidate and two or more opponents. The challengers may find it in their mutual interest to cooperate in some fashion, such as modifying their plans about what primaries to contest, to slow or stop the front-runner. If that task is accomplished, however, (and even if it is not), the incentives to maintain cooperation are removed, and the challengers will again become competitors. That is, coalitions in this game are hard to attain and impossible to maintain. Nonetheless, there are some indications that the potential for coordinated action existed in 1976. Typically, these instances illustrated the difficulties of actually coordinating plans of action.

Very early, many Democrats feared a strong Wallace campaign. Were he to become a strong candidate, he would have had to do it by a direct appeal in the primaries. To stop him, then, would have required stopping him at the polls. He was expected to be a formidable adversary in many primaries; certainly one who could harm others' candidacies. Witcover, for example, wrote:

But if Wallace was generally perceived as a threat by the other candidates, the confident Carter, as we have seen, viewed him as an opportunity . . . [A] confrontation with Wallace in Florida had been projected since 1972 as the critical make-or-break exercise. . . . Carter knew that if he could rid the Democratic Party of the pesky Wallace, liberals, blacks and other Southern Democrats weary of being perceived in the Wallace image would all be in his debt.[15]

All candidates except Shapp initially decided to let Florida be the Carter-Wallace showdown, hoping that Carter could in fact rid them of the "pesky" Wallace. Thus, an implicit coalition was forged. Jackson, however, decided to mount a major last-minute effort in Florida. Circumstances had changed, especially Carter's strong initial showings. He, not Wallace, was the man to be stopped. Writing *before* the New Hampshire primary, Evans and Novak discussed the formation of an implicit "alliance of political strangers" (Jackson, Wallace, and Florida's Governor Rubin Askew) for the Florida primary. They wrote that the alliance was forming for the purpose of "slowing the amazing momentum being built up by Jimmy Carter's quest for the Democratic presidential nomination."[16]

Brown, Church, and Udall agreed to divide the remaining key primaries in the late-challenger phase so that only one of them faced Carter each time. Church stated, "[Carter's] trying to lead a wagon through a series of mountain passes, and there's a different candidate waiting to ambush him at each one."[17] Said Witcover:

> According to John Gabusi, Udall's campaign manager, key figures in the Church, Brown, and Udall campaigns discussed the best allocation of resources after the Pennsylvania primary. "Udall stayed out of Nebraska," Gabusi said later, "to give Church a shot at it," and Brown's Maryland plans inevitably led Udall to focus on Michigan. There, Carter charged that a "secret deal" had been made. . . . All the Carter foes naturally denied any collusion.[18]

To Gabusi's chagrin, Udall also decided to pull out of Oregon, at his brother's suggestion, and leave it up to Brown and Church to defeat Carter.

The impossibility of maintaining such an implicit or explicit coalition is illustrated by the behavior of Udall and Church in Ohio. It had become clear that, if Carter won in Ohio, the nomination was his. Since the two challengers would divide much of the same vote, Carter could win a plurality against two opponents that he might not win against only one. Thus, both Udall's and Church's chances would have been improved if only one of them challenged Carter. However, the chance of the one who beat Carter in the last primary, were it to happen, would be better than that of the person who withdrew. Therefore, both called upon the other to withdraw. Neither did—and Carter won (albeit with a majority). As Witcover relates:

> Church's decision to campaign in Ohio had caused much bitterness in Udall's camp. Some of Udall's people believed they had a deal that Church would stay out . . . as Church said later, "it had served my purposes to choose states where Udall wasn't entered. I decided against entering Wisconsin, where I had no chance and he did; I didn't go into Connecticut for the same reason. Ohio was the first place I decided to try where Mo Udall also was deeply involved.[19]

A final example was the possibility of a Humphrey-Brown coalition. If the idea of such a coalition existed in the minds of the two principals, it would have illustrated a quite different set of circumstances. Here, the prize was divisible. Humphrey would have been the presidential nominee, and Brown would have received either the vice-presidential nomination or other benefits related to future presidential campaigns. Thus, there were grounds for more than a temporary coalition. Whether or not there was a coalition between the principals, there was among others advocating a Humphrey-Brown ticket. This coalition was clearest in New Jersey, where a slate of candidates for delegate endorsed both Humphrey and Brown before the primary. The endorsement of two candidates was an unprecedented move, and one that did not distinguish one candidate as preferred for the presidential nomination, the other for the vice-presidential slot. James P. Dugan, New Jersey state party chairman and architect of the strategy, said that it was the first time that one primary vote "offered a complete Democratic national ticket." The reason for the rather arcane maneuvering was that neither Humphrey nor Brown was explicitly cooperating, nor did either directly seek anything but the presidential nomination. However, on June 2nd, the *New York Times* noted that the two "toured New Jersey today in a final, cooperative effort to stop . . . Carter."[20]

Policy Competition: The Winnowing Phase

A third way of looking at multicandidate contests is in terms of policy competition. This subject will be looked at in detail in the next chapter, but one aspect of it, the winnowing process, is relevant here.

In a field of many competitors, candidates appear to adopt a secondary goal in the initial phases of the campaign: survival. How, then, does one become a survivor of the first few phases? Clearly, a victory is sufficient but not necessary. What appears to be necessary is to do as well as or better than one's rivals for some defined constituency. Thus, Carter and Wallace competed in Florida and North Carolina to become *the* southern candidate. More commonly, one tries to become *the* representative of a policy-based constituency. Becoming *the* southern candidate clearly entails a substantial focus on policy, among other things. Region and policy are closely aligned in the traditional Democratic Party coalition.

It is common for candidates and media alike to divide the candidates into three policy groups: the liberals, the conservatives, and the moderates. The active candidates at the beginning of the Democratic Party campaign in 1976 consisted of one conservative (Wallace), two centrists (Jackson and Carter), and numerous liberals. Jackson and Carter remained viable by winning an early primary outright, and of course Carter had demonstrated surprising strength in the early caucuses. Wallace was beaten by Carter along regional lines. There remained the competition among the many liberal candidates.

The competing liberals were Bayh, Harris, Shapp, Shriver, and Udall. In December 1975, New York's New Democratic Coalition, a liberal group, met to endorse a liberal Democratic candidate. Bayh campaigned there strenuously, as did Harris and Udall (although Udall's efforts have been called less tenacious and "essentially stop-Bayh drives"). On the last ballot, Bayh fell short of the required 60% by .026%, and no endorsement was issued.

The liberal competition moved to the opening caucuses. Bayh, Harris, and Udall competed with Carter in Iowa. Udall said of his campaign there "I think my campaign is catching on and doing well *in other states*, and we expect to *survive* here." Witcover adds that "The great irony in Udall's entry in Iowa to muddle the picture, and prevent Bayh from jumping to the forefront of the liberal pack, was the fact that Bayh himself had entered Iowa to hold Udall back."[21] The two leading "candidates" in Iowa were uncommitted delegates and Carter, followed by Bayh, Harris, and Udall, all winning small percentages. Harris' 10% was sufficient for him to proclaim that "Iowa started the winnowing-out process, and we've been winnowed in."[22]

The first primaries, of course, were the real winnowing process. While Carter won the New Hampshire primary, Udall won the liberal vote, essentially ending Harris's chances. Udall's second-place finish to Jackson the next week finished Bayh's campaign. Shriver and Shapp hung on for one or two primaries, but their chances had also ended in New England. Udall was the surviving liberal (or "progressive," as he preferred) until the middle of May.

The implication of the winnowing process seems to be that, in a complex field, candidates and media personnel alike look for simplifying devices such as broad policy or regional characteristics. A large field of competitors is narrowed to a handful by competition for survival within some such major category. As Udall showed, survival does not require a first-place showing; rather, one looks for dominance within one's own group. Winning is better than surviving, but surviving is certainly better than being forced to withdraw.

One crucial aspect of policy is the voters' response to variations among candidates' policy positions. Steven Brams begins his study of "The Primaries: Who Survives the Hurdles?" by arguing the "primacy of issues" in primary elections.[23] Certainly, this general perspective underlies the rationale for the more liberal Ford expecting to do well in more liberal Republican states and the more conservative Reagan expecting to do well in more conservative areas. So too, does the rationale of several liberal Democratic candidates dividing up the same votes rest on the presumption of the centrality, if not primacy, of issues in the electorate.

Clearly, the importance of public policy concerns in elections, whether primary or general elections, is much broader than simply determining what primaries are good or bad ones for a candidate. Much of the practical as well as theoretical and normative importance of electoral mechanisms of all sorts is based on the selection of policy directions to be followed directly (e.g., via referendum) or indirectly (e.g., via selection of new office holders). These concerns motivate the study of policy competition in the next chapter.

7 Competition over Policy

The most important functions of elections in a democracy are to select competent leaders and to affect the direction of public policy. Thus far, the focus has been on the candidate. Lurking in the shadows, however, has been some notion that public policy is relevant. The purpose of this chapter is to bring the question of policy competition to the fore. In this chapter, I shall examine the rationale underlying the positions candidates take (or fail to take) on issues in preconvention campaigns.

Candidates contesting for support by competing over public policy have three questions to address. The first is, What positions should the candidate take on issues? The second is related to the first. Should the candidate take a specific position, or not? That is, under what conditions should a rational candidate be ambiguous or fuzzy about issues, as Carter's opponents claimed he was? The answers to these questions are often beyond the control of the candidates. Many, for example, have taken (or have had to take) positions on issues long before seriously contemplating a run for the presidential nomination. On the other hand, candidates may be better able to control the *emphasis* placed on issues in the public debate. The third question is, What issues should a candidate emphasize or discuss at all? Presumably, candidates attempt to emphasize issues which will gain them support and a competitive advantage.

Candidates undoubtedly try to manipulate their positions on the issues, the relative clarity of their positions, and the relative emphasis they place on issues. They are not the only players in this game, however. The media must report their strategies to the electorate, and the media's own goals and constraints affect their coverage. Moreover, the public at large must perceive the candidates' strategies. Either group can affect the ability of the candidate to pursue a chosen strategy effectively. Ellen McCormack, for example, was simply unable to gain sufficient media attention to get her pro-life message to the electorate. Her inability to obtain substantial popular support, (in primaries, e.g.) in turn meant that the media did not have to pay much attention to her campaign. The cyclical phenomenon described in chapter 5 applies in this context as well. More generally, the weight of evidence in political science shows that the public possesses little information about issues, often has weak or nonexistent preferences, rarely pays attention to detailed policy statements, and frequently misperceives the candidates' positions.[1] The roles played by these other actors must be taken into account by the candidates. One view of the candidates is that they are entrepreneurs attempting to sell the electorate a policy package by taking or by failing to take positions or that they are attempting to sell a policy agenda by what they discuss or fail to discuss.

Candidates take positions on a large number of issues. A request for the positions of a candidate will elicit weighty piles of documents relating to virtually every conceivable aspect of public policy, from the most technical positions on agricultural policy or B-1 bombers to general statements about inflation and unemployment. While their position papers are available to all, the presumption is that few will read them— only those very few devoted to party politics or to specific issues. Further, the media are expected to provide relatively little coverage of these public pronouncements. Thus, candidates can expect to be able to appeal to specific and small constituencies on detailed policy grounds and yet maintain a strategy that deemphasizes the same issues to the general public. The candidates' ability to pursue this apparently contradictory, two-pronged strategy is grounded on their recognition of the roles of the media and the general public.

The General Position of the Candidates

As usual in the 1976 nomination campaigns, the Republican campaign represented one extreme, the Democratic campaign the other. As we shall see shortly, there is a major theoretical difference between a two-candidate race and a multicandidate race in respect to the strategic nature of policy competition. A second major difference between the two parties in 1976 was that Reagan and Ford were unusually constrained in their choice of policies. Both candidates had assumed positions on many issues: Ford because he was the incumbent, and Reagan because of his well-articulated and well-known conservatism. Thus, their positions were more or less given prior to the campaign. Their strategic options revolved more around what issues to discuss and emphasize, and less around what positions to take. Ambiguity was a strategy rarely available to them.

Many Democrats were also constrained in respect to the positions they could adopt. However, some, notably Carter and Brown, had greater room to maneuver and, indeed, enough flexibility to be ambiguous. The complications of the multicandidate competition also dictate a different type of strategy. Thus, a larger set of strategies was available to the Democrats.

A general overview of the positions of several of the candidates of both parties, an overview especially relevant when analyzing the views of an often inattentive public, is presented in figure 7.1. That figure is based on a CBS/*New York Times* poll of a national sample conducted early in February 1976. Respondents were asked to respond to nine public issues (aid to minorities, abortion, federal provision of jobs, federal provision of social services, balancing the federal budget, busing,

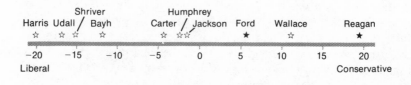

Figure 7.1   **Liberal-Conservative Continuum: Self-Ratings of Supporters of Candidates.** Data were taken from the CBS/*New York Times* poll, reported in the *New York Times*, 13 February 1976, p. 36.

pollution, détente, and military spending) and then to place themselves on a general ideological scale, from conservative to liberal. Figure 7.1 is a summary of each candidate's supporters' responses. The scale corresponds remarkably well to the media's perception of where the candidates themselves would be located on such a scale. This correspondence implies that people do indeed tend to support the candidate whose policies are most like their own. Ford was perceived as a moderate conservative, Reagan as a strong conservative. Wallace, was viewed as the most conservative Democrat, Jackson and Carter as centrists, and the other Democrats as a more liberal bloc. As the *Times* reported, "the candidates do seem to draw their main support from logical ideological constituencies."[2]

This general ideological orientation of the various candidates will guide our analysis of the questions: What positions should a candidate adopt on issues? And, given that many candidates were constrained a priori, What were the consequences of the positions the candidates adopted?

Republican Issue Strategies and Their Consequences

Two-candidate elections have been modeled mathematically in terms of policy competition. The "spatial model" of electoral competition, originated by Anthony Downs, is the best known of this literature.[3] The essential argument is this: Suppose there are two candidates competing for votes. Suppose, further, that citizens respond by supporting the candidate whose positions are more similar to their own preferences. What positions should candidates offer to the electorate? Where an answer to this question is possible, the answer is always the same. Each candidate should offer a central and, often, the most central position possible.[4] Thus, the dominance of moderation in electoral politics is predicted, giving theoretical justification to Wallace's oft-repeated claim that there's not a dime's worth of difference between the two candidates. Without exception, in the past decades, the more central of the two candidates in the general presidential election won, generally in direct proportion to the extent to which he was more moderate on issues. Benjamin Page, however, has shown that it is rare for either candidate to adopt a pure, moderate position.[5] Rather, the Republican candidate is generally right of center and the Democratic candidate usually assumes a more liberal stance. Why is there this tendency?

Downs's model and its subsequent elaborations seem most applicable to the general election. As will be seen shortly, their general conclusions break down completely when there are more than two candidates. However, even in a two-candidate nomination campaign there is one crucial difference from the Downsian model: the winner is selected as the nominee, not as the president. The nominee has to wage a second campaign. Thus, the candidate's behavior in the first campaign, especially that concerned with matters of public policy, must be affected by the final goal of becoming president. In Downs's model, a candidate in the preconvention campaign might want to adopt positions that are moderate within that party. Such a position, however, might prove disastrous in the general election. On the other hand, it might prove equally disastrous to adopt a moderate position in relation to the preferences of the general electorate, since the candidate would risk rejection by his party in the nomination campaign. The resolution of this dilemma leads to the observed divergence from the exact policy center. This dilemma, of course, is similar to the citizen's dilemma, which was described in chapter 4. Should he or she support the candidate who offers preferable policies or the one more likely to be elected?

The 1964 and 1968 Republican campaigns illustrate this dilemma. For long portions of the 1964 campaign, the two active candidates were Nelson Rockefeller, then governor of New York, and Senator Barry Goldwater, the eventual nominee. Goldwater was a conservative senator who appealed directly to the interests of conservative Republicans. Rockefeller's strongest claim was that he was a Republican who could win in November, a refrain he emphasized in his 1968 campaign against the more conservative Richard Nixon as well. In effect, he was telling Republican partisans, "If you give a little on policy grounds and support me, I'll be more likely to win the election than Goldwater, and you will not have an even less desirable president. Wouldn't you rather have me than Johnson (or Humphrey, or an even more liberal Democrat in 1968)?" The Gallup polls in 1968 bore him out his claim—until the very last poll prior to the Republican convention.[6] Goldwater's and Nixon's claims were that they better represented the opinion of most Republicans than did Rockefeller. Gallup Poll evidence bore *them* out, as well.

The potential tradeoff for candidates and partisans alike, then, is issues or ideology for electability. The candidates' tradeoff, that is, parallels that advanced in chapter 4 about the potential voters' tradeoff and is based on the same logic. Aranson and Ordeshook extended the Downsian framework to study this tradeoff. Their general conclusion was that, if party members use as criteria both the issues and electability, the best position for a candidate is some place between the policy center of his party and that of the electorate as a whole. The candidate cannot stray too far from the preferences of the party without becoming vulnerable to a candidate at the party's center. At the same time, a candidate who is directly at the party's center can be defeated by a rival who is a bit less ideologically pure, but a more likely winner in the general election. Their conclusion, then, is that Downs's prediction of moderation by both candidates in the general election must be modified. Candidates must often stray from the center to win their party's nomination. This explains, in large part, why the Democratic and Republican candidates are more liberal and more conservative, respectively, than each other and than Downs suggests. Just how far from the center a successful candidate will stray depends upon the weight the participants in primaries and caucuses place on issues versus electability, as well as on the candidate's ability to mobilize policy and other groups in the party.[7]

This tradeoff is exacerbated by the fact that party activists, those most likely to participate in the nomination campaign, tend to be more extreme than their inactive counterparts, especially in the Republican party.[8] Effectively, then, the active Republicans are more conservative and the active Democrats more liberal on many issues than the larger group of all party identifiers.

What does this analysis tell us about recent Republican nomination campaigns that were two-candidate affairs in whole or major part? The 1952 nomination struggle between Senator Robert Taft, known as "Mr. Conservative," and a more electable General Eisenhower fits the general pattern well, with a slight edge for electability. In 1964, Goldwater was ideologically very pure, perhaps even more conservative than his party, on average. Rockefeller, however, was just too liberal for most Republicans. His highest Gallup Poll standing among Republicans in 1964 was but 16%, and that was in January–February. By early June, he trailed Goldwater by 11 points, 21% to 10%. His fate in the 1968 election was much the same. Nixon was the first choice of most Republicans (in the last two polls, March and June, Nixon and Rockefeller were chosen by 60% and 24% and 60% and 23%, respectively), yet Rockefeller did better against Democratic opponents until the very end. In either case, it appears that Rockefeller just strayed too far left in the eyes of his party.

The 1976 Republican campaign also pitted a pure conservative against one less so. Ford was the choice of most Republicans through-out the campaign, but the gap was often small. In trial heats against a major Democratic hopeful, Ford proved to be slightly more electable than Reagan, and he was consistently so for the duration of the cam-paign, as the spatial view in figure 7.1 suggests. Reagan's strength lay in the greater activity of conservative Republicans faithful to him. These two narrow advantages, Reagan's strength among activists and Ford's electability, essentially balanced out and resulted in a very tight race.

The variations in Ford's and Reagan's chances to win the nomina-tion, slight though they might have been, were reflected in the variations in Gallup Poll standings reported in chapter 5. This reflection is to be expected when party identifiers are determining their preference in part on grounds of electability. While Reagan drew his support from the more conservative Republicans, primarily, and Ford from the less conserva-tive, the porportionate division of these groups shifted, at least margin-ally, as first one and then the other candidate appeared more electable.

The presence of Reagan as a strong contender had its effect on Ford in the longer term, however. Had Reagan not been an active candidate, Ford would have been able to play only one game, that of the general election policy competition. This freedom, granted to Johnson in 1964 and Nixon in 1972, was used to advantage in the general election. Rea-gan's candidacy, on the other hand, hampered Ford. He simply could not afford to stray too far from his party's policy center. Moreover, since he had to campaign against Reagan, he was unable to advance his themes for the general election until later. Given the razor-thin edge by which Carter won in November, it might be that the drag of Reagan's competition, which denied Ford the necessary room to maneuver, cost him the general election.

Democratic Positions: Ambiguity

If the Republicans' ability to adopt positions was relatively constrained, does this imply that the Democrats were unconstrained? The answer is, generally, no. The flexibility of most Democrats was also limited. The general public might have been unaware of the details of the positions of most candidates, but the attentive public was not. Certainly, the media personnel who followed the individual campaigns were aware of past positions of the candidates they covered; even when they were not, they had the incentive and the ability to find out where the candidate stood. It is the rare presidential contender who arrives on the scene unencumbered by past statements and actions as well as personal preferences about policy. After all, most candidates have held high public office, generally a national office. Even governors must often stake out positions on national issues, and generating the kind of background necessary to initiate an attempt at the presidency usually requires speaking out in public forums. Nonetheless, those few candidates who were relatively unconstrained by prior commitments could be relatively ambiguous.

Carter, for example, had held a major elective office for only one term, and that as governor of a state not ordinarily in the limelight. Further, he began his campaign much more quietly than most and focused on building grass-roots organizations rather than on gaining media attention. In fact, obtaining media attention prior to the Iowa caucuses was difficult for him. Thus, he was less constrained than his early rivals. It was less than coincidental that he and he alone would be accused of "fuzziness" and "wishy-washyness" on issues, and that the media coverage of his stands on issues was an attempt to *discern*, rather than *report* the policies he espoused.

Brown, too, was relatively unconstrained for much the same reasons, having been elected governor of California only two years earlier. In principle, he, also, was not invulnerable to charges of fuzziness. Indeed, he made a virtue of appearing enigmatic, and, in part for this reason, was not criticized for fuzziness. Thus, the two candidates least constrained by past behavior were also the two whose policy positions were most difficult to ascertain; a fact they appeared to capitalize on.

Is there a reason for this apparent attempt to retain an aura of ambiguity by the two least constrained candidates? Brams studied this question in the context of a multicandidate preconvention campaign. He demonstrated that, even if a campaign focuses on but a single dimension, there is no dominant position for any one of many candidates, as there is for both candidates in a two-candidate race. He discussed the effect of the entrance of a third or fourth candidate into a two-candidate race:

There are *no* positions in a two-candidate race . . . in which *at least one* of the two candidates cannot be beaten by a third (or fourth) candidate. . . . Indeed, it is easy to show that *whatever* positions two candidates adopt (not necessarily the same), one will always be vulnerable to a third candidate; if the other is not, he will be vulnerable to a fourth candidate. . . . There is, in fact, *always* a place along a left–right continuum at which a new candidate can locate himself that will displace one or more nearby candidates.[9]

An ambiguous strategy is developed in response to the inability to derive a single "best" position to adopt on issues. Of course, there is no guarantee that there is a "best" position even for two candidates in a multi-issue campaign.[10]

Shepsle developed a formal model of the strategy of ambiguity. He proposed that candidates who have the flexibility and who find themselves with no optimal issue position to propose (a situation that Brams demonstrates is endemic to multicandidate contests) should not adopt a precise position. Rather, they should communicate to the voters that they are offering a range of options on a given issue. For example, a Democrat might argue that expenditures for a given social service should be increased, without saying by exactly how much. The attentive voter, then, would know *approximately* where the candidate stands but would not know *exactly* where.[11]

The opposite of an ambiguous position was McGovern's tax reform proposal in 1972. The basic idea was to use income tax to provide greater financial security to the poor. McGovern specifically stated that $1,000 would be made available to all. This unambiguous proposal was open to easy attack. Hubert Humphrey, among others, criticized the proposal, apparently with telling effect, in such primaries as California. Humphrey, of course, would not have desired to or been able to criticize a less specific proposal. Indeed, had it been stated ambiguously enough, Humphrey probably would have supported the program. An ambiguous position was taken in 1976 by candidates who endorsed the spirit of the Humphrey-Hawkins full employment bill, then before Congress, without supporting the specific legislation.

The advantage of an ambiguous or fuzzy strategy is that the candidate may be able to appeal to a larger proportion of the electorate. Carter, for example, had great appeal among some of the more liberal *and* more conservative Democrats, winning surprisingly large support from blacks and from southern whites. The advantage of an ambiguous strategy is that it may not alienate votes on policy grounds. Carter's position on abortion was, roughly, that he personally opposed it except in life-endangering situations but that he also opposed a constitutional amendment prohibiting it. This position (the one most frequently called wishy-washy) alienated no one but the most committed "pro-lifers" and pro-abortionists. He stood to lose a greater number of voters by taking a clearer position at either extreme.

The disadvantage of fuzziness is that it lays the candidate open to charges of refusing to take stands and of pusillanimity generally. Carter had to face such charges. He did not suffer greatly in the preconvention campaign, however, for several reasons. First, the charges of fuzziness were made by the two Republicans, not by the Democrats. Thus, they could be dismissed by Democratic voters as partisan charges. Second, even the Republicans' attacks were not initiated until Carter had become the front runner and Jackson had been eliminated from contention. Udall, whose candidacy was at best marginal by this time, did not want to hurt his slim chances even further by appearing to be another McGovern. Rather, he needed to be perceived as a moderately liberal alternative and could not afford to carve out specific liberal programs with which to attack Carter's ambiguity. Carter's main opposition, then, came from Brown who, like himself, was avoiding concrete proposals. Third, there was no issue (or, at least, none was found) that provided Carter's opponents with a convenient point of attack. Thus, he was able to pursue his relatively ambiguous strategy. Later, we will see that this particular strategy was as consistent with Page's concept of emphasis as it was with Shepsle's notion of ambiguity.

Democratic Positions: Competition

If we take the general positioning of the candidates in figure 7.1 as an accurate accounting and add Brown and Church to the group of more liberal Democrats, we can return to Brams's analysis and investigate the consequences of these positionings.

Brams argues for the three-part division of candidates into "liberal," "moderate," and "conservative." As we did in the previous chapter, he argues that candidates initially compete within their policy bloc to achieve dominance as *the* liberal, conservative, or moderate; only later is there direct confrontation between the representatives of each bloc. It is this first level of competition that he claims results in the early winnowing of so many candidates. He concludes that a moderate liberal will emerge as *the* liberal, on the grounds that the least liberal member of that group will be the most likely to succeed. The competition among conservatives will usually be won by the moderately conservative candidate.[12]

In the 1976 Democratic campaign, there was, of course, only one conservative. Among the liberals, we have seen that Udall emerged victorious, when Brams's analysis would suggest that Birch Bayh was the more likely victor (if figure 7.1 is to be believed). Bayh's failure was perhaps the biggest surprise of the early campaign, excepting only Carter's emergence. The explanation is that Bayh competed for much the same voters as Jackson, concentrating not only on the Massachusetts and New York primaries, but also seeking union support and related traditional Democratic votes. Further, he campaigned as the "best politician" available, rather than as, say, the best liberal. Thus, Bayh was squeezed from the left (by Udall) and the right (by Carter and Jackson) instead of, as the most moderate liberal, squeezing the other liberals to his left. Brams argues that this squeeze from both sides is often an insurmountable difficulty for the middle person in a three-candidate race. (Perhaps, he suggests, this squeeze helped McGovern, and presumably Wallace, at the expense of the more moderate Humphrey in 1972.) What happened, then, was that Bayh played the wrong game by competing on the wrong grounds, and was consequently beaten for resources and in votes. It was, after all, his losses to Carter and Udall in New Hampshire and to Jackson and Udall in Massachusetts that ended his campaign.

Jackson and Carter, apparently natural competitors for the moderate vote, survived the winnowing phase by concentrating on different states. As was shown in chapters 5 and 6, Carter emphasized New Hampshire and Florida; Jackson, Massachusetts. Therefore, neither lost to the other in a contest bearing on their basic campaign strategy until the first phase of the competition was completed. This analysis reaffirms the importance of the New York and Pennsylvania primaries to Jackson and Carter. These primaries were the first major head-on clashes among these moderates.

The tradeoff between electability and policy facing Republicans was not absent on the Democratic side. Indeed, Brams's analysis of the winnowing process is based on selecting the best representative of one policy faction. That representative is the one who has shown the greatest promise of winning the general election. Udall became the liberal survivor because he defeated Bayh and the other liberals. While Udall did not win any primaries outright, he did better than any of his liberal opponents. Quite simply, liberal voters, thus, turned to him because there was no viable liberal alternative. The New York and Pennsylvania primaries can be interpreted as head-to-head confrontations between Jackson and Carter (even though Udall competed in both and finished ahead of Carter in New York). Carter defeated Wallace for the more conservative southern vote and then defeated Jackson for the support of the Democratic center. He did so by giving every appearance of being more electable than each of these two, in turn.

The tradeoff between electability and policy is demonstrated in the massive shifts of preferences of Democrats during the campaign. These changes in popularity, as measured by the Gallup Poll, much more prominent on the Democratic side and clearly tied to electoral success, reflect the importance of electability in attaining the nomination.

Up to this point, I have argued that the flexibility of most candidates was restricted. In general, their positions were fixed before the campaign began, because of prior stands and personal inclinations. Most candidates simply had to play their policy cards as dealt. Their flexibility lay more in choosing where to compete on the issues and against whom, and less in which positions to adopt. Those few candidates who were relatively unencumbered by prior positions, such as Carter and Brown, often avoided specific commitments. While this strategy has advantages and disadvantages, the situation in 1976 appeared to favor the advantages.

Emphasis on Issues

If candidates have relatively little ability to develop issue strategies in the sense considered so far, there remains the possibility of attempting to manipulate the relative emphasis placed on various issues during the campaign. Evidence will be produced to argue two propositions. First, each candidate develops a general strategy based on the set of issues that he believes will aid his candidacy most. Second, these issues changed during the campaign. In particular, the campaigns are fought publicly in individual primaries, for the most part, and candidates can emphasize issues that they expect will appeal most directly to the particular constituency whose primary is imminent. Therefore, we should be able to trace the general themes of each candidate and observe the variations in emphasis as a function of the sequencing of the primaries.

A third theme that will become evident is that the candidates have a great deal of control over which issues are extensively covered in the media. In the last chapter, it was seen that the candidates could control the media in the sense of making a state primary seem crucial or unimportant to their fortunes. Here, it will be seen that they also control the reporting of issues, at least to the extent that it is their own actions (purposeful or occasionally accidental) that lead to some issues being reported and not others.

If candidates are generally constrained in terms of what issues they can adopt, what can we expect in terms of the issues they choose to emphasize? Variations in emphasis are designed to raise the *salience* of that issue to the electorate. Suppose there are two issues and two candidates, one whose given position is more in line with the electorate's on one issue, the other on the other issue. Each candidate will attempt to raise the salience of "his" issue so that voters are more likely to vote on the basis of that policy dimension rather than on the basis of the dimension which favors the opponent's chances. That is, the candidates will become the entrepreneurs of their special appeal. A classic example is Humphrey's attempt, in the 1968 general election, to appeal for the support of union members and others who favored Wallace on social or "hard-hat" issues, Vietnam, and the like by emphasizing traditional Democratic economic issues. Apparently, this strategy worked, as Wallace's support eroded and Humphrey's increased. Often such issues are chosen as the general theme that underlies each candidate's campaign.

We can also expect that candidates will not emphasize issues on which their competitors are known to have similar positions. As we shall see, this was the situation of the two Republicans on many domestic issues. If the candidate does not have something distinctive to offer, there is little electoral advantage to stressing that issue.

Many issues are partisan in orientation, dividing Democrat from Republican. Such traditional issues as the degree of government intervention in economic and social affairs evokes general agreement among most Republican and most Democratic leaders, but the two groups of party leaders often have opposite views. One reason that issues may seem to play a lesser role in preconvention campaigns is that intraparty divisions are often much smaller than interparty divisions. There are notable exceptions, of course, such as the cross-cutting effects of Vietnam in 1968. The difference between McCarthy and Kennedy on the one hand and Johnson and Humphrey on the other were more profound than the difference between Humphrey and Nixon. As a result, electoral choice could have been based much more heavily on the issue of Vietnam in the Democratic nomination campaign than in the general election. Obviously, as well, George Wallace was very different from George McGovern, Morris Udall, or even Hubert Humphrey and Henry Jackson, and Barry Goldwater was very different from Nelson Rockefeller. These exceptions do not belie the general point that intraparty divisions are usually much smaller than interparty differences.

Another exception to the above argument should be noted. Even when the competition is in basic agreement about a given policy, speaking out early and often on that issue can be an effective tactic. A candidate may be able to co-opt the issue, making it perceived more as "his" issue than anyone else's. The voter may reason that the candidate who places greater emphasis on the issue may be expected to expend more effort to achieve that policy once in office. That is, the candidate gives the issue a higher priority, or appears to do so.

It has been noted earlier (e.g., in chapter 6), that candidates have game plans or scenarios for forming winning nomination coalitions, such as Jackson's appeal to blue-collar workers. What is relevant here, though, is that he also emphasized those issues most likely to win the support of those citizens. The general themes sounded by each candidate are designed with this central core of hoped-for support in mind.

The development of issue strategies occurs over time, and we should expect dynamic elements to enter in several ways. First, some issues appear not to catch on with the public, while others appear to do so. Therefore, we should expect the emphasis on issues to change. A good example will be seen with Reagan's position on welfare. Second, if an opponent's issue does catch on, the candidate may be forced to react to it. Ford had to do so on several foreign-policy issues. Third, there may be a natural evolution as certain situations arise independently of the campaign. Finally, since primaries occur in a sequence and each state has a different constituency, candidates will tailor their emphasis to that particular electorate, as well as to the particular candidates who are opposing them in that primary.

Another expectation is based on the fact that preconvention campaigns are intraparty affairs. The kinds of concerns addressed should reveal stark differences between the two parties. Republicans will compete for Republican votes on Republican-style issues, and Democrats will emphasize traditional Democratic concerns. It is not until a candidate has defeated all opposition that he can generate themes useful in the general election. Until that time, the candidate must be concerned with his immediate opposition.

The strategy of emphasis is theoretically tied to the strategy of ambiguity. Benjamin Page has developed a theory of "emphasis allocation." Shepsle viewed ambiguity in terms of ranges of positions on issues. Page posits an alternative model, one in which candidates simply do not discuss certain issues. By talking about some issues and not others, candidates can manipulate the salience of issues in the electorate. This model is consistent with the one developed here. One of Page's major conclusions is that "the emphasis theory predicts that candidates place all their emphasis on consensus issues and say nothing about issues of conflict."[13]

Our evidence will support this contention—and Page's notion of emphasis allocation—but only in part. It is true that the Republican candidates discussed issues on which most Republicans would have a relatively consensual position vis-à-vis Democrats and that most Democrats discussed issues that were traditional Democratic appeals. However, there are important exceptions. The candidates usually did attempt to differentiate themselves from their opponents. Reagan, for example, argued for quite different directions in foreign policy than Ford, and the conflictual nature of his appeals was reflected in intense debates during the Republican Party's platform hearings. The Panama Canal Treaty renegotiation issue that Reagan emphasized generated conflict that outlived the 1976 campaign and pitted Republican against Republican. We shall see evidence both for and against the emphasis allocation theory throughout our analysis.

The Measurement of Emphasis on Issues

The data to measure the emphasis placed on issues were derived from three daily newspapers. The first two are national papers, *The New York Times* and *Washington Post*. The *Lansing State Journal* was also clipped daily to obtain a record of what a medium-sized newspaper reported (often, therefore, what wire services reported). The daily coverage of the Republican campaign was followed from January 1st until the 1976 Republican Convention opened and was cumulated weekly (ending on Tuesdays to coincide with most primary election dates). The Democratic coverage ran from January 1 to the week after the last primary and was recorded in a similar fashion. Since the purpose was to record what a generally inattentive public might notice, only major, often headline, stories about issues were included. Thus, although my other analyses of news reportage were exhaustive, this count purposefully was not.

My basic concern was to aggregate the stories by the type of issue reported. Secondarily, stories were classified according to the candidate or candidates, if any, who were the central figures in the story. The expectation of differences between the parties was realized, and slightly different categories had to be constructed to reflect this disparity.

Domestic policy was divided into eight types of issues and these categories were used as uniformly as possible. However, the frequency and content of the eight categories varied substantially by party. One category applicable to both parties was economic and tax policy. Various federal social services—such as education, labor, health insurance, mass transit, and aid to the cities—were mentioned frequently by Democrats. On the Republican side, only social security was mentioned at all frequently, and even that was rare. Welfare and Reagan's proposed transfer of responsibility for welfare to the state and local level, however, received much attention. Neither of these two issues seemed important to the Democrats except in isolated instances. Both issues were retained as separate categories for the Republican analysis. An early Democratic (especially Carter) issue was bureaucratic reform. Although it quickly receded, it was made a category for that party. The questions of energy and environmental issues were raised occasionally in both parties, but more frequently by Democrats. It was more common for Democrats to support conservation and other environmental concerns and to oppose oil conglomerates and nuclear power plants. The Republicans were more likely to argue the opposite on energy matters. Both parties raised agricultural issues rarely, and only Democrats considered farm labor issues. The last Democratic category consisted of problems related to minorities—ethnics, blacks, the poor, and women. Such issues were rarer on the Republican side, and fully half of these were raised by groups other than the candidates (e.g., blacks and ERA groups who attacked the stance of the Republican candidates). However, the question of busing became a short-lived but hot Republican issue. There was also an "other" category of scattered concerns for both parties.

Democrats discussed foreign and defense policies so rarely that only those two general categories were necessary. On the Republican side, defense was one category, but foreign affairs was divided into three. The role of Nixon and his policy of détente, Kissinger's stewardship of foreign affairs, and general questions about the Soviet Union made up one category; the Panama Canal and treaties were a second; and "other foreign" was the third. Notable in the "other" category was a spate of articles about Rhodesia.

The distribution of the types of stories is shown in table 7.1. Given nine fewer weeks of coverage of the Democratic campaign, approximately the same number of stories were recorded for each party, but the types of issues were dramatically different. While barely one-fifth of the Democratic stories were about foreign policy and defense, over half the Republican stories concerned these matters. Indeed, Kissinger alone figured in almost as many Republican stories as there were all Democratic foreign-affairs stories combined.

Issues Emphasized by Republicans

The stories reported in table 7.1 that could be classified as from or directly about Ford or Reagan are divided in table 7.2. The number of stories is less than in table 7.1 because some stories were attributable to neither candidate and some were attributable to both.

Two points are noteworthy. First, the large proportion of the Republican issue stories *could* be attributed to one candidate or the other (117 of 171). Second, substantially more stories concerned Ford than Reagan, over a 2:1 ratio. There are two reasons for this unexpected result.

One is the advantage of incumbency. Presidents are always covered extensively in the media as they perform the duties of their office. One of the president's major duties has become to initiate as well as execute public policy. Incumbents running for another term in office are quick to capitalize on this resource as an electoral tool. Ford was no exception, using bill signings and vetoes, statements to Congress, and the like as a major part of his campaign strategy. This strategy is so usual that its title, "White House strategy" (or its 1976 name, "Rose Garden strategy") is commonly understood.

Reagan was in the position of most candidates. In general, it is their day-to-day travels that are reported by the media, and candidates develop a stock speech that is repeated with few changes from one stop to another. The speech can contain only a relatively small number of themes. Only rarely do candidates have the time or the forum to pre-

Table 7.1 Newspaper Coverage of Issues Emphasized by the Two Parties, 1976

Republicans

Issues	No. of Stories	Percentage of all stories about Republican Campaign
Foreign & defense policy	105	52.5
Defense	(20)	(10.0)
Détente, Kissinger, USSR	(32)	(16.0)
Panama Canal	(20)	(10.0)
Other foreign	(33)	(16.5)
Domestic policy	95	47.5
Economy & taxation	(13)	(6.5)
Busing & school segregation	(18)	(9.0)
Welfare: $90-billion reform	(9)	(4.5)
Social security	(4)	(2.0)
Energy & environment	(8)	(4.0)
Agriculture	(7)	(3.5)
Minorities, etc.	(9)	(4.5)
Other domestic	(27)	(13.5)
Total	200	100.0

Democrats

Issues	No. of Stories	Percentage of all stories about Democratic Campaign
Foreign & defense policy	33	19.3
Defense	(6)	(3.5)
Foreign policy	(27)	(15.8)
Domestic policy	138	80.7
Economy & taxation	(20)	(11.7)
Busing & school segregation	(18)	(10.5)
Federal social services	(21)	(12.3)
Bureaucracy reform	(5)	(2.9)
Energy & environment	(13)	(7.6)
Agriculture	(5)	(2.9)
Minorities, etc.	(28)	(16.4)
Other domestic	(28)	(16.4)
Total	171	100.0

SOURCE: Based on analysis of stories in the *New York Times*, *Washington Post*, and *Lansing State Journal*, from 1 January 1976 to the national party convention for the Republicans, to two weeks after the primaries for the Democrats.

Table 7.2 Issues Emphasized by Ford and Reagan, 1976

Issues	Ford Stories		Reagan Stories		All Republican Stories	
	No.	Percentage	No.	Percentage	No.	Percentage
Foreign and Defense Policy	65	55.6	32	59.3	105	52.5
Defense	(13)	(11.1)	(5)	(9.3)	(20)	(10.0)
Détente, Kissinger, USSR	(20)	(17.1)	(12)	(22.2)	(32)	(16.0)
Panama Canal	(11)	(9.4)	(7)	(13.0)	(20)	(10.0)
Other foreign	(21)	(17.9)	(8)	(14.8)	(33)	(16.5)
Domestic Policy	52	44.4	22	40.7	95	47.5
Economy & taxation	(8)	(6.8)	(2)	(3.7)	(13)	(6.5)
Busing & school segregation	(15)	(12.8)	(7)	(13.0)	(18)	(9.0)
Welfare & $90-billion program	(3)	(2.6)	(4)	(7.4)	(9)	(4.5)
Social security	(2)	(1.7)	(1)	(1.9)	(4)	(2.0)
Energy & environment	(2)	(1.7)	(4)	(7.4)	(8)	(4.0)
Agriculture	(3)	(2.6)	(0)	(0)	(7)	(3.5)
Minorities, etc.	(6)	(5.1)	(0)	(0)	(9)	(4.5)
Other domestic	(13)	(11.1)	(4)	(7.4)	(27)	(13.5)
Total	117	100.0	54	100.0	200	100.0

SOURCE: Based on analysis of stories in the *New York Times*, *Washington Post*, and *Lansing State Journal*, from 1 January 1976 to the national party conventions.

sent a new, major address, and reporters can write or broadcast only so many stories about their set speeches. This is a fact of life for candidates at all levels and in both primary and general election campaigns. The structure of a protracted campaign virtually necessitates a stock speech; yet the media must provide protracted coverage. The complaints that little attention is paid to the issues may rest in large part on this basis. Reagan could say only so much new about issues in the 170 or so days of active campaigning for the Republican nomination.

The second reason for the disparity between the number of Ford and Reagan stories is that Reagan was most often on the offensive and Ford on the defensive. Often a small number of stories initiated by Reagan required a larger number of responses by Ford. For example, over half the stories about Reagan's stand against Kissinger were about Reagan's national television address and immediate follow-ups. This sort of forum is so penetrating that only this one address was virtually all Reagan needed to say on the subject, while Ford was forced to spend a longer period of time in reaction. The media play up such situations; any apparent weakness provides a basis for continual questioning by reporters in their regular meetings with candidates or press secretaries.

Turning now to more specific questions, recall our expectation that the issues themselves flowed from a general, nationally oriented perspective, but that the raising of specific issues was timed with an eye on imminent primaries.

Reagan began his campaign by emphasizing some domestic issues. In particular, he was concerned with welfare and with promoting the so-called $90 billion welfare reform. He proposed to shift the responsibility for welfare to the state and local levels at a saving, he claimed, of $90 billion. This issue tapped a standard conservative and Republican Party theme of reduction of central government control. However, the $90 billion saving became something of a symbolic tag line that could be tellingly attacked by Ford, his supporters, and the media, much as McGovern's $1,000 income tax return proposal was easily rebutted in 1972. Reagan was forced from an offensive to a defensive posture. Seven of the nine recorded stories on welfare occurred during the New Hampshire campaign, one in the week immediately following. There was only one story after that. Much the same happened with the Social Security issue, when Reagan was also forced on the defensive. Few stories about Social Security from the Republican perspective postdated New Hampshire.

Reagan also had the problem of running a campaign against an opponent whose basic domestic policy positions were just not that different.
The distinction between Ford and Reagan on most domestic issues paled
in comparison with the difference between either of them and the host
of liberal Democrats.

Finally, Reagan's two issues, especially Social Security, simply would
not set well with voters in the following competed primary, in Florida two weeks later. In 1964, Goldwater had paid the price of sounding
anti-Social Security in Florida, with its heavy concentration of elderly
voters, and his mistake was not to be repeated.

Reagan developed a second complex of issues that was much more
suited to both his national and his Florida campaign: foreign policy.
At the national level, many conservatives were disenchanted (to say
the least) with Kissinger's foreign policy, with Nixon's handling of relations with the Soviet Union, and especially with détente. Ford's policy
was aligned with Nixon's in all of these areas. Here, a sharper distinction between Ford and Reagan could be drawn, an offensive position
could be maintained, and there was a receptive audience. Republicans,
in particular, were likely to be receptive to these appeals. These issues
first surfaced in Florida and were emphasized by Reagan in his television address soon thereafter. The reasoning was made clear in the quotation in chapter 2, p. 45. Sears and Wirthlin approached Reagan the
morning after the New Hampshire primary, to persuade him to discuss
foreign policy in Florida on three grounds: (1) getting the press to for-
get the $90 billion plan; (2) trying to make Ford react and perhaps
make an error; and (3) to offer a "more clear-cut contrast" between
Reagan and Ford then could be made on "any domestic issue."

The Panama Canal and the then-current renegotiation of our treaty
with Panama was an issue of much the same order. Ford was in the
position of defending the so-called "giveaway." It was anathema to most
conservative ideologues, and Florida Republicans were among them. As
Witcover wrote:

> The issue of American rights over the canal, long in dispute between
> the Panamanian and American governments and long the subject of
> negotiation, was hardly a matter of primary concern to Americans
> in 1976. But it was a kind of litmus test for patriotism among conser-
> vatives, as Reagan knew, and certainly it was when it was discussed
> —as Reagan invariably did—in terms of American's unalienable
> rights . . . For a while, the Panama Canal pitch was not much of

an applause-getter. But then one day, before a retirement community in Sun City, near Tampa, Reagan cranked it out, and out of the blue, bedlam broke loose. "Reagan, who knows his audiences very well, was so taken aback that he lost his balance," [Reagan's southern coordinator, David A. Keene said]. After that, references to the canal were sure-fire cheerlines.[14]

References to all foreign and defense categories were heavy in the week of the Florida primary for the first time and continued to be so throughout the remainder of the campaign, as Reagan made these issues cornerstones of his national policy campaign.

Kissinger, détente, defense, and the Panama Canal Treaty issues differ in several respects from many domestic issues. First, the key words are as much symbols or slogans as they are substantive concerns with specific policy options. To illustrate, Ford declared that his policy with the Soviet Union would no longer be called détente, even though the actual policy would be unchanged. Second, to the extent that there were distinct choices, they tended to be general directions of policy ("we are becoming the second strongest power military, and we must be first,") or there were exactly two choices (Kissinger would either have a foreign policy role in the next administration or he would not, the Panama Canal Treaty would either be renegotiated or it would not). Third, foreign policy and defense are of concern to a relatively small proportion of the public. Evidence from all previous elections indicates that it is the extremely rare instance in which votes are cast on such policy grounds. The action in issue voting is in domestic policy. It was just this type of appeal—inspecific, symbolic, concerned with direction of policies in general rather than specific programs—that led Page to his theory of emphasis allocation. The contrasts between Reagan on welfare and foreign affairs support Page's case.

Occasionally, of course, outside events intrude. Roughly one-quarter of all "other foreign" stories, and all but one of those that appeared just before the last primaries, were concerned with Ford's initiative in response to a stray comment by Reagan. Reagan stated that he might consider sending troops to Rhodesia to help quell armed conflict over racial policies there. Reagan's initial comments were made during the week of the Texas, Alabama, Georgia, and Indiana primaries. Ford's initiative was focused primarily on California voters.

Ford did not press the Rhodesia comment in the more conservative states where Reagan's comments were made, or in Ohio or New Jersey,

whose primaries were held on June 8th, like California's. Recall that
Ford was trying to pin Reagan in California to keep him from competing effectively in Ohio. Ford used televised commercials and attacks
on Reagan on Rhodesia and on school busing to keep Reagan concerned
in California while he concentrated on Ohio. What the Rhodesian comment provided Ford was a specific way of bolstering his counterclaim
that Reagan was "irresponsible" about foreign policy, to voters who
would be receptive to the charge that Reagan might precipitate another
Vietnam style U.S. military adventure. Again, the characteristics of
most foreign policy concerns were present, the symbolism, the lack of
specific proposals, etc.

The emphasis on domestic policies differed substantially from those
on foreign policies. As noted, the differences between the two candidates were much more difficult to portray in the domestic concerns.
However, issues of a more concrete nature were argued, and the particular policies raised were tailored much more directly to the specific
primary at hand. Agricultural issues were raised in Illinois, North Carolina, and Nebraska, but rarely anywhere else. Concern about minorities,
an issue developed largely in reaction to Carter's "ethnic purity" comment, was confined exclusively to the time of the Pennsylvania primary
and to Ford alone (Reagan was inactive in that primary). There was
only scattered concern about energy and the environment—except in the
Michigan campaign (debate was focused on energy in the automobile
state) and in the Texas campaign (where concern was expressed about
the oil-depletion allowance). The busing issue, which arose in the Democratic Party in Massachusetts, was not debated by the Republicans
until much later, largely because the candidates did not campaign in
Massachusetts, where busing was a controversial issue. Of the 18 Republican stories about busing and school segregation, 15 appeared in
the two weeks before the California primary. Busing was somewhat of
a hot issue there, especially since the Los Angeles busing plan was in
the courts at that time. Much as he did with the Rhodesia issue, Ford
attempted to appeal to California voters on this issue with the purpose
of tying Reagan to that state and keeping him from Ohio. While the
issue had little impact on voters (there was hardly any difference between the two candidates' positions), the strategy proved effective.

The only domestic issue recurrently emphasized was the economy and
taxation. Even this issue was concentrated early in the campaign; 6 of

the 13 stories dealt with tax policy in light of Reagan's $90 billion trans-
fer program, an issue that disappeared before Ford's victory phase did.

Stories in the large "other domestic" category were scattered over
many issues. Many of these were predictable: gun control in Texas, the
seeking of stronger drug penalties, also in Texas; importation of manu-
factured goods, in manufacturing states; and the like.

Beginning the week after the Pennsylvania primary, when Carter vanquished his last active rivals, and growing throughout the rest of the
campaign was a new type of issue. Both Republican candidates began
to attack Carter as fuzzy or wishy-washy on issues. Earlier, with the
exception of but a few scattered reactions, such as to Carter's "ethnic
purity" remark, the Republicans had fought their own campaign. As
Carter emerged as the likely Democratic nominee, both Republicans
began to take a little time to attack him on issues, almost exclusively in
terms of fuzziness (and their charge concerned Carter's approach to issues, rather than specific policies). Until that time, neither Ford nor
Reagan desired to commit themselves to interparty policy debates, and
even when they did, specific policies were not questioned. The two candidates were locked in such a tight struggle for the nomination that they
did not have the latitude even to begin to establish the general campaign
themes that the eventual nominee would have to muster in short order
—and that Carter was able to initiate over several months.

In general, few concrete policies were discussed during the Republican preconvention campaign. It was a campaign dominated, like few
others, by foreign policy issues that bore very little on the sorts of concerns on which most voters base their decisions. The foreign policy advantage was held by Reagan because he was able to be on the offensive
and keep Ford generally on the defensive. This point seems particularly
crucial when it is recalled that the people who did react to these foreign
policy concerns were the intense, vocal minority of conservative Republican activists. Our description appears to fit the emphasis allocation
theory. The major difference lies in the necessity for each candidate to
try to differentiate himself from his opponent. A strategy of emphasizing
only consensual issues, ones on which neither candidate differs, let alone
the public, simply cannot be maintained. Nonetheless, the general picture
of shifting emphasis, of vagueness introduced into some issues by simple
neglect and into others by refusing to *take* a specific position and, in-

stead, attacking the opponent's specific position, meshes well with the theory of emphasis allocation as a basis of ambiguity.

Issues Emphasized by Democrats

The analysis of the Democratic campaign tells much the same story, but about a quite different set of issues. Like the Republicans, the Democrats emphasized issues that long had been cornerstones of the party's philosophy and its coalition. Like the Republicans, each Democratic candidate established general themes for the campaign and modified them appropriately for each primary constituency. Like Ford and Reagan, the Democrats emphasized direction of policy and avoided advocating specific programs.

Each candidate's allocation of emphasis is shown in table 7.3. The full distribution of Carter's emphasis is shown in that table. The major concentrations of most of his opponents are also indicated. The summary of the concerns of all candidates but Carter includes Bayh, Harris, Shapp, and Shriver in addition to the candidates listed. Some newspaper reports about issues could not be attributed to a specific candidate.

Carter, like most Democrats, deemphasized foreign and defense policy. Only Jackson and Church had much to say about foreign policy. Jackson's emphasis, a cornerstone of his candidacy, will be discussed shortly. Much of Church's emphasis derived from his role as chairman of a Senate subcommittee investigating CIA practices, a role that continued through much of the 1976 preconvention campaign and delayed his own active campaign.

Issues Emphasized by Carter's Opponents

As a general rule, Carter's opponents discussed many of the same issues as he. The economy and taxation are major issues in all campaigns, and these candidates provided no exceptions. Democrats generally emphasize issues related to the coalition forged in the New Deal, and most candidates in 1976 discussed minority issues and federal social services. The interparty differences in these two areas are stark. Democrats were much more likely to campaign for federal programs related to education, labor, aid to cities, mass transit, and government health insurance. The Republicans emphasized more typically Republican concerns, such as welfare and Social Security. Concern for the minorities was not a major Republican theme, but in the Democratic Party, the candidates actively cam-

Table 7.3 Issues Emphasized by Democratic Candidates, 1976

Issue	Carter Stories		Other Candidates							All Democratic Stories	
	No.	Per-centage	No. Brown	No. Church	No. Jackson	No. Udall	No. Wallace	No. All but Carter	Percentage All but Carter	No.	Per-centage
Foreign & defense policy	5	8.1						16	20.7	33	19.3
Defense	(1)	(1.6)						(1)	(1.3)	(6)	(3.5)
Foreign Policy	(4)	(6.5)		5	9			(15)	(19.5)	(27)	(15.8)
Domestic policy	57	91.9						61	79.2	138	80.7
Economy & taxation	(10)	(16.1)	3		3	5		(14)	(18.2)	(20)	(11.7)
Busing & social segregation	(3)	(4.8)			4	2	3	(9)	(11.7)	(18)	(10.5)
Federal social services	(15)	(24.2)			5	7	2	(16)	(20.8)	(21)	(12.3)
Bureaucratic reform	(5)	(8.1)						(0)	(0)	(5)	(2.9)
Energy & environment	(1)	(1.6)	4					(8)	(10.4)	(13)	(7.6)
Agriculture	(3)	(4.8)		3		2		(3)	(3.9)	(5)	(2.9)
Minorities, etc.	(14)	(22.6)						(8)	(10.4)	(28)	(16.4)
Other domestic	(6)	(9.7)						(3)	(3.9)	(28)	(16.4)
Total	62	100.0						77	100.0	171	100.0

paigned for programs of concern to blacks, the poor, women, and Jews. The large concentration of Carter stories in this category can be traced to his "ethnic purity" remarks and his subsequent elaboration.

In contrast to Carter, the other Democrats discussed environmental issues and busing, and did not make major points about bureaucratic reform. Carter was able to avoid the busing issue (in part because his campaign in Massachusetts was a last-minute affair), at least more than his competitors. Note that the symmetry of the two-man Republican campaign was not as clear-cut in the multicandidate Democratic campaign, because each of the many candidates articulated a unique theme or set of related policies. (This distinction between the two campaigns bears out the argument in chapter 6.)

Henry Jackson, a powerful senior senator, may be classified as a "traditional Democratic liberal"—that is, often liberal on bread-and-butter domestic issues and an advocate of a strong foreign policy. Constrained by his personal beliefs and prior actions, Jackson advanced general themes in 1976 consistent with this characterization of him. Foreign policy was the cornerstone of his campaign, differentiating him from his opponents. Key words in headlines reflect his stance: JACKSON— FORD'S NAVY PLANS IMPERIL SECURITY, CHALLENGES DETENTE, SCORES PLANNED SALES TO EGYPT, COLD WARRIOR, AGAINST KISSINGER. His foreign and defense policies were similar to Reagan's in that they were attacks on the incumbent. Added to the anti-Kissinger and anti-détente themes was a major concern (virtually his exclusively in 1976) with the Middle East.

If Reagan's foreign policy initiatives were successful, why weren't Jackson's? The answer lies in the constituency to which the appeals were directed. Republican conservatives were likely to sympathize with Reagan's statements, Democrats simply were not responsive. Jackson, as entrepreneur, cornered a very small market.

Jackson's Middle East policies were different. He raised them primarily in two states, Florida and New York. These states have heavy concentrations of Jewish (and hence Democratic) voters, and his appeals were directed to them. The Middle East presented Jackson with an issue on which his stance was well known long before 1976, on which he hoped to find large blocs of sympathetic voters, and on which he was able to blend both his foreign-policy expertise and his domestic interest in forging a new New Deal coalition.

Jackson's domestic policies also fitted into his general theme. The key words in these headlines reflected the scattered themes that have long been emphasized by Democrats: Jackson on URBAN ISSUES, CITIES, HEALTH PROGRAMS, JOBS, ENERGY, and JACKSON—MOVING LEFT.

Two specific issues that Jackson discussed illustrate the influence of the specific constituency of each primary. The New York primary was crucial for him, as it was for Bayh, and eventually, for Carter and Udall. Each of these four raised the issue of aid to New York City or its school system when campaigning there.

Jackson, like Udall, Wallace and, to a lesser extent, Carter, was concerned about the busing of school children to promote desegregation. None of them was strongly for it. Indeed, Udall in the context of the busing issue said that he preferred to be called a "progressive" rather than a "liberal." Of the 18 Democratic stories on busing, 11 were published prior to the Massachusetts primary; 8 in the two weeks preceding it. Four more busing stories can be attributed to Carter's reaction to the Republican emphasis on busing in the California primary. The facts that busing was a major issue in Massachusetts, that the primary was contested vigorously on the Democratic side, and that Wallace was still considered a major threat, explain virtually all of the emphasis placed on this issue by Jackson and his opponents.

Udall, in his competition for dominance among the group of liberal candidates, emphasized standard Democratic liberal concerns. Key words in headlines illustrate the point well; Udall on MASS TRANSIT AID, FEMINIST ISSUES (ERA and child care), EMPLOYMENT (specifically the full employment Humphrey-Hawkins bill), HEALTH INSURANCE, OPEN HOUSING and FEDERAL PUBLIC HOUSING, JOB PLAN, and GUN CONTROL (he was for it). His change from "liberal" to "progressive" in the context of busing in Massachusetts is related. Udall was attempting to be portrayed as a moderate, or at least as not too extreme a liberal. Not only was he attempting to avoid the problems of McGovern in 1972 but (consistent with Brams's spatial analysis), he was attempting to moderate his liberal stance.

The basic change in Udall's strategy was from sounding his own themes to doing so in the context of criticizing Carter. This move is consistent, of course, with the thrust of the campaign. Carter was the odds-on favorite for the nomination and, as we saw in the last chapter, Udall was aligned with others in trying to slow him down. The change is a dramatic one. Before the New York and Wisconsin primaries, no Udall story was primarily an attack on Carter. After that date, virtually all Udall stories were aimed at Carter: Udall on Carter's position on open and federal public housing, on Carter's position (or at that time lack thereof) on the Humphrey-Hawkins employment bill, and on Carter and a proposed federal takeover of some welfare programs.

The other challengers for the nomination survived too few primaries to produce general themes and then modify them substantially. The general themes of each were reflected, however, in the few issue-related articles published about them. For example, Bayh (aiming at the New York primary) was the subject of a few stories about abortion, opposition to allowing the Concorde to land in New York, and opposition to Ford's policies with respect to New York City. Stories about Wallace focused heavily on busing in his Massachusetts campaign, anti-abortion measures, and scattered but predictable concerns. Stories about Church concerned his CIA investigation, women's rights, gun control, and so forth. Stories about Brown were focused on economics (his "small is beautiful" pitch) and environmental matters, notably his ambiguous position on limiting nuclear plants. One headline read: BROWN REMAINS NON-COMMITTAL ON BID TO LIMIT NUCLEAR PLANTS. The media placed much more emphasis on "the Brown phenomenon," meaning his dramatic rise in the primaries, than on his policies. The three major issue stories about Harris illustrate his liberal "People's Campaign": HARRIS WANTS TAX ON CAPITAL GAINS, HITS OIL GIANTS, and WANTS HALT IN THE BUILDING OF ATOMIC POWER PLANTS. All three were printed after he was "winnowed in" in Iowa, but before the New Hampshire primary, when he was effectively winnowed out again.

Issues Emphasized by Carter

Carter's was the only Democratic campaign similar to Ford's and Reagan's in terms of length of time in the limelight. Thus, there was a similar number of issue-related stories from and about him. The particular issues addressed were, of course, different, but there were a number of similarities with the two Republicans.

Carter began the campaign, much like Reagan, with a theme he dropped quickly. Carter announced his desire to reduce the size of the federal bureaucracy, much as he reminded people he did as governor. This issue is a complex one when gone into in any detail, and one more in keeping with standard Republican than Democratic philosophy. As Carter began to address specific liberal constituencies and to advocate more federal programs, his arguments for trimming the bureaucracy became awkward and he dropped them. There was only one preconvention reference to bureaucratic reform after the fourth week of the primaries. Carter's references to federal social services supplanted the bureaucratic reform theme and were concentrated in the weeks of the New York primary campaign (federal aid to New York City), the Pennsylvania primary (several references to government health insurance), and during the California, New Jersey, and especially the Ohio primaries. Significantly, 6 of 15 stories about Carter's concern for social programs were printed the week *after* the last primary, as he moved to unify the party and shift his attention to the general election.

The majority of stories about Carter's stand on minority issues appeared during just one week, the week after the New York and Wisconsin primaries. During those campaigns, Carter uttered his "ethnic purity" remark, claiming that urban neighborhoods should be encouraged to maintain their ethnic heritage. The remark went unnoticed until after those two primaries, but was picked up with a vengeance thereafter. The term "ethnic purity" was loaded with symbolic content and was open to attack. It was not so much the content of Carter's statement as the terminology that sounded so bad. After dissembling in defense of the remark, Carter issued an apology that led to the end of the controversy. Carter was lucky. The remark became salient after one set of primaries and was no longer publicized in the last two weeks before the next primary, Pennsylvania's; thus, time was able to heal any serious wounds. Moreover, Democrats generally did not attack Carter for his comments. Indeed, several came to his defense publicly. And the black electorate, presumably those most likely to react negatively to the phrase (and a key constituency in Pennsylvania) had nowhere else to turn. Neither Jackson nor Udall had much success in obtaining the support of blacks. Carter, however, had, in part due to the campaigning of such black leaders as Andrew Young and the Rev. Martin Luther King, Sr. Carter's ability to hold onto the black vote in Pennsylvania cemented the death of "ethnic purity" as an issue.

The few stories about Carter's foreign policy, mostly attacks on Ford's policies, were scattered until the week of the Michigan and Maryland primaries. At that point, Carter foresaw victory and began to shift from an internal to an interparty campaign.

From the week after Pennsylvania to the end of the primary season, Carter's positions on issues received little publicity. The emergence of foreign policy concerns, slight though it was, accounted for virtually all such reports, except for agriculture issues (in Nebraska) and a few others. However, during the last week of the primaries and the week following there were 27 stories (over 40% of the total of such stories) about Carter's positions. In part, this concentration was due to the interest of the media in the Democratic winner. Some of the stories cited groups backing Carter, but others were generated by Carter himself, as he moved to unify his party and advance issues that might prove useful in the general election. The heavy concentration of stories about federal social services has been noted already; there were also stories about minority issues. There were, for example, stories about Carter's position on health insurance, ERA, energy, regulation of industry, transportation, aid to cities, and education. At this time, he also picked up a theme from Jackson, one that he had not emphasized previously: the Middle East. Like Jackson, Carter used this issue to combine policy with an appeal to a traditionally Democratic group. One of Carter's major statements of his Middle Eastern policy and support of Israel was reported in a story headlined CARTER GETS AN OVATION AFTER ASSURING JEWS IN NEW JERSEY ON HIS RELIGIOUS VIEWS. The general picture of Carter's position on issues, then, is of an outsider to the traditional Democratic Party moving ever closer to its mainstream, until at last, in his attempts to unify and solidify the Party around his banner, he sounded very like the typical Democratic nominee. His acceptance speech culminated this shift, and was reported widely in just these terms.

Conclusions

I began this chapter by posing three questions about the use of issues in preconvention competition: What positions should be taken? Should a candidate be specific or ambiguous? Which issues should be emphasized and which not? All three involve slightly different but fundamentally related aspects of policy competition. Two basic questions remain. First, what bearing, if any, does the policy competition in the spring have on the competition in the fall? Second, and more important, what long-term effect does policy competition in preconvention campaigns have on policy in the United States? This question will be discussed in chapter 8.

Competition based on the issues in the 1976 preconvention campaign had remarkably little effect on the issues raised in the general election. One fundamental reason for this discontinuity is the shift of the contest from two rather independent intraparty affairs to one interparty race. Partisan differences that were irrelevant in the spring become very relevant in the fall. Second, the protagonists are different. In 1976, this meant that there were no relative extremists, no Reagan, Harris, Udall, or Wallace. Rather, there were two candidates nearer their respective party centers.

The Republican campaign illustrates these two points. Reagan and Ford were competing in the spring for the support of Republicans, a relatively conservative group. Realistically, they were competing for the support of a minority of Republicans, a minority that was more conservative than most Republicans and more attuned to specific matters of policy. Foreign affairs were more important to them than to most groups in this society. Moreover, Reagan could criticize Ford's policy on the Panama Canal. In the fall, Carter had neither the incentive nor the inclination to challenge Ford's policies. As a result, the Canal issue went entirely unmentioned after the Republican Convention.

What strikes one the most is that the issues in the preconvention campaigns were remarkably distinct from those the public believed to be the most important. The Gallup Poll surveyed public opinion in late April 1976 and in late October 1976. The results, shown in table 7.4, demonstrate that the economy was by far the central issue in the minds of the citizens.

Moreover, identifiers of both parties agreed, although they differed substantially over which aspect of the economy was more problematic, particularly in the context of the partisan fall campaign. The contrasts between the problems concerning the public and those to which the candidates spoke in the preconvention campaigns (see table 7.1) are stark. Even the Democrats discussed foreign affairs far more than its apparent relevance to the public. Both parties discussed economic affairs much less than the public's concern about them warranted (even though table 7.1 includes the issue of taxation, not included in the Gallup Poll tabulation).

Although Ford and Carter did discuss foreign and defense policy extensively in the fall, they emphasized economic issues far more than in the spring. Gallup reported that, in early October 1976, 45% of the

Table 7.4   The Citizens' View of the Most Important Issue, 1976:
Distribution of Responses to the Question, "What Do You Think
Is the *Most* Important Problem Facing the Country Today?"

Issue	Percentage of Total	Percentage of Democrats	Percentage of Republicans	Percentage of Independents
Spring 1976				
High cost of living	38	39	38	36
Unemployment	24	27	19	25
Dissatisfaction with government	13	13	8	15
Crime	8	7	11	8
Foreign affairs	5	4	6	5
Fall 1976				
High cost of living	47	46	51	45
Unemployment	31	40	22	24
Dissatisfaction with government	6	6	3	8
Crime	6	6	7	7
Foreign affairs	6	4	10	7

SOURCE: *Gallup Opinion Indices*, Report 131 (June 1976), p. 25; and 137 (December 1976), p. 29. The surveys were conducted from April 23 to 26 and from October 22 to 25, 1976.

Emphasis in question was in the original. The five areas reported above include all listed in the Indices in which one of the four categories of respondents exceeded 5% selecting that area (except, of course, the "all others" category).

sample polled cited inflation, and 33% unemployment, as the most important problem.[15] By late October, the percentages were 47% and 31%, respectively. Thus, not only was there a remarkable disjuncture between what the candidates emphasized in the spring and in the fall, but the fall campaign was based on issues that were much more important to the bulk of the electorate. Indeed, in the fall, the economy was virtually the *only* "most important problem" reported in the polls.

The sharp discontinuity between preconvention and postconvention issue emphases should not be construed as evidence that the spring campaigns did not bear materially on the candidates' campaigns on issues in the fall. For example, Carter was forced to drop his bureaucratic reform message early in the spring; consequently, he was unable to develop this theme as well in the fall as he might have. His movement toward typically Democratic concerns in the preconvention campaign undoubtedly helped shape the public's view that he was, or had become, a typical Democrat. Ford's long and close struggle to defeat Reagan had several important consequences that Carter was able to avoid. Ford was forced to continue the intraparty competition in the convention itself and was unable to generate his general election campaign themes until much later than Carter. His very low standing, vis-à-vis Carter, in the polls around the time of the conventions is attributable, in part, to the tougher competition he faced. He also faced a divided party in the convention, divided over policy as well as personality, while Carter had a month to unify his party before his convention opened. Finally, because Reagan's offensive posture kept Ford on the defensive most of the time, he was unable to set his own agenda even in the intraparty competition. Thus, the differences between the preconvention campaigns had a very real effect on the candidates ultimately selected to compete for the presidency and on their room to maneuver during the final portion of the campaign.

The general point that a major opponent or issue in the nomination campaign can force a candidate to modify his behavior in the fall campaign is exemplified by Humphrey in 1968. The strong antiwar sentiment in his party led him to modify his position on the Vietnam War (in the Salt Lake City speech discussed in chapter 5) so he could appeal to erstwhile McCarthy and Kennedy supporters. It was feared that otherwise, the left would not vote for the Democratic nominee. There is evidence of this point in the effect of Reagan and his conservatism on Ford's behavior in 1976. Faced with strong opposition from a conservative, Ford did in fact offer more conservative positions in the election year, at least by one important measure. The president, on legislation about which he took a public position, was in more frequent agreement with the conservative coalition in Congress (defined by roll call votes in which a majority of Republicans and southern Democrats opposed a majority of other Democrats) in 1976 than in 1974 and 1975. Ford's position was in agreement with the conservative coalition in at least one chamber of Congress 83.3% of the time in 1974 and 1975. In 1976, the level of agreement rose to 96.9%—all but one instance. The effect of Reagan's emphasis on foreign affairs is also visible. Ford's agreement with the conservative coalition rose from 79% in the preceding two years to 100% in the election year (the comparable figures for domestic policy are 87.8% and 95.4%, respectively).[16]

Benjamin Page has studied in detail the positions candidates present to the electorate in the general election campaign. His analysis, like mine, rests on rational-choice models in general and on spatial models in particular. He contrasts two sorts of theoretical results: those that predict that both candidates will converge to the center ("public opinion" theories) and those which predict that, while the midpoint of public opinion exerts some pull on the candidates, the two candidates nonetheless will fail to converge completely at the center ("party cleavage" theories). More particularly, he argues that candidates will fail to converge on those issues that have long divided and that continue to divide both the leaders and the identifiers of the two parties. His empirical findings are strongly supportive of party cleavage theories. Rarely were the candidates he analyzed unaffected by the pull of votes to be won by taking policy positions at the center of the entire electorate. At the same time, none of the candidates adopted a central position on all issues. Their divergences were closely related to differences in opinion between party identifiers in the electorate. That is, the candidates did not take central positions on issues that divided the electorate; Democratic candidates took positions more consistent with potential Democratic voters, and Republican candidates aligned with Republican supporters. Typically, these issues were ones that had divided partisans for years, even decades.[17]

A variety of factors helps explain this divergence. For example, a Democratic candidate might be a Democrat precisely because his or her own preferences are consistent with the party's position. A very important set of factors leading to this divergence, however, is related to the nomination campaign. To be successful, a candidate must win the support of the mass of the party identifiers (to win votes in primary elections), of party activists (e.g., those willing to donate money or time to a candidate of that party), and of party leaders (including those partisans willing to attend the national convention as delegates). As a result, the pressures of the nomination campaign might be expected to separate the candidates of the two parties precisely on those issues that divide the parties. The development of Jimmy Carter's issue strategies as he sought the nomination is a clear example of the effect of these forces.

Jimmy Carter began his quest for the nomination as one outside the established Democratic Party. Indeed he made a virtue of this fact, capitalizing on what could have been a liability. He had never served in Washington, and he ran initially on what many perceived as an anti-Washington platform. He was a southerner, and his early strategy was to present himself as a viable southern alternative to those who supported Wallace. He had headed a relatively small bureaucracy, and he claimed that he had reformed and streamlined it substantially. He had relatively little experience in national politics, and he argued that he was not beholden to special interests or to entrenched elites.

These campaign themes proved effective in the early phase of the campaign. He used them to distinguish himself from many competitors like Jackson and Bayh, who had long been connected with Washington. Nonetheless, these very themes engendered suspicion in those who had played major roles in national Democratic politics for many years. That he was an outsider led some to wonder how he could manage the massive, contradictory Democratic coalition. That he was inexperienced in Washington politics and that he had not worked with most Democrats in power led some to question how successful he would be in dealing with Congress and the federal bureaucracy. That he was a southerner led some to wonder how attuned he would be to the needs and interests of such traditionally Democratic groups as labor. That he was inexperienced in foreign affairs and a fundamental southern Baptist led some to hesitate about his dedication to such standard Democratic groups and issues as the Jewish constituency and support for Israel. That he was presenting himself as a southern alternative to Wallace led many liberal groups to hesitate to embrace him.

The analysis of the issues Jimmy Carter discussed over the course of the nomination campaign tells a clear story. He and he alone discussed such issues as reforms of the bureaucracy early in the campaign. As he emerged as front runner he dropped such appeals and began to emphasize issues in the Democratic mainstream. In an attempt to unify the party and assuage the uncertainties of traditional Democratic leaders and partisans, he spent more and more time discussing health, jobs, and related issues. By June and July, reporters began to perceive him as a standard Democrat. As a result, he entered the general election with policy positions (and a public perception of his positions) completely in line with the party cleavage theories outlined by Page. Page discovered little evidence of a shift in the positions of candidates on the issues in presidential campaigns from 1964 to 1972. Jimmy Carter is a candidate whose treatment of the issues changed rather broadly and fundamentally during the preconvention campaign. But it was a change not so much in the positions adopted as a wholesale change in emphasis.

8   Conclusions and Implications

The three basic themes of this book are that the rules of the preconvention campaign influence the candidates' behavior; that the candidates are rational actors seeking the best means to their ends within this complex of institutional rules; and that the dynamics of the six or so months of the preconvention campaign affect the candidates, their behavior, and their success or failure. In the remainder of this book, I have attempted to demonstrate the veracity of these themes.

The purpose of this chapter is to step back a bit from the details of the argument and the 1976 campaign and to consider some of the more general questions my view of the preconvention campaign raises. First, a number of specific aspects of a candidate's campaign have been modeled. These various aspects are not independent. Just how do the pieces fit together to create a more unified accounting of candidates' decision making in the preconvention campaign? Second, the arguments in this book have been based primarily on a single election year, evaluated retrospectively. If the arguments are plausible, they should tell us something about other campaigns occurring under somewhat different circumstances. What, if anything, can the arguments made here tell us about what to expect or to look for in 1980? Do likely candidates in 1980 possess characteristics similar to those found in 1976? The Democratic Party has proposed new rules, some of them intended for the 1980 campaign. What consequences will these new— or, for that matter, proposed and possible—changes in the institutional context have on future campaigns? Third, how does the nature of policy competition in the preconvention campaign affect the victorious president and, hence, the country? Finally, what does this view of nomination politics tell us about the nature of the men likely to become major party nominees, and thus about the nature of our presidents?

Toward a Unified Theory of the Preconvention Campaign

The central chapters of this book can be divided roughly in two. Chapters 2 to 4 contain the background: of the candidates, of the institution, and of the citizen as participant. Chapters 5 to 7 present the strategic problem, how the candidates mold the background to achieve their ends: that is, by exploiting the dynamic forces, and by deciding which primaries to contest, which issues to emphasize, and which policies to advocate. Once a candidate decides to seek the nomination, explores the rules and laws of the campaign setting, and evaluates the participating citizen, the strategies to pursue are not separable pieces but related elements of a unified decision-making process.

That the same events recurred in each chapter illustrates, in itself, that each decision a candidate reaches is related to all others. Reagan's decisions about the time of the North Carolina primary exemplify the point. First, his financial resources were depleted. Second, his popularity and prospects for the nomination were waning. While his victory in North Carolina was both slight and surprising, it provided him with the base from which to launch a reversal of his fortunes. It appeared likely that the Wisconsin primary would result in a narrow defeat that would reduce the gain made in North Carolina. His decision to withdraw from the Wisconsin race capitalized on an informal norm of the media (candidates are not considered defeated if they say they are not contesting a given primary, at least outside their central core). Reagan's decision to withdraw deprived Ford of his best outcome (defeating an active opponent), thus illustrating the relationship between one candidate's strategy, the other's, and the outcome. Reagan simply moved attention to the next competed primary, in Texas, a more congenial state.

Reagan's decision to address the nation instead of competing in Wisconsin on a daily basis accomplished several things. His televised address allowed him to acquire sorely needed money. It enabled him to appeal directly to the national electorate and perhaps reverse his declining fortunes (e.g., as reflected in the Gallup Poll of Republicans). It also provided him with a forum for changing the policy emphasis of his campaign. He had found a receptive audience in Florida but had not gained national attention to his new emphasis on foreign affairs. Before his direct appeal to the nation, the average citizen was aware only of Reagan's welfare plan, if of any policy. By criticizing Ford's foreign policy, Reagan captured the attention of all the media for several days. He moved from a defensive to an offensive posture, put Ford on the defensive, and alerted Texans about "a policy you can support and an issue on which you probably don't agree with Ford." In short, at one stroke, Reagan was able to change his strategy in a variety of related contexts.

Rarely can we observe such a dramatic change in campaign strategy, one which demonstrates so vividly the close relationship among the myriad aspects of *a* campaign strategy. This does not mean that the typical strategy is not as closely intertwined; it means only that it is usually more difficult to perceive the relationships.

Let us use the decision to contest a primary as a focal point. To contest a primary means that the candidate expends resources and risks failure in the hope of gaining delegates and momentum. Failing to compete in a primary ordinarily means foregoing but a very few delegates from that state. But it preserves resources for later events *and* avoids the risk of losing momentum. In the two-candidate race, one candidate can eliminate the dynamic effect of a primary simply by failing to contest it. In the multicandidate race, one candidate can minimize the prospects of a negative dynamic for himself, but he cannot guarantee that other candidates will not obtain the costs or benefits of the dynamic. This is a clear distinction between two-candidate and multicandidate campaigns. In the first case, both candidates have greater or more direct control over the dynamics. As a result, they are both more likely to compete in primaries when the outcome is likely to be close. In the second case, individual candidates have less control of the situation. As a result, they are more likely to lay their candidacies on the line in a small set of selected states—those whose electorate comes closest to their perception of the central core or heart of their campaign. Also, since the candidate's perception of the central core is more or less public, defeats outside the central core are not as serious. Carter's defeats in Massachusetts and Nebraska, like Jackson's in Florida, were not as important as Wallace's in Florida or Bayh's in Massachusetts. Or, in the two-candidate race, as Ford's defeat in Texas and Indiana or Reagan's in Michigan.

It is the nature of the policy emphasis and appeal of the candidate that defines his central core, which primaries are expected to be close and which noncompetitive, what their expectations should be, and the like. Candidates begin the campaign with a past history of policy stands, with personal preferences about policy, and with a plan about which issues to emphasize and which to deemphasize. This strategy changes during the course of the campaign. The first way it varies is the tailoring of issues to emphasize the concerns of the electorate whose primary is imminent (busing in the Democratic primary in Massachusetts, for example). This variation is natural and predictable. Reagan's move towards foreign policy illustrates a second time-related variation. Quite simply, he needed a new focus which would distinguish him from his opponent and yet find a receptive audience. His first attempt failed on objective grounds (i.e., appeared not to find a receptive audience in New Hampshire, in the media, or in the nation.) This led him and his staff to seek a second focus to help change electoral and resource dynamics.

Carter's changed focus illustrates a third type of variation. His issue strategy evolved rather than changed abruptly. It evolved as his initial objectives were met, enabling him to appeal to the party as a whole. By the end of the campaign, he was stressing traditionally Democratic themes to solidify his support in the party and to unify it under his banner. This evolution required some of his initial appeals (e.g., for bureaucratic reform) to give way to the necessity of appealing to the many constituent groups of the Democratic Party. The luxury of stressing traditional Republican themes in the same fashion was never available to Ford, because he was never clearly the dominant candidate. Indeed, the Reagan-Ford policy competition ended only after the Republican Convention itself was well under way.

In sum, policy, resource, delegate, and vote gathering strategies are inexorably intertwined. Where a candidate competes is a decision made in light of the dynamics of the campaign. Does he have sufficient resources on hand to conduct the type and extent of campaign desired? Can he expect to receive sufficient support in the state to replenish those resources? Are his chances in the state improved through prior success?

What kind of campaign is to be conducted? What appeals should the candidate make? Is there an audience receptive to these appeals? All these aspects of setting strategy are part and parcel of the decision. When strategy is changed, are these changes designed to affect resource dynamics, to change or to broaden the appeal to the electorate, or to win more delegates? Ordinarily, a change in strategy is designed to change all three. The revealed weakness of a strategy generally means that the expected electoral support was not there, that the delegates were not won, as expected, that his appeal as a candidate was not as great as hoped, and that he was not and will not be able to generate the resources he planned to receive to continue his quest for the nomination. A campaign strategy, that is, consists of making a variety of related choices.

1980 and Beyond

At this writing, the 1980 presidential campaign is just beginning to unfold. The cast of candidates likely to try for the nomination is assembling, and the Democratic Party has modified the rules governing its preconvention campaign. In this section, I shall examine the set of possible candidates to see if they are consistent with the model developed in chapter 2. Then I shall speculate about the consequences of some new, proposed, and possible changes of the rules on the conduct of preconvention campaigns in 1980 and beyond.

Who Might Run in 1980

The campaign for the 1980 Democratic nomination will be quite different than those of the 1970s. An incumbent president seeking reelection is a major hindrance to the proliferation of candidacies common in the absence of an incumbent seeking renomination.

Incumbents have such reservoirs of resources (broadly defined) that their initial probability of nomination is very high. Ford, in 1976, was a good example. He was the first incumbent to have no experience at running a national campaign, to have tested himself electorally only in one congressional district, and to have assumed the vice presidency by appointment and the presidency upon Nixon's resignation. Yet his decision to run for the nomination effectively ruled out the opposition of all but the strongest opponent. The power of incumbency can also be measured by considering the odds of Ford's defeating Reagan, regardless of how narrowly, had Ford not been president.

At this writing, the only important challengers to Carter are Kennedy and Brown. Kennedy's massive and long-held popularity places him in a category all his own, perhaps as even a stronger competitor to Carter than Reagan was to Ford in 1976. The prospects of a Brown candidacy seem dimmer. It is, of course, what has been called the Brown phenomenon, his gathering of momentum as Carter swept to victory in 1976, that makes it at all plausible that he can attain the nomination. Judged by the criteria developed in chapter 2, both Brown and Kennedy possess very few liabilities.

The Republican campaign is more similar to the Democratic ones of the 1970s. With no incumbent, there is a much larger field of candidates. Reagan is running again and is considered the initial leader. (Ford is "available" much like Humphrey was in 1976, and, much like Humphrey, he may be forced to campaign actively or forego his nomination hopes.) The most prominently mentioned others, all of whom have declared their candidacies, include: John Anderson, a moderate congressman from Illinois; Howard Baker of Tennessee, Republican leader in the Senate; George Bush, a former congressman from Texas, former head of the CIA, diplomat to the People's Republic of China, former Republican national chairman, and a senatorial candidate from Texas (defeated by Lloyd Bentsen in 1970); John Connally, former Democratic governor of Texas and holder of several positions in the Nixon administration; Philip Crane, a conservative congressman from Illinois; and Senator Robert Dole of Kansas. I shall take these seven as the core set of possible candidates, although some may join and others leave this list before the campaign ends.[1]

The candidacies of these seven men are consistent with some of the hypotheses tested in chapter 2. Many come from a strong electoral base. The offices of senator or governor are the elective offices held currently or immediately preceding by four of them. Three—Anderson, Crane, and Bush—have not held an office with a strong electoral base, but they hold or held the next elective office down the opportunity structure, U.S. Representative. Bush and Connally held high appointive office between their last elective office and the 1980 campaign.

Of the three that currently hold no office, only one, Bush, can be said to have left office under less than favorable circumstances, or at least was defeated in his senatorial campaign. What was first noticeable in 1976, indeed, may be a trend. There does appear to be a tendency for candidates who currently hold on office to emerge, quite possibly due to the rigors of the complex preconvention campaign. The first three hypotheses in chapter 2 are not contradicted.

The fourth hypothesis concerns reelection status. Three of the possible four candidates must stand for reelection in 1980: Anderson, Crane, and Dole. Anderson and Crane, of course, are in the same position as Udall or any other member of Congress. Dole is not. It is not certain that he can run for renomination after learning his fate at the convention. Thus, the reelection hypothesis is not well supported.

Only three of these Republicans have proven to be risk takers. The four who have not demonstrated a proclivity for risk taking are Anderson, Dole, Crane, and Connally. John Connally's partisan conversion might be argued as evidence that he has risk-taking propensities, but he has not demonstrated them in the terms set forth in chapter 2. John Anderson's outspoken liberalism might be considered a sign of risk taking in the Republican Party, if not by my measure. Dole is in a position not unlike Shriver's in 1976. Both were defeated vice-presidential nominees four years earlier. Perhaps having had that nomination may compensate for the lack of at least demonstrated risk-taking attitudes. Crane is a conservative ideolog who is now considered a long shot. He may be running less for the presidential nomination than for future goals (later office or an attempt to assume the mantle of conservative spokesman when Reagan, who is now 67, relinquishes it). Whatever the case, the risk-taking hypothesis is not supported.

New Rules and Their Consequences

On June 9, 1979, the Democratic National Committee adopted a series of rules for the selection of delegates proposed by the party's rule revision panel, the Winograd Commission.[2] The rules adopted contained four major provisions, one a modification of a change enacted at the 1976 national convention.

In 1976, the convention approved that all delegations must be selected by proportional allocation. The effect of this rule, compared to other formulas, is to encourage candidates who do not expect to win a primary or caucus outright to enter the fray (see chapted 6). The debate in 1979 centered on the threshold, i.e., the percentage of the vote below which no delegates could be won. In 1976, Reagan lost all the delegates in Rhode Island because he received about 30% of the vote when the threshold was 33⅓%. The higher the threshold, the more closely a proportional primary approximates a winner-take-all primary.

The plan finally approved contained two parts. In all caucus states, and in the selection of delegates at-large in all states that hold primaries, the threshold must be between 15% and 20%. The exact figure is to be determined by the individual state. As a consequence, unsuccessful or fringe candidates will now find it difficult to win delegates to the convention. In states that hold primaries and select delegates at any sub-state level, the threshold is to be proportional to the number of delegates selected in the unit. Since many districts selected three delegates in 1976, their threshold would have been 33⅓%, like the Rhode Island Republican primary. However, the proposal was amended to make 25% the maximum threshold. The general effect will be to set the threshold between 20% and 25%. This plan reflects the continued debate between those who, in 1976 and earlier, wanted to allow winner-take-all provisions and those who did not. In 1976, the Democratic loophole was the compromise. In 1979, those supporting winner-take-all or loophole provisions lost further ground. For example, if the Democratic vote in the 1976 Massachusetts primary had been uniformly distributed throughout the state, and its districts selected four delegates each, all delegates would have been uncommitted, because Jackson, the plurality winner, failed to reach the threshold figure of 25%. The result of this provision will be something close to national uniformity (on the Democratic side, at least) with all states employing something in between a purely proportional formula and a loophole or plurality-within-district formula. A proposal that was tabled until the 1980 convention would have permitted a district to select only one delegate. If approved and enacted, any primary using this plan would revert to a loophole or winner-take-all primary, where "all" is one delegate.

Warren Weaver, Jr. has reported on the results of the Democratic Party's Compliance Review Commission, headed by Peter Kelley, whose mission was to implement the ban on loophole type primaries enacted at the 1976 convention (I have not been able to ascertain its relationship to the Winograd Commission). Weaver states that the commission proposed formulas with the following consequences: "If only one candidate reaches the threshold, the next highest vote-getter is awarded

one delegate automatically, to prevent a winner-take-all situation," even
at the district level. Thus, if one candidate receives 99% of the vote
and an opponent 1%, the winner of 1% of the vote would receive one
delegate. Also, "if no candidate reaches the threshold, delegates are distributed among the winner and all candidates who came within 10 percent of his share of the vote."[3]

The most important consequences of the enacted provisions are to
make the allocation rule only a marginal consideration for most candidates, under most circumstances, but to be less discouraging to candidates with bleak prospects of a first-place victory than winner-take-all
primaries.

A second major alteration was a shortening of the primary season.
In 1976, delegate selection procedures stretched over five months on the
Democratic side and seven on the Republican. The new rule for Democrats is that they are to be limited to three months: the second Tuesday
in March through the second Tuesday in June. When it takes full effect,
this change will reduce the primary season by about two weeks but will
reduce the caucus season more substantially. This provision, then, continues the Democratic attempt to make caucuses more primary-like. The
plan is to confine all caucus procedures to the primary season. The immediate consequence will be to make them less newsworthy and less
integral to candidates' plans. In 1976, the early Democratic caucuses,
such as Iowa, and the late Republican ones, such as Missouri, attracted
the attention of the media and the candidates (and helped start Carter
and stop Bentsen) because there was no proximate primary. Such caucuses drew the largest turnouts, something less likely to happen under
the new rule.

New Hampshire's primary (and other early primaries and caucuses)
may be exempted from this plan. If and when New Hampshire is forced
to move its primary date, it seems unlikely that it can retain its status
as the very first primary state. If, let us say, the New Hampshire and
Massachusetts primaries are held on the same date, New Hampshire
will lose its unique status. Its primary will be overshadowed by its neigh-
bor's or by that of any other larger state, in terms of attention—from the
media (see chapter 3) and from the candidates (see chapter 6). One
other consequence may be to reduce the permeability of the nomination
process to the outsider, to the little-known candidate, to the long shot.
As a very small state, New Hampshire can be worked by a grass-roots
campaign that costs relatively little money but relatively much time.

Effort can substitute for media attention, money, and name recognition. Jimmy Carter would have found it more difficult to attain the nomination had he needed to win an early primary in a larger state through a more media oriented campaign.

Let us suppose that the delegate selection process is shortened further. At the extreme, if all primaries were held on one day, the result would be, in effect, a national primary. A series of regional primaries, or just many simultaneous primaries in all regions, might be a middle ground. Cramming thirty or more primaries into a very short period would have many consequences.

The preceding argument, that the nominating process will become less permeable to all but established, well-known figures, would be intensified by the reduced role of dynamic forces. At the extreme, with a single national primary, the dynamic forces would be quite different. That is not to say, of course, that there could be no dynamic forces. We saw that Humphrey's 1968 general election campaign suffered from them and then benefited from them. Popularity would still be measured by the Gallup Poll over the course of the winter and spring. Such measures of popularity could serve as a vote surrogate, as in the general election. They would not, however, be reinforced by primary votes, news coverage, and television primary night specials, presumably reducing their impact. By becoming less salient to the average citizen, the polls would affect the acquisition of resources less powerfully. The rises and falls of candidates would be less common and less dramatic. As a consequence, initial levels of support would be more determinate of final outcomes.

Dynamic forces would be affected further by the shortened time. It takes time for the full effect of a victory in a primary to be realized. A highly visible victory may increase the candidate's ability to collect money, but it is technically difficult to capitalize on this ability quickly. It takes time for the full effect of a surprising success to be realized by the electorate, let alone to be taken advantage of by the candidate. The citizen will have less time to assimilate the unfolding information and to reach or change decisions and behavior. In 1976, the first few primaries were spread over a relatively large portion of the primary season. Thus, the result of the individual primary could be assimilated more fully. Again, the most obvious consequence of a muting of the dynamics of the preconvention campaign would be to reduce its permeability.

The effect of a short primary season on the organization of campaigns might be great. Campaigning in thirty or more states in a very short period of time is an even more complex task than now, and it would tend to favor those with the largest initial resources.

The candidates would have less time to prove themselves, to learn during the course of the campaign (most candidates, after all, have run few if any national campaigns), and to modify or change their strategy. Both Republicans, for example, benefited from experience gathered during the campaign. Reagan was able to make substantial changes in strategy. Ford's campaign went through several reorganizations and several campaign directors. The shorter the period involved, the less time there is for the candidates and their campaign committees to develop, learn, or adapt—and even if adaptation is possible—for it to be demonstrated fast enough.

The citizen is in a similar situation. One view of the current nominating process is that it provides the citizen with an opportunity to acquire information and to observe the actions and reactions of the candidates as campaigners, as politicians, and as leaders of a large organization. The shorter the length of a campaign, the less time the citizen has to learn about the candidates and how they react to the demands and rigors of a campaign. There would also be less time for the candidates to articulate well-rounded programs. Currently, as the campaign moves from one state to another, the candidates have the opportunity to raise different issues in different locales. The shorter the campaign period, the less time there will be for a candidate to discuss, say, social security in Florida, agricultural issues in Nebraska, and energy policies in Texas, etc. There would also be less opportunity for the media to present the candidates' views on the various issues. Once the shorter period begins, the media will be under even greater pressure to concentrate on the horse-race aspects of the campaign. In short, the briefer the campaign, the lesser its role as a proving ground for the candidates and as a learning situation for the citizens.

One final example of the consequences of a proposed rule change concerns the oft-proposed regional primary.

The idea of a regional primary is that several adjoining states hold their primaries simultaneously to simplify the campaign. There were some regional-type primaries in 1976. Massachusetts and Vermont held their primaries on the same date; so did Oregon, Idaho, and Nevada. In 1980, Connecticut will hold a primary on the same date as the other two New England states and the Oregon, Idaho, and Nevada primaries will again be coordinated. The oil states of Texas, Louisiana, Arkansas, and Oklahoma considered holding their primaries at the same time. However, the uncertainty of Texas's primary date makes that coordination unlikely. There has been some bizarre politicking (including several legislators, "Killer Bees," in hiding while Texas Rangers searched for them), and Texans have so far failed to resolve their primary procedures. All told, as many as 36 states may hold primaries in 1980, although some have legislated voluntary party primaries. The most obvious effect of regional primaries would be to induce bias into the system, a bias created by the increased proportion of relatively homogeneous portions of the electorate who play their role in nomination politics simultaneously.

Consider the 1976 Republican campaign. Ford was expected to do well in the northeast, Reagan in the south and west, and both to have more equal chances in the midwest and the border states. Clearly, regional primaries would have had tremendous consequences on the campaign. If the northeast held its primary first, followed by the midwest, the border states, the south, and then the west, Ford would have had the advantage. Reagan would have had the advantage had the order been reversed. Whatever, the sequence, that sequence would favor some kinds of candidates and campaigns over others. To be sure, the present ordering of the system is not neutral. However, regional primaries would concentrate relatively more homogeneous electorates than the 1976 system, which began in New England, moved to the South, to the Midwest, to the South, to the Midwest, to the East, and back to the South again for the Texas primary.

The Implications of Policy Competition

In chapter 7, it was argued that there was a sharp disjuncture between policies advanced during the nomination and the general election campaigns. In part, this discontinuity is natural. In the preconvention campaign, the competition is between candidates of the same party and, as long as the nomination remains competitive, directed at partisans of that party. The candidates must differentiate themselves from competitors from the same party and must win the support of their party identifiers. The general election campaign, on the other hand, is an interparty affair, conducted to influence the electorate as a whole. Ordinarily the nominee must hold the bulk of his party, attempt to win the growing independent vote, and cut into the other candidate's party support as best he can. The competition, therefore, is simply one Democrat versus one Republican. When there are many nomination candidates, they stress their own themes and proposals and attempt to place them high on the public agenda. Such a preconvention campaign presents the electorate with more alternatives and more disparate views of even the same policies. This diversity may be considered good, presenting a fuller menu of policies to the public, or bad, sounding cacophonous. At any rate, the preconvention campaign is different from the fall campaign.

John Kessel has termed this discontinuity a change of political "seasons."[4] He identified three seasons: the nomination, the electoral, and the executive (i.e., after the president is in office). Each season is different. In general, he found the first and last more alike, particularly in respect to the amount of public policy discussion. In the 1972 general election campaign, he found more emphasis on group politics, national unity, and the blending of themes into a more unified whole. In the other two seasons, he found a "relatively clean, policy oriented pattern" that was more dominated by policy and more distinctly divided into specific policy domains. My findings are not inconsistent with his. I have already discussed some of the consequences of the preconvention campaign on the postconvention contest. But what of the third, and, for the workings of democracy, most important season?

Contrary to conventional wisdom, campaign promises are not idle rhetoric. The limited research available shows that executives do attempt to act upon their campaign pledges. Kessel cites evidence that governors elected between 1944 and 1964 carried out almost 80% of their campaign pledges and that Johnson and Nixon redeemed about 60% of theirs.[5] Carter has been more self-conscious about this than most. Of course, political reality prohibits the direct translation of promise into policy. Ordinarily, however, the attempt is made and the programs enunciated in campaigns tend to appear on the incumbent's legislative and executive agendas.

The evolution of Carter from outsider to insider, along with the heightened emphasis on economic problems after the convention, assume added importance in this context. His policy in office resembles more his campaign in June, July, and November than it does his campaign in January or February. Nonetheless, some issues placed on the agenda even before the conventions have had a substantial impact on national policy.

The Panama Canal issue that Reagan raised is the most obvious example. Neither Ford nor Carter discussed the Canal much after Reagan was eliminated, in part because it was an issue on which they differed little and in part because the conservatives that Reagan addressed were not a key to either's electoral hopes. Nevertheless, the forces that Reagan unleashed (and was barely able to control himself) were felt long after his defeat, very nearly led to defeat of the treaties, and may yet be felt again. Howard Baker's agonizing decision to support the treaties, for example, was a key to their passage; it will make it difficult for him to avoid the wrath of treaty opponents, who are heavily concentrated among conservative Republicans.

Carter's preconvention campaign speeches about minorities and federal social services provide another example. Since the majority of Carter's references to minorities (as tabulated in chapter 7) concerned his "ethnic purity" remark, it is fair to say that he deemphasized these areas until he moved to unify the party late in the spring. Until then, he concentrated on the economy, the bureaucracy, and the like. His behavior in office is more like his early than his late campaign: the conflicts between programs and budget have been resolved more heavily in favor of the budget than the traditional Democratic Presidents. Black leaders such as Vernon Jordan and liberals such as Ted Kennedy observed this point very early in Carter's administration.

One of the key economic issues in early 1976 was the so-called "full employment," or Humphrey-Hawkins, bill. The bill was a symbolic indication that its supporters favored fuller employment rather than less inflation. Carter did not take a position on the bill, *per se*, until after his nomination; even then, he endorsed only portions of what had become a substantially modified proposal. His conduct in office has been consistent with his conduct in the campaign. Obviously, reality has played an important role in his decisions; nonetheless, Carter's campaign is not irrelevant to an understanding of his behavior.

Finally, and possibly most important, many themes that were prominent in the preconvention campaign are now absent from view or greatly reduced in salience. A large part of the explanation is that the candidates who articulated many of those concerns are no longer in a position to influence public opinion or the conduct of the presidency. As I noted in chapter 7, the candidates' emphasis in the preconvention campaign correlated weakly with the public view of important problems. Without an attentive and concerned public and an active and highly visible spokesman, the emphases of the defeated contestants recede. That the Panama Canal issue remained salient was due to the simple facts that the treaties had to be decided one way or the other and to the existence of an intense, vocal minority who had spokesmen and advocates in key positions.

The Nature of the Candidate Who Survives

A presidential election can be thought of as an attempt to survive. The candidate who does so longest wins the presidency. This book has been addressed to the questions of who survives longest and why.

The largest screening device occurs first, as individuals decide whether or not to run for president. In general, this screening eliminates those who are not white, male, Christian, and who do not have policies that are at best close to the mainstream. Second, most nonpoliticians and most politicians who have not already won high elective office are virtually eliminated at the outset. Third, the year of the election tends to reduce the set of candidates further, by eliminating most of those just elected to high office for the first time and those who must stand for reelection. Also, if a presidential incumbent decides to run for reelection, that also reduces the chances of those in the same party who do not possess unusual qualifications. When an incumbent seeks reelection, the two parties will have quite different fields of contenders. This timing is more or less fortuitous. Whether or not, say, a senator must stand for reelection is more a matter of luck than an inherently political factor. However, the political implications for, say, a member of Congress are clear, as they are for those states that have moved the gubernatorial election to a nonpresidential year.

A fourth factor is the recent proliferation of primaries and related reforms. The preconvention campaign has become more arduous, complex, and resource-demanding. This, combined with its increased importance, has made it more difficult and costly for potential candidates with time-consuming positions to make the attempt. Frank Church's need to chair the CIA hearings is one example. Governors, solely responsible for the conduct of that branch of government, are at a greater disadvantage than legislators, and those candidates who hold office are at a greater disadvantage than those who do not.

Fifth, and related to the foregoing factors, the individuals who seek the office of president tend to be risk takers. In part because they are more ambitious than others, most candidates are willing to take a high-risk gamble. The successful candidate, that is, is usually strongly motivated by the desire for success and is willing to take chances with his own career. Any relationship between this willingness and the conduct of such a person, once in office, remains to be discovered.

The five factors just discussed have to do with the first screening: the voluntary decision to run for the nomination. The preconvention campaign screens out most of the remaining candidates. Success in this sphere is also partly a matter of luck. There is some luck early in the campaign, just as there is luck in terms of institutional arrangements (e.g., the timing of particularly favorable or unfavorable primaries). However, most of one's luck involves the competition. Who else has chosen to run for the nomination? In 1976, had Humphrey run actively, Jackson's chances might have been diminished further. Had Kennedy run, all other Democrats might have seen their prospects reduced greatly. Had Wallace not run, Carter's campaign would have been designed differently, and the Florida primary would have played a different role. Had Udall not run, Bayh or some other liberal's chances would have been improved. Had Reagan not run, Ford could have begun his general election campaign in January instead of August. In 1980, Bush may be the only moderate Republican in the New Hampshire primary. If four or five other candidates divide the conservative vote between them, Reagan could be hurt and Bush helped. But if Anderson, Baker, or other moderates contest that primary, Bush's prospects for survival in New Hampshire would be reduced.

Success in the nomination campaign is based in part on a series of givens—including the opponents and the rules—over which a candidate has little control. In that sense, these givens are luck, just as it was luck that placed McGovern in charge of the commission to revise delegate selection procedures for 1972. But there is far more to success than luck.

The successful candidates are more likely than not to have the following characteristics. First, they must have a theme that finds a responsive audience in the electorate. The electorate, in its component parts, *is* the major determinant. Carter's theme of trust was better suited to the Democratic electorate in 1976 than Bayh's theme "the politicians' politician." Foreign policy was a theme better suited to the Republican electorate in

1976 than massive welfare reform. Second, the candidates and staffs who better understand the rules of the game will play the game better and, thus, are more likely to succeed. Third, the candidates and the central staffs must be capable of managing a complex organization that is national in focus but can also operate in fifty different states. Fourth, successful candidates must be able to learn from and adapt to changing circumstances. Most candidates have never run a national campaign organization and are, in this sense, amateurs. Moreover, we have seen that each campaign evolved over time. The strategy that was successful in February was not the same strategy that was successful in June: the resource bases differed, the electorate differed, the competition and delegate standings differed, and so did the policies that were emphasized.

In short, the successful candidate tends to be one who is personally ambitious, who is politically experienced, who can develop a powerful campaign organization, who can learn the rules and procedures of a complex campaign, who is a good decision maker, whose approach is flexible as circumstances rapidly change, and, who, in the final analysis, is most adept at reading the preferences of the electorate, who can present himself with the least error throughout a long and difficult campaign, and who can do so in a competitive situation in which the opponents are attempting to reach the same goals.

If this characterization of the successful candidate is correct, and if this list is similar to the list of attributes we desire in our presidents, so be it. If not, either we must change the circumstances that lead individuals to become active candidates for the presidency or we must change the nature of nomination politics.

Appendix of Tables

217   **Appendix**

Table 1   Republican Party Primary Rules

State	Date	Size of Dele- gation	No. C.D.	No. A.L.	No. Appt.	Ballot Type	Method	Length of Bind	Party Regis- tration
AL	May 4	37	21	16	0	Slots	Plurality	0	No
AR	May 25	27	12	15	0	Direct	PR	1	No
CA	June 8	167	0	167	0	Direct	WTA	2	Yes
DC	May 4a	14	12	0	2	Direct	?	2	Yes
FL	Mar. 9	66	45	21b	0	Direct	Loophole	2	Yes
GA	May 4	48	30	18	0	Direct	Loophole	2	No
ID	May 25	21	0	17	4	Direct	PR	1	No
IL	Mar. 16	101	96	0	5	Separate	Plurality	0	No
IN	May 4	54	33	21	0	Direct	Loophole	1	No
KY	May 25	37	0	37	0	Direct	PR	1	Yes
MD	May 18	43	24	19	0	Direct	Loophole	2	Yes
MA	Mar. 2	43	36	7	0	Direct	PR	4	Yes
MI	May 18	84	0	84	0	Direct	PR	2	No
MT	June 1c								
NB	May 11	25	25	0	0	Separate	Plurality	2	Yes
NV	May 25	18	0	18	0	Direct	PR	2	Yes
NH	Feb. 24	21	6	15	0	Separate	Plurality	4	Yes
NJ	June 8	67	60	7	0	Delegates	Plurality	0	No
NY	Apr. 6	154	117	0	37	Delegates	Plurality	0	Yes
NC	Mar. 23	54	0	54	0	Direct	PR	1	Yes
OH	June 8	97	69	28	0	Direct	Loophole	0	No
OR	May 25	30	30	0	0	Direct	PR	2	Yes
PA	Apr. 27	103	84	0	19	Delegates	Plurality	0	Yes
RI	June 1	19	19	0	0	Direct	PR	1	Yes
SD	June 1	20	6	14	0	Direct	PR	3	Yes
TN	May 25	43	24	19	0	Direct	PR	2	No
TX	May 1	100	96	0	4	Slots	Plurality	3	No
WV	May 11	28	12	16	0	Delegates	Plurality	0	Yes
WI	Apr. 6	45	36	9	0	Direct	Loophole	4	No

NOTE: *C.D.* means delegates chosen at a substate level, typically apportioned over Congressional Districts; *A.L.* means delegates chosen at large, or statewide; *Appt.* means delegates selected by the state party's executive committee or similar body. There are four *ballot types*: *Slots* means that citizens cast several ballots, one for each delegate running in a district or statewide, these delegates being listed under their presidential preference; *Direct* means that citizens vote their presidential preference, and this vote is used to select delegates; *Separate* means that citizens vote separately for delegates and for their presidential preference; *Delegates* means that citizens vote for delegates whose presidential preference is not indicated on the ballot. *Methods* are tabulated: *Plurality* means that the delegates who win are those who receive a plurality of the votes cast; *PR* means that allocation of delegates is proportional to the vote received by presidential candidates in the appropriate unit; PR means that allocation of delegates is proportional to the statewide vote received by presidential candidates, even if delegates are selected in C.D.'s; *WTA* is a statewide, winner-take-all vote (California Republicans only); *Loophole* means winner-take-all at the C.D. level only. *Length of Bind* means the number of national convention ballots in which delegates are bound to vote a can-

Table 1 (Notes, continued)
didate (e.g., 0 is a nonbinding primary). Most states also include an "or until released" condition. Some have other conditions (e.g., "or until the candidate receives fewer than 15% of the convention votes"). *Party Registration*: "Yes" means that voters express a party preference in registering to vote and can vote only in that party's primary; "No" means that voters do not register by party and, hence, denotes a cross-over primary.

aPrimary not held in 1976 because only Ford filed a slate of delegates and write-in votes were not permitted. bFive of the 21 are bonus delegates, one being awarded to the presidential candidate for each three Congressional Districts carried. cBeauty contest primary in Republican Party only. See table 3 for caucus rules.

Table 2   Democratic Party Primary Rules

State	Date	Size of Dele-gation	No. C.D.	No. A.L.	No. Appt.	Ballot Type	Method	Length of Bind	Party Regis-tration
AL	May 4	35	27	8	0	Slots	PL/PR	1	No
AR	May 25	26	24	2	0	Direct	PR	1	No
CA	June 8	280	210	70	0	Direct	PR	4	Yes
DC	May 4	17	13	4	0	Direct	PR	2	Yes
FL	Mar. 9	81	61	20	0	Direct	PR	2	Yes
GA	May 4	50	38	12	0	Slots	PL/PR	2	No
ID	May 25	16	13	3	0	Direct	PR	0	No
IL	Mar. 16	169	155	14	0	Separate	PL/PR	0	No
IN	May 4	75	57	18	0	Direct	PR	1	No
KY	May 25	46	35	11	0	Direct	PR	1	Yes
MD	May 18	53	40	13	0	Separate	PL/PR	0	Yes
MA	Mar. 2	104	78	26	0	Direct	PR	1	Yes
MI	May 18	133	100	33	0	Direct	PR	2	No
MT	June 1	17	16	1	0	Direct	PR	0	No
NB	May 11	23	23	0	0	Separate	PL	2	Yes
NV	May 25	11	0	11	0	Direct	PR	2	Yes
NH	Feb. 24	17	17	0	0	Separate	PL	4	Yes
NJ	June 8	108	81	27	0	Separate	PL/PR	0	No
NY	Apr. 6	274	205	69	0	Separate	PL/PR	1	Yes
NC	Mar. 23	61	46	15	0	Direct	PR	1	Yes
OH	June 8	152	114	38	0	Separate	PL/PR	0	No
OR	May 25	34	34	0	0	Direct	PR	2	Yes
PA	Apr. 27	178	134	44	0	Separate	PL/PR	1	Yes
RI	June 1	22	18	4	0	Direct	PR	1	Yes
SD	June 1	17	13	4	0	Separate	PR	3	Yes
TN	May 25	46	37	9	0	Direct	PR	2	No
TX	May 1	130	98	32	0	Separate	PL	3	No
WV	May 11	33	25	8	0	Delegates	PL/PR	0	Yes
WI	Apr. 6	68	58	10	0	Direct	PR	4	No

For explanation of column heads, see notes to table 1. A *Method* of a different type, *PL/PR*, is introduced in this table. It means that the plurality method is used for C.D. delegates and the PR method is used for A.L. delegates.

Table 3 Republican Party Caucus Rules

State	Size of Delegation	Length of Bind	No. of Steps in Caucus	State Conv. Dels. Selected No.	Date	C.D. Dels. Selected No.	Date	County Conv. Date	Ward or Precinct Meetings Date
AK	19	?	3	16	5/22	3	5/22[a]	?	?
AZ	29	?	3	17	4/24	12	4/24[b]	4/24[e]	
CO	31	?	4	16	7/10	15	6/5,19; 7/9	5/13–6/2	5/3
CT	35	?	3	17	7/16	18	7/15[c]		5/4[c]
DE	17	?	2	17	6/19				6/5[c]
HI	19	?	3	13	5/15[d]	6	5/15		1/27
IA	36	0	4	18	6/19	18	6/18	2/28	1/19
KS	34	?	4	7	5/22	27	5/8	4/8	3/25
LA	41	0	2	17	6/5	24	5/8		
ME	20	?	3	14	5/4	6	5/1	1/9	
MN	42	?	4	18	6/24	24	4/24	3/13	2/24
MS	30	?	4	15	4/10	15	4/10[b]	3/27	3/27
MO	49	?	4	19	6/12	30	5/6	4/24[f]	4/19
MT	20	0	2	0	6/26	20	6/26[b]	6/1	
NM	21	?	3	15	6/26	6	6/26[b]		4/23
ND	18	?	2	15	7/8	3	7/8[a]	5/1	
OK	36	?	4	18	5/15	18	5/8	4/24	4/5
SC	36	0	4	18	4/24	18	4/5	3/22	3/12
UT	20	?	4	14	7/17	6	7/17[b]	6/15[f]	5/17
VT	18	0	2	15	5/22	3	5/22[a]		4/22
VA	51	?	3	21	6/5	30	5/14	1–5/76	
WA	38	?	4	17	6/19	21	6/18[b]	4/2	3/2
WY	17	?	3	17	5/8			3/1–3/15	2/4

[a]Although all delegates are chosen at the state convention, three delegates are designated as "CD." [b]Although all delegates are selected at the state convention, the procedure followed is: (1) the state convention divides into congressional district subcaucuses at which each congressional district selects its delegates; and (2) the state convention reconvenes and chooses the at large (statewide) delegates. [c]A vote at the precinct level is conducted to elect representatives to congressional district/state convention. [d]The delegates selected at the state convention are regional delegates, where "region" is a unit smaller than a Congressional District (often an island). [e]County conventions must meet up to 20 days prior to April 24. [f]This date is approximate.

Table 4   Democratic Party Caucus Rules

State	Size of Delegation	Length of Bind	No. of Steps in Caucus	State Conv. Dels. Selected No.	Date	C.D. Dels. Selected No.	Date	County Conv. Date	Ward or Precinct Meetings Date
AK	10	?	2		4/23[a]	10	3/12		2/10
AZ	25[i]	?	3			20	5/8		4/24[b]
CO	35	?	4	4	6/26	31	5/22	5/13–6/2	5/3
CT	51[i]	?	2			51	6/12		5/11[b]
DE	12	2	2	12	6/11				6/5[b]
HI	17	1	3	4	5/28	13	5/28[d,e]		3/9
IA	47	?	4	7	5/29	40	4/10	3/6	1/19
KS	34[i]	?	3			27	5/1	4/3	
LA	41[i]	1	3			32	5/1[f]		5/1[b]
ME	20	0	2	0	5/9	20	5/9[d]		2/1
MN	65	0	4	16	6/6	49	4/24	3/13	2/24
MS	24	2	4	5	2/29[g]	19	2/21	2/14	1/24
MO	71	0	4	17	6/12	54	5/25	5/11	4/20
NM	20	?	3		5/15[a]	20	5/15	4/29	4/22
ND	13	?	?	13	approx. 6/24			4/27	?
OK	37	4	4	9	4/4	28	3/20	2/28	2/7
SC	31	4	4	7	3/31	24	3/31[d]	3/8	2/28
UT	18	?	4	3	6/15	15	6/15[d]	App. 6/10	3/17
VT	12	0	2	12	5/22				4/22
VA	54	?	2	0	5/29[h]	54	5/22		4/3
WA	53	2	4	13	6/13[c]	40	5/22	4/10	3/2
WY	10	?	2	10	5/8			3/14	

[a]State convention ratifies delegate selection made by C.D. (or other) caucuses. [b]First step in caucus procedure entails statewide balloting, or "quasi-primary." In CT and LA, this vote determines national convention delegate distribution. In AZ and DE the vote selects caucus participants who then select national delegation independently. [c]At-large delegates selected by caucus of C.D. delegates. [d]Although all delegates are selected at the state convention, the procedure followed is: (1) state convention divides into C.D. subcaucuses where each district selects its delegates; and (2) state convention reconvenes and chooses at-large delegates. [e]C.D. vs. A.L. breakdown (in absence of other information) on 75% allocation rule that governs most multi-C.D. states. [f]Results of quasi-primary employed to determine distribution of C.D. delegates. [g]At-large delegates are elected by State Executive Committee during state convention; distribution of at-large delegates must reflect distribution of C.D. delegates. [h]State convention plays no role in selection of delegates. [i]Includes delegates elected by committee: 5 in AZ (5/15); 7 in KS (6/5); and 9 in LA (5/8).

Table 5   Republican Party Primary Results

Primary	Date	Turnout	Ford Vote (%)	Reagan Vote (%)	Other Uncom- mitted (%)	Ford Dels.	Reagan Dels.	Uncom- mitted Dels.
NH	2/24	111,677	49.4	48.0	2.6	18	3	0
MA	3/2	193,411	59.6	32.9	3.1	28	15	0
FL	3/9	609,819	52.8	47.2		43	23	0
IL	3/16	775,893	58.9	40.1		75	11	15
NC	3/23	193,727	45.9	52.4	1.7	25	28	1
NY	4/6					0	0	154[b]
WI	4/6	591,812	55.3	44.4	0.3	45	0	0
PA	4/27	796,660	92.1	5.1	2.8	0	0	103[b]
TX	5/1	464,742	32.7	66.8	0.5	0	100	0
AL	5/4	53,404	33.9	66.1		0	37	0
DC	5/4					14	0	0
GA	5/4	188,472	31.7	68.3		0	48	0
IN	5/4	631,292	48.7	51.3		9	45	0
NB	5/11	208,414	45.4	54.4	0.2	7	18	0
WV	5/11	155,692	56.8	43.2		0	0	28[b]
MD	5/18	165,971	57.9	42.1		43	0	0
MI	5/18	1,062,826	64.9	34.3	0.8	55	29	0
AR	5/25	32,541	35.6	62.9	1.5	10	17	0
ID	5/25	89,793	24.9	74.3	0.8	5	16	0
KY	5/25	133,516	50.9	46.9	1.4	19	18	0
NV	5/25	47,748	28.8	66.2	5.0	5	13	0
TN	5/25	242,729	49.8	49.0	1.3	21	22	0
OR	5/25	298,524	50.3	45.8	3.9	16	14	0
RI	6/1	14,352	65.3	31.2	3.5	19	0	0
SD	6/1	84,077	44.0	51.2	4.8	9	11	0
CA	6/8	2,450,491	34.5	65.5		0	167	0
NJ[a]	6/8	296,122	72.1	27.9		0	0	67[b]
OH	6/8	964,939	56.6	43.4		91	6	0

Primaries are ordered by date to aid in evaluating the dynamics of campaign. D.C. primary was not held.

[a]The vote percentages are based on delegate votes, because only Ford was on the presidential preference ballot. [b]Selected, by state party rule, as formally uncommitted even though most supported Ford.

Table 6   Democratic Party Primary Results

State	Date	Turnout	Brown	Carter	Church	Jackson	Udall	Wallace	Uncommitted	Undeclared Candidates
NH	2/24	82,381		28.4%		2.3%[a]	22.7%	1.3%[a]		
MA	3/2	747,634		13.6		22.0	17.4	16.5	1.3%	
FL	3/9	1,300,330		34.5	0.4%[a]	23.9	2.1	30.5	2.9	0.4%
IL[b]	3/16	1,311,914		48.1				27.6		
NC	3/23	604,842		53.6		4.3	2.3	34.7	3.8	1.3
NY	4/6	?								
WI	4/6	740,528		36.6		6.4	35.6	12.5	1.0	1.6
PA	4/27	1,385,241		37.0		24.6	18.7	11.3		4.1
TX	5/1	?		47.6				17.5		22.2[c]
AL	5/4	612,027	1.5%	25.5	0.9		1.8	48.9	13.7	5.5
DC	5/4	24,674		39.7			26.0		32.7[d]	
GA	5/4	502,471		83.4	0.5	0.7	1.9	11.5		0.5
IN	5/4	614,389		68.0		11.7		15.2		5.2
NB	5/11	175,013		37.6	38.5	1.5	2.7	3.2		15.8
WV	5/11	372,577						11.0		89.0[e]
MD	5/18	591,746	48.4	37.1		2.4	5.5	4.1		2.5
MI	5/18	708,696		43.4		1.5	43.1	6.9	2.2	2.9
AR	5/25	501,800		62.9		1.9	7.5	16.5	11.4	
ID	5/25	74,405	2.0[a]	11.9	78.7	0.7	1.3			5.0
KY	5/25	306,006		59.4	9.0	2.7	10.9	16.8	3.9	6.3
NV	5/25	75,242	52.7	22.3	2.4	2.5	3.0	3.3	6.1	
TN	5/25	334,926	0.6[a]	77.6		1.7	3.7	10.9	1.8	
OR	5/25	432,626	24.7[a]	26.7	33.6	1.2	2.7	1.3		8.6
MT	6/1	106,841		24.6	59.4	2.7	6.3	3.4	3.6	4.1
RI	6/1	60,348		30.2	27.2	1.3	4.2	0.8	31.5[g]	9.8
SD	6/1	58,671		41.2		1.0	33.0	2.4	13.4	0.5
CA	6/8	3,408,788	59.1	20.4	7.3	1.1	5.0	3.0	2.3	
NJ[f]	6/8	360,839		58.4	13.6	8.8		8.6		6.0
OH	6/8	1,134,374		52.2	13.9	3.2	21.0	5.7	4.0	

Table 6   Notes

Other declared candidates and states in which they exceeded 5% of the vote are as follows: Bayh, 15.2% in N.H.; Harris, 10.8% in N.H., 7.4% in Mass., 7.5% in Ill.; McCormack, none; Sanford, none; Shapp, none; Shriver, 8.2% in N.H., 7.1% in Mass., 16.3% in Ill.

[a]Write-in vote. [b]Vote percentages listed are from presidential preference vote. [c]Bentsen, of Texas. [d]There were two slates of uncommitted delegates: Fauntroy (21.6%) and Washington (11.1%). [e]"Other" was Sen. Robert Byrd. [f]Presidential preference balloting reported. [g]An uncommitted slate that favored Brown received most of the votes and delegates in R.I.

Table 7   Democratic Party Primary Results: Delegates Awarded

State	Brown	Carter	Church	Jackson	Udall	Wallace	Uncom-mitted	Undeclared Candidates
NH	0	15	0	0	2	0	0	0
MA	0	16	0	30	21	21	0	1
FL	0	34	0	21	0	26	0	0
IL	0	53	0	0	0	3	18	95[a]
NC	0	36	0	0	0	25	0	0
NY	0	35	0	104	70	0	65	0
WI	0	25	0	7	25	10	0	1
PA	0	68	0	23	20	2	46	0
TX	2	112	0	0	0	1	9	6[b]
AL	0	3	0	0	0	27	5	0
DC	0	6	0	0	0	0	6[c]	0
GA	0	50	0	0	0	0	0	0
IN	0	51	0	0	0	10	14	0
NB	0	8	15	0	0	0	0	0
WV	0	0	0	0	0	0	33[d]	0
MD	0	32	0	10	7	0	4	0
MI	0	69	0	0	58	0	4	0
AR	0	17	0	0	1	5	3	0
ID	0	2	14	0	0	0	0	0
KY	0	38	0	0	2	6	0	0
NV	6	3	1	0	0	0	1	0
TN	0	36	0	0	0	1	9	0
OR	10	11	13	0	0	0	0	0
MT	0	4	11	0	0	0	2	0
RI	0	7	7	0	0	0	8	0
SD	0	9	0	0	7	0	1	0
CA	204	67	7	0	2	0	0	0
NJ	0	25	0	0	0	0	83	0
OH	0	126	0	0	20	0	0	6[e]

Other declared candidates and states in which they won at least 1 delegate are as follows: Bayh, 1 in Mass.; Harris, 6 in Mass.; McCormack, 1 in Mass., 1 in Wisc.; Shapp, 1 in Mass., 19 in Pa.; Shriver, 7 in Mass.

[a]85 for Stevenson, 4 for Walker, 6 for Humphrey. [b]Bentsen, of Texas. [c]5 for Rep. Fauntroy, 1 for Mayor Washington. [d]Presumably, Sen. Robert Byrd won all delegates. [e]Rep. Louis Stokes, whose slate swept the 21st C.D.

Table 8   Republican Party Caucus Results: Delegates Awarded

State	Ford	Reagan	Uncommitted	State	Ford	Reagan	Uncommitted
AK	17	0	2	MO	16	30	3
AZ	2	27	0	MT	0	20	0
CO	4	26	1	NM	0	21	0
CT	35	0	0	ND	12	4	2
DE	13	0	4	OK	0	36	0
HI	0	0	19	SC	4	26	6
IA	19	17	0	UT	0	20	0
KS	29	4	1	VT	18	0	0
LA	0	36	5	VA	6	36	9
ME	15	4	1	WA	7	31	0
MN	32	6	4	WY	0	0	17
MS	0	0	30				

Table 9   Democratic Party Caucus Results: Delegates Awarded

State	Brown	Carter	Church	Harris	Jackson	Udall	Wallace	Uncommitted	Other
AK	0	0	0	0	0	0	0	10	0
AZ	0	5	0	0	0	19	1	0	0
CO[d]	11	15	3	0	0	6	0	0	0
CT	0	19	0	0	8	16	0	8	0
DE	0	10	0	0	0	0	0	2	0
HI	0	0	0	0	1	1	0	15	0
IA	0	20	0	2	0	12	0	13	0
KS	0	16	0	0	1	3	0	14	0
LA	0	13	0	0	0	0	9	19	0
ME	0	9	0	0	0	5	0	6	0
MN	0	0	0	0	0	0	0	17	48[a]
MS	0	5	0	0	0	0	11	4	4[b]
MO	0	39	0	0	1	3	0	27	1[c]
NM	0	8	0	0	0	6	0	4	0
ND	0	0	0	0	0	0	0	0	0
OK	0	12	0	7	0	0	0	18	0
SC	0	9	1	0	0	0	8	13	0
UT[d]	5	10	1	0	0	0	0	1	1
VT	2	3	0	0	0	3	0	4	0
VA	0	23	0	0	0	7	0	24	0
WA	0	0	0	0	32	7	0	14	0
WY	1	1	0	0	0	1	0	7	0

[a]Other is Humphrey. [b]Other is Shriver. [c]Other is McCormack. [d]No final breakdown available; the totals are votes as cast at the convention. In Utah, there was 1 vote for Shapp and 1 for Chavez.

Table 10   Democratic Party Caucus Results: First Round

State	Date	Est. Turnout	Brown	Carter	Church	Harris	Jackson	Udall	Wallace	Uncommitted	Other
AK	2/10	1,000		4.0%			6.0%			90.0%	
AZ	4/24	27,500		10.3	1.6%		5.5	70.9%	6.9%	2.9	1.2%[a]
CO[b]	5/3	106,604	7.0%	23.2	13.5		1.0	14.5		34.2	
CT[c]	5/11			33.2		0.2%	17.8	30.8		12.8	5.2[a]
DE											
HI	3/9	3,000		2.4			2.8	4.9		85.1	4.2
IA	1/19	45,000		27.6		9.9	1.1	6.0		37.1	16.5[d]
KS	4/3	120,000		36.1		1.8	6.5	4.5		50.2	
LA[e]	5/1	6,500		28.7		2.5			24.6	7.8	33.9[f]
ME	2/1	58,000		25.8		3.8		3.8		64.4	2.2[g]
MN	2/24	60,000				4.2		1.2		41.6	51.4[h]
MS	1/24	20,000		14.0		1.1	2.2		43.9	27.5	12.3[i]
MO	4/20			13.4				5.3	2.2	66.0	4.7[j]
NM	4/22			28.5				33.2		37.0	
ND	4/27			2.6				2.0	11.5	66.1	7.7[h]
OK	2/7	65,000		18.5		17.0				35.7	12.0[k]
SC	2/28	63,000		22.9	1.6				27.6	48.0	
UT	3/17										
VT	4/22	20,000	4.3	14.2		1.2		11.3		67.0	1.6[h]
VA	4/3	20,000		30.0				8.9	2.5	57.8	
WA	3/2	60,000		1.0			57.5	8.2	1.0	30.3	
WY	3/14	600		3.7		1.4	1.7	5.1		87.0	

[a]Other is McCormack. [b]Percentages compiled by CO State Dem. Comm. from randomly selected sample precincts. [c]Percentages based on statewide balloting (at town level) to elect delegates to C. D. conventions. [d]Bayh, 13.2%; Shriver, 3.3%. [e]32 C.D. delegates awarded on basis of vote in "quasi-primary" on May 1st. [f]Governor Edwards of LA. [g]Bayh, 1.0%; Shriver, 0.8%; Humphrey, 0.4%. [h]Humphrey. [i]Shriver. [j]McCormack, 2.5%; Humphrey, 2.2%. [k]Bentsen.

Table 11   Financial Expenditures and Visits of Republican Candidates

State	Total Expenditures Amount	Rank	Total Visits Days	Rank	Composite Rank	Individual Expenditure Limits
AL	$ 150,137	17	4	12	15	$ 425,752
AK	26,937	44	0	40	44	218,200
AZ	64,879	31	1	33	32	258,698
AR	91,664	26	1	33	28	252,973
CA	1,977,201	1	37	1	1	2,590,470
CO	129,804	20	2	21	18	302,338
CT	50,196	37	0	40	42	379,144
DE	7,944	50	0	40	47	218,200
DC	97,073	25	0	40	35	152,740
FL	1,634,977	2	25	2	2	1,050,851
GA	215,494	14	6	9	11	575,001
HI	18,551	47	0	40	46	218,200
ID	55,114	34	2	21	27	218,200
IL	1,366,815	4	19	4	3	1,336,082
IN	473,726	8	9	7	7	628,591
IA	112,095	23	2	21	20	345,105
KS	50,229	36	1	33	37	277,900
KY	187,477	16	2	21	17	404,281
LA	25,344	45	3	15	30	432,036
ME	22,221	46	0	40	45	218,200
MD	131,620	19	0	40	28	490,863
MA	313,418	11	0	40	24	715,172
MI	378,201	10	8	8	9	1,072,671
MN	77,374	28	3	15	19	465,028
MS	33,642	43	2	21	32	265,157
MO	149,891	18	5	11	15	580,063
MT	38,081	41	1	33	40	218,200
NB	198,035	15	4	12	12	218,200
NV	119,682	21	2	21	18	218,200
NH	418,534	9	24	3	6	218,200
NJ	71,866	29	2	21	23	890,605
NM	43,267	39	1	33	38	218,200
NY	117,037	22	1	33	27	2,231,051
NC	881,552	5	14	5	5	625,156
ND	11,240	48	2	21	37	218,200
OH	504,349	7	4	12	10	1,284,238
OK	56,007	33	1	33	36	330,966
OR	242,359	12	3	15	12	280,343
PA	103,597	24	2	21	21	1,459,845
RI	58,123	32	0	40	38	218,200
SC	52,273	35	0	40	41	327,125
SD	36,147	42	0	40	43	218,200
TN	231,918	13	3	15	14	505,351
TX	1,519,132	3	14	5	3	1,435,756

Table 11 (continued)

State	Total Expenditures		Total Visits		Composite Rank	Individual Expenditure Limits
	Amount	Rank	Days	Rank		
UT	39,003	40	2	21	31	218,200
VT	7,671	51	0	40	48	218,200
VA	49,426	38	3	15	26	598,566
WA	83,607	27	2	21	22	429,418
WV	66,175	30	2	21	24	219,073
WI	529,772	6	6	9	7	547,071
WY	8,769	49	3	15	32	218,200

Source: Mandated maximum expenditures in state, corrected for inflation, taken from *Congressional Quarterly Weekly Report*, 13 March 1976, p. 554. Total limits are $10,910,000 per candidate, with up to $2,182,000 in addition allowed for fundraising and other special costs.

Italics indicate caucus states. Figures are the sum of the expenditures and visits by Reagan and Ford, calculated as discussed in chap. 3. Each entry should be halved to be comparable to the Democratic figures in table 12. *Composite rank* was determined by summing expenditures and visits.

Table 12   Financial Expenditures and Visits of Declared Democratic
Candidates

State	Average Expenditures		Average Visits		Composite Rank
	Amount	Rank	Days	Rank	
AL	$ 71,891.40	16	0.20	40	27
AK	303.67	50	0.00	43	50
AZ	28,955.33	35	0.50	33	35
AR	35,909.40	31	1.60	25	27
CA	387,610.00	1	3.60	13	7
CO	47,407.40	25	0.20	40	33
CT	54,957.00	19	1.80	22	21
DE	22,319.40	43	0.00	43	46
DC	31,993.20	32	1.60	25	29
FL	264,765.00	4	8.50	4	3
GA	58,013.20	18	1.80	22	19
HI	292.75	51	0.00	43	51
ID	28,547.60	36	0.40	36	36
IL	93,916.43	13	4.43	10	12
IN	53,855.20	21	2.00	21	22
IA	49,021.00	23	4.00	11	15
KS	17,611.29	46	0.29	38	43
KY	49,024.20	22	1.80	22	23
LA	27,020.33	38	1.17	29	34
ME	15,657.67	48	0.44	35	42
MD	137,339.20	8	4.80	8	8
MA	313,514.38	3	17.00	1	1
MI	94,734.40	12	5.40	7	10
MN	19,547.38	45	0.00	43	47
MS	40,559.00	27	1.33	28	26
MO	40,288.00	28	0.67	32	31
MT	27,944.00	37	0.00	43	41
NB	54,609.40	20	3.10	15	17
NV	39,547.40	29	1.00	30	30
NH	112,687.62	10	10.00	3	6
NJ	136,655.40	9	3.80	12	11
NM	23,347.33	40	0.33	37	38
NY	331,463.09	2	11.43	2	1
NC	79,553.00	15	2.29	20	17
ND	17,272.00	47	0.00	43	48
OH	216,107.60	6	7.20	6	5
OK	48,805.71	24	3.00	16	19
OR	104,504.40	11	2.80	17	13
PA	245,809.73	5	8.00	5	4
RI	61,799.20	17	2.80	17	15
SC	31,891.50	33	0.88	31	32
SD	36,010.60	30	2.40	19	24
TN	45,870.80	26	1.60	25	25
TX	89,874.67	14	3.33	14	13

Table 12 (continued)

State	Average Expenditures		Average Visits		Composite Rank
	Amount	Rank	Days	Rank	
UT	23,637.00	39	0.20	40	40
VT	21,030.25	44	0.50	33	38
VA	30,412.43	34	0.29	38	36
WA	22,694.63	42	0.00	43	45
WV	22,995.20	41	0.00	43	43
WI	140,093.58	7	4.57	9	8
WY	14,311.14	49	0.00	43	49

Italics indicate caucus states. The number of active candidates is based on the procedures discussed in chap. 3. The date used for the primary is its date, while the date used for the caucus is the date of the first step. The entries are the sum of expenditures and visitation days spent in that state, divided by the number of candidates active on the appropriate date. *Declared* covers the 13 candidacies (sse chap. 2). For expenditure limits, see table 11.

Table 13 Newspaper Coverage of States

| State | Wash. Post Stories | | N.Y. Times Stories | | Combined Rank |
	No.	Rank	No.	Rank	
AL	0.43	33	1.14	32	29
AK	0.00	46	0.09	51	51
AZ	0.00	46	0.75	40	45
AR	0.86	24	0.57	47	37
CA	2.43	5	4.77	5	5
CO	1.00	17	2.43	16	15
CT	0.71	27	4.29	7	25
DE	0.14	44	1.86	23	33
DC	1.43	12	0.71	41	43
FL	2.90	3	4.70	6	3
GA	0.57	31	1.57	29	28
HI	0.10	45	0.70	44	47
ID	0.43	33	0.71	41	40
IL	1.00	17	3.67	11	13
IN	1.43	12	2.43	16	13
IA	0.91	23	2.00	20	20
KS	0.00	46	0.67	45	48
KY	1.00	17	0.86	38	26
LA	0.50	32	1.00	35	33
ME	0.18	43	0.27	50	50
MD	3.57	1	2.00	20	19
MA	1.30	15	4.10	8	10
MI	1.43	12	3.00	13	11
MN	0.40	36	1.70	27	29
MS	0.81	25	2.72	14	17
MO	0.68	30	1.62	28	27
MT[a]	0.71	27	1.71	26	23
NB	1.57	9	2.14	18	12
NV	0.71	27	0.43	49	41
NH	1.50	10	3.90	9	7
NJ	1.71	7	10.14	2	6
NM	0.25	40	1.25	31	37
NY	2.44	4	14.33	1	2
NC	1.00	17	1.89	22	17
ND	0.38	37	1.00	35	39
OH	3.00	2	5.00	4	1
OK	0.22	42	1.78	25	33
OR	1.00	17	1.57	29	21
PA	1.88	6	8.12	3	3
RI	0.43	33	1.14	32	31
SC	0.00	46	1.80	24	36
SD	0.29	38	0.71	41	42
TN	1.29	16	1.14	32	22
TX	1.50	10	3.88	10	8
UT	0.29	38	2.57	15	23

Table 13 (continued)

State	Wash. Post Stories		N.Y. Times Stories		Combined Rank
	No.	Rank	No.	Rank	
VT	0.25	40	0.50	48	46
VA	0.78	26	0.78	39	31
WA	0.00	46	0.90	37	44
WV	1.00	17	2.14	18	16
WI	1.67	8	3.44	12	8
WY	0.00	46	0.67	45	48

Italics indicate caucus states. The number of newspaper stories about a state was derived by dividing them by the number of active candidates, i.e., the number of active Democrats (see table 12, note) plus the two Republicans. Since the national newspapers are also local newspapers, they report nearby events in greater detail. For the composite rankings, the following exceptions were made: For CT, NY, and NJ the *Washington Post* rank was doubled; for MD and DC *New York Times* ranking was doubled.

[a]MT was a primary state for the Democrats and a caucus state for the Republicans (whose primary was a beauty contest).

Table 14   Visitation Days Spent in Primary States by Major Candidates

	Republicans		Democrats					
State	Ford	Reagan	Brown	Carter	Church	Jackson	Udall	Wallace
NH	4	20	0	15	0	0	22	0
MS	0	0	0	8	0	28	29	22
FL	5	20	0	17	0	21	0	19
IL	5	14	0	7	0	2	2	7
NC	2	12	0	5	0	2	0	7
NY	0	1	6	17	0	32	26	1
WI	2	4	0	9	0	2	15	8
PA	0	2	0	14	0	15	15	3
TX	6	8	2	5	0	0	0	6
AL	1	3	0	1	0	0	0	0
DC	0	0	3	6	0	0	0	2
GA	2	4	0	0	0	0	1	2
IN	5	4	0	6	0	2	0	3
NB	3	1	0	2	12	1	0	0
WV	0	2	0	0	0	0	0	0
MD	1	0	13	5	0	1	2	1
MI	5	3	0	6	0	2	14	5
AR	0	1	0	0	0	0	1	5
ID	0	2	0	1	1	0	0	0
KY	1	1	0	0	0	1	4	4
NV	1	1	3	2	0	0	0	0
TN	1	2	0	1	0	0	2	5
OR	2	1	5	5	9	0	0	0
MT	0	1	0	0	0	0	0	0
RI	0	0	4	2	5	2	0	1
SD	0	0	0	2	0	0	5	0
CA	6	31	0	4	5	0	1	5
NJ	1	1	4	8	0	1	5	0
OH	3	1	0	10	5	2	16	1

Gathered from candidates' itineraries or media reports, (see Chap. 3). States are ordered by date of primary to facilitate interpretation of the dynamics of the campaign.

Table 15   Days Spent in Caucus States by Major Candidates

State	Republicans		Democrats					
	Ford	Reagan	Brown	Carter	Church	Jackson	Udall	Wallace
AZ	0	1	0	0	0	0	2	1
CO	0	2	1	0	0	0	0	0
CT	0	0	0	1	0	1	6	0
DE	0	0	0	0	0	0	0	0
HI	0	0	0	0	0	0	0	0
IA	0	2	0	7	0	3	10	0
KS	0	1	0	0	0	1	0	0
LA	1	2	2	1	0	0	0	1
ME	0	0	0	1	0	0	1	0
MN	0	3	0	0	0	0	0	0
MS	1	1	0	1	0	0	0	2
MO	3	2	0	2	0	0	0	0
MT[a]	0	1	0	0	0	0	0	0
NM	0	1	0	0	0	0	2	0
ND	0	2	0	0	0	0	0	0
OK	0	1	0	1	0	0	0	0
SC	0	0	0	2	0	0	0	3
UT	0	2	0	0	1	0	0	0
VT	0	0	0	1	0	0	1	0
VA	1	1	0	2	0	0	0	0
WA	0	2	0	0	0	0	0	0
WY	0	3	0	0	0	0	0	0

See note, table 14.

[a]Caucus state for Republicans; primary state for Democrats.

Table 16   Monthly Financial Contributions by Individuals to Major
                      Candidates

Month	Republicans		Democrats					
	Ford	Reagan	Brown	Carter	Church	Jackson	Udall	Wallace
Jan.	1.20[a]	0.66		0.12	0.08	1.02	0.07	0.28
Feb.	2.05	1.86		0.38	0.25	0.11	0.35	0.32
Mar.	2.50	1.12	0.03	0.61	0.20	0.99	0.55	0.14
Apr.	1.22	1.96	0.21	0.73	0.11	0.43	0.32	0.27
May	2.53	2.58	0.65	1.50	0.35	0.40	0.68	0.23
June	1.38	1.25	0.48	2.33	0.36	0.14	0.33	0.48

Excluded are federal matching funds, PAC contributions, and income from sales
(e.g., tickets to rock concerts).

[a]All figures are in millions of dollars.

Table 17   *New York Times* Weekly Coverage: Percentage of
Party's Stories about Major Candidates

	Republicans[a]	Democrats[b]					
Week	Ford	Brown	Carter	Church	Jackson	Udall	Wallace
1/14–1/20	62%	0	17	3	7	10	17
1/21–1/27	62	3	24	0	7	7	10
1/28–2/3	64	0	25	0	33	5	20
2/4–2/10	62	0	17	0	4	8	17
2/11–2/17	29	0	19	0	19	4	23
2/18–2/24	59	2	22	0	10	13	8
2/25–3/2	59	0	25	1	15	13	13
3/3–3/9	67	0	24	1	29	13	20
3/10–3/16	58	2	33	0	17	10	17
3/17–3/23	64	2	33	4	19	13	17
3/24–3/30	60	0	33	0	31	26	8
3/31–4/6	48	2	36	0	25	25	5
4/7–4/13	50	2	38	2	17	19	11
4/14–4/20	59	10	53	0	23	10	3
4/21–4/27	49	1	43	4	29	19	4
4/28–5/4	56	4	56	2	21	8	8
5/5–5/11	50	0	59	0	5	23	14
5/12–5/18	50	23	42	9	2	19	5
5/19–5/25	52	29	37	17	0	17	0
5/26–6/1	52	25	41	19	0	9	6
6/2–6/8	52	25	42	11	0	18	3
6/9–6/15	52	16	54	10	0	13	7
6/16–6/22	56	13	83	0	0	0	4
6/23–6/30[c]	55	6	94	0	0	0	0
7/1–7/7	68						
7/8–7/14	65						
7/15–7/21	52						
7/22–7/28	51						
7/29–8/4	53						

Weeks based on Tuesdays, as all but the Texas primary were held on Tuesdays. Note that the first step in the Iowa caucuses was held in the week of 1/14–1/20, where coverage became large enough to calculate percentages. The New Hampshire (and first) primary was held 2/24, the last primaries on 6/8.

[a]Calculation based on number of stories about Ford (as discussed in text) divided by the sum of the number about Ford and the number about Reagan; hence Reagan % = 100 − Ford %. [b]Calculation based on number of stories about each Democratic candidate divided by the sum of the number of stories about each declared candidate. [c]Calculations about Democrats stopped in this week, as Brown "acquiesced" to Carter's nomination.

Table 18   *Washington Post* Weekly Coverage: Percentage of
Party's Stories about Major Candidates

Week	Republicans	Democrats					
	Ford	Brown	Carter	Church	Jackson	Udall	Wallace
2/18–2/24	62%	0	26	0	26	11	16
2/25–3/2	46	0	24	0	15	21	9
3/3–3/9	47	0	19	0	27	19	12
3/10–3/16	55	4	35	0	19	23	12
3/17–3/23	43	0	41	4	9	18	23
3/24–3/30	58	5	42	0	16	16	21
3/31–4/6	46	4	34	0	20	25	11
4/7–4/13	57	0	41	0	22	19	12
4/14–4/20	44	0	57	0	7	14	21
4/21–4/27	55	4	43	7	36	7	4
4/28–5/4	58	18	57	4	7	7	7
5/5–5/11	48	17	50	8	6	14	6
5/12–5/18	46	20	50	10	2	10	8
5/19–5/25	44	24	36	16	0	20	4
5/26–6/1	46	8	40	24	8	12	8
6/2–6/8	48	5	71	10	0	14	0
6/9–6/15	50	16	62	8	0	15	0
6/16–6/22	50	0	100	0	0	0	0
6/23–6/30	57	0	100	0	0	0	0
7/1–7/7	67						
7/8–7/14	62						
7/15–7/21	33						
7/22–7/28	56						
7/29–8/4	54						

See table 17, notes. There were too few stories from 1/14 through 2/17 to provide meaningful weekly percentages.

Sources

Carol F. Casey, *Procedures for Selection of Delegates to the Democratic and Re-publican 1976 National Conventions: A Survey of Applicable State Laws and Party Rules* (Washington, D.C.: Library of Congress, Congressional Research Service, 1976).

Congressional Quarterly Weekly Report (Washington, D.C.: Congressional Quarterly): V 34, Nos. 1–34 (January–August, 1976).

Thomas M. Durbin, Rita Ann Reimer, and Thomas B. Ripy, *Nomination and Election of the President and Vice President of the United States: Including the Manner of Selecting Delegates to National Political Conventions* (Washington, D.C.: Library of Congress, Congressional Research Service, 1976).

Federal Elections Commission, *1976 Presidential Campaign Receipts and Expenditures*, F.E.C. Disclosure Series No. 7 (Washington, D.C., 1977), and related reports.

Warren J. Mitofsky and Catherine C. Krein, eds., *Campaign '76: A Reference of Official Vote Returns* (New York: Arno, 1977).

Republican National Committee, *1976 Republican National Convention: Delegate Selection Procedures* (Washington, D.C., 1976).

The basic sources for most rules and many of the results of individual delegate selection procedures were direct reports from the individual state party organizations or the state governments.

Notes

Chapter 1

1. Robert L. Peabody, Norman J. Ornstein, and David W. Rohde, "The United States Senate as a Presidential Incubator: Many Are Called but Few Are Chosen," *Political Science Quarterly* 91, no. 2 (Summer 1976):237–58.

2. This point is argued eloquently in Robert A. Dahl's brilliant *A Preface to Democratic Theory* (Chicago: University of Chicago, 1965).

3. Numerous histories of our political parties and of the evolution of national party conventions exist, such as Arthur M. Schlesinger, Jr., ed., *History of U.S. Political Parties*, 4 vols. (New York: Bowker, 1973); and Richard C. Bain and Judith H. Parris, *Convention Decisions and Voting Records* (Washington, D.C.: Brookings Institution, 1973). Perhaps the best available book on the entire nomination process, including the party conventions, is William R. Keech and Donald R. Matthews, *The Party's Choice* (Washington, D.C.: Brookings Institution, 1976). See also the massive compendium *Guide to U.S. Elections* (Washington, D.C.: Congressional Quarterly, 1976 and 1976 update).

4. The best book on the presidential primary, including an historical account, is James W. Davis, *Presidential Primaries: Road to the White House* (New York: Crowell, 1967).

5. The presidential primary was made possible by the efforts of such progressive Republicans as Senators Robert LaFollette (Wisconsin) and Jonathan Bourne (Oregon). The Democratic Party has led the recent reforms. The Republican Party has played a much lesser role over the last decade or so. It has not been completely immune to change, however. For a review of its efforts, see Charles Longley, "Party Reform and the Republican Party" (Paper delivered at the Annual Meeting of the American Political Science Association, 1978, New York).

6. On the decline of partisan loyalties, see Paul R. Abramson, "Generational Change and the Decline of Party Identification in America," *American Political Science Review* 70 (June 1976), pp. 469–79; and Norman H. Nie, Sidney Verba, and John R. Petrocik, *The Changing American Voter* (Cambridge: Harvard University, 1976). Walter Dean Burnham discusses the decline of party as organization as well as repository of the electorate's loyalties in, for example, *Critical Elections and the Mainsprings of American Politics* (New York: Norton, 1970); and "American Politics in the 1970's: Beyond Party?" chapter 10 in *The American Party*

Systems: Stages of Political Development, ed. William Nisbet Chambers and Walter Dean Burnham, 2d ed. (New York: Norton, 1975).

7. On rational choice in general and the elements of decision making, see William H. Riker and Peter C. Ordeshook, *An Introduction to Positive Political Theory* (Englewood Cliffs, N.J.: Prentice-Hall, 1973), especially chaps. 1 and 2 and sources cited therein.

8. For details, see ibid., chap. 2; and R. Duncan Luce and Howard Raiffa, *Games and Decisions* (New York: Wiley, 1957).

9. Riker and Ordeshook, *An Introduction,* Luce and Raiffa, op. cit.

10. The standard typology of decision-making settings is presented in Luce and Raiffa, op cit.

11. An example of the application of such procedures to a relevant decision, namely the choice of voting or abstaining, is found in John A. Ferejohn and Morris P. Fiorina, "The Paradox of Not Voting: A Decision-Theoretic Analysis," *American Political Science Review* 68 (June 1974):525–36.

12. Kenneth J. Arrow, *Social Choice and Individual Values,* 2d ed. (New Haven: Yale University, 1963).

13. This theme is expressed best in Kenneth A. Shepsle's recent works, such as "Institutional Structure and Policy Choice: Some Comparative Statics of Amendment Control Procedures" (Paper delivered at the Conference on Political Science and the Study of Public Policy, Hickory Corners, Michigan, May 15–17, 1978); and "Institutional Arrangements and Equilibrium in Multidimensional Voting Models," *American Journal of Political Science* 23, 1 (February 1979):27–59.

14. Bo H. Bjurulf and Richard G. Niemi "Strategic Voting in Scandinavian Parliaments," *Scandinavian Political Studies* 1, New Series, no. 1 (1978):5–22.

15. This "seasonal" terminology, which will reappear in the last chapter, is taken from John H. Kessel, "The Seasons of Presidential Politics," *Social Science Quarterly* 58, no. 3 (December 1977):418–34.

Chapter 2

1. Joseph Schlesinger, *Ambition and Politics: Political Careers in the United States* (Chicago: Rand McNally, 1966), p. 1.

2. David W. Rohde, "Risk-Bearing and Progressive Ambition: The Case of Members of the United States House of Representatives," *American Journal of Political Science* 23, 1 (February 1979):1–26. See also Gordon Black, "A Theory of Political Ambition: Career Choices and the Role of Structural Incentives," *American Political Science Review* 66 (March 1972):144–59.

3. See Jules Witcover, *Marathon: The Pursuit of the Presidency, 1972–1976* (New York: Viking, 1977), p. 364.

4. Peabody, Ornstein, and Rohde, op. cit., pp. 237–58; table 3, p. 249.

5. Barbara Hinckley, Richard Hofstetter, and John Kessel, "Information and the Vote: A Comparative Election Study," *American Politics Quarterly* 2, no. 2 (April 1974):131–58. They also cite some of the advantages governors have over senators.

6. Udall is quoted in the *Congressional Quarterly Weekly Report,* 22 June 1974, p. 1,628.

7. Michael Barone, Grant Ujifusa, and Douglas Matthews, *The Almanac of American Politics: 1976* (New York: Dutton, 1975), p. 188.

8. Rohde, op. cit.

9. Actually, these data do not test hypothesis 6 directly, since it states that a larger percentage of high risk takers will run for higher office than the rest who

are similarly situated. One interpretation of "similarly situated" would be that more high risk takers will run for the presidential nomination than non–high risk takers who have the same liability score. A direct test of this hypothesis spreads the already thin data even further. However, the results are consistent with this hypothesis:

	Liability Score						
	0	1	2	3	4	5	
% of high risk takers who were declared or potential candidates in 1976	60%	20%	43%	20%	0%	0%	
	5	10	7	5	1	1	N (denominator)
% of non–high risk takers who were declared or potential candidates in 1976	0%	33%	0%	17%	0%		
	5	3	5	6	1	0	N
% of high risk takers who were declared candidates 1968–76	60%	20%	14%	20%	0%	0%	
	5	10	7	5	1	1	N
% of non–high risk takers who were declared candidates 1968–76	0%	0%	0%	0%	0%		
	5	3	5	6	1	0	N

10. Anthony Downs, *An Economic Theory of Democracy* (New York: Harper & Row, 1957), p. 28.

11. William Riker, *The Theory of Political Coalitions* (New Haven: Yale University, 1962), p. 22.

12. Joseph Schlesinger, "The Primary Goals of Political Parties: A Clarification of Positive Theory," *American Political Science Review* 69 (September 1975):843.

13. Witcover, op. cit., p. 387.

14. Ibid., p. 398.

15. *Christian Science Monitor*, 23 March 1976.

16. See John Aldrich, "The Goals of Candidates in Elections: Some Modifications and Extensions" (Michigan State University, 1977), mimeographed. There, the candidates' utility functions are formalized, and the conditions under which office seeking is compatible with other goals are derived.

Chapter 3

1. These and most figures reported in this section are from Herbert E. Alexander, *Financing Politics: Money, Elections and Political Reform* (Washington, D.C.: Congressional Quarterly, 1976). See also the sources cited in his bibliography.

2. The 1971 Acts and 1974 and 1976 Amendments are summarized in ibid., appendix, pp. 268–81.

3. David Adamany and George Agree, "Election Campaign Financing: The 1974 Reforms," *Political Science Quarterly* 90 (Summer 1975):201–19, especially 205–8. The figures on the percentages of voters making campaign contributions are taken from John H. Aldrich and David W. Rohde, "Law and Political Behavior: Some Effects of Federal Campaign Finance Reform on the Federal Electorate" (Michigan State University, 1978), mimeographed. The figures on the donations to Nixon's campaign are from Alexander, op. cit., pp. 112–26.

4. This evolution of the primary was described in chap. 1. See also James W. Davis, *Presidential Primaries: The Road to the White House* (New York: Crowell, 1967).

5. See, for example, Douglas W. Rae, *The Political Consequences of Electoral Laws*, rev. ed. (New Haven: Yale University, 1971).

6. Michael J. Robinson with the assistance of Karen A. McPherson, "Television News and the Presidential Nomination Process" (Catholic University, Washington, D.C., 1977), quoted in his footnote 2, p. 2.

7. Thomas E. Patterson and Robert D. McClure, *The Unseeing Eye: The Myth of Television Power in National Politics* (New York: Putnam's, 1976), pp. 34–42.

8. Robinson, op. cit.

9. *Congressional Quarterly Weekly Report*, 6 March 1976, p. 503.

10. Sanford was quoted in the *New York Times*, 27 January 1976, p. 21.

11. Witcover, op. cit., p. 31.

Chapter 4

1. Good overviews of the issues involved in interpreting the voter's behavior can be found in Angus Campbell, Philip Converse, Warren Miller, and Donald Stokes classics, *The American Voter* (New York: Wiley, 1960); and *Elections and the Political Order* (New York: Wiley, 1966). Two major, more recent works are Norman Nie, Sidney Verba, and John Petrocik, *The Changing American Voter* (Cambridge: Harvard University, 1976), and Philip Converse, "Public Opinion and Voting Behavior," chap. 2 in *Handbook of Political Science*, ed. Fred I. Greenstein and Nelson W. Polsby, (Reading, Mass.: Addison-Wesley, 1975) vol. 4, *Nongovernmental Politics*. The areas of disagreement are presented well in Richard G. Niemi and Herbert F. Weisberg, eds., *Controversies in American Voting Behavior* (San Francisco: Freeman, 1976).

2. The logic of the turnout decision is developed formally in Downs, op. cit., especially pp. 260–76 and chap. 14; Gordon Tullock, *Towards a Mathematics of Politics* (Ann Arbor: University of Michigan, 1967), especially chap. 7; William H. Riker and Peter C. Ordeshook, "A Theory of the Calculus of Voting," *American Political Science Review*, March 1968, pp. 25–42; John Ferejohn and Morris Fiorina, "The Paradox of Not Voting: A Decision Theoretic Analysis," *American Political Science Review* 68 (June 1974):525–36; and John Aldrich, "Some Problems in Testing Two Rational Models of Participation," *American Journal of Political Science* 20 (November 1976):713–33. Richard Niemi argues that the costs of voting in presidential elections have been "tremendously exaggerated," in "Costs of Voting and Nonvoting," *Public Choice*, Fall 1976, pp. 115–19.

3. These two forms of abstention are reviewed in Otto A. Davis, Melvin J. Hinich, and Peter C. Ordeshook, "An Expository Development of a Mathematical Model of the Electoral Process," *American Political Science Review*, June 1970, pp. 426–48, and Riker and Ordeshook, *An Introduction*, especially chaps. 11 and 12. An empirical test of the two forms of abstention can be found in Richard A. Brody and Benjamin I. Page, "Indifference, Alienation and Rational Decisions," *Public Choice*, Summer 1973, pp. 1–17.

4. Herbert F. Weisberg, "Rational Abstention Due to Satisfaction" (Paper delivered to the Midwest Political Science Association, Chicago, 1977).

5. Austin Ranney, *Participation in American Presidential Nominations: 1976* (Washington, D.C.: American Enterprise Institute for Public Policy Research, 1977), p. 15 and table 2, p. 16.

6. Witcover, op. cit., p. 216.

7. Ranney, op. cit., p. 15.

8. New York did not assemble voting data on a statewide basis. Only the Democratic primary was held in the District of Columbia. Therefore, only 28 of the 30 primary states can be analyzed. In addition, Ohio and Wisconsin did not keep statewide registration figures, so that only 26 primary states can be included in our discussion. The data are reported in ibid., pp. 21–26 and tables 3 and 4.

9. Ibid., p. 33.

10. Detailed state-by-state results proved surprisingly difficult to obtain, especially for caucus states. In fact, except for actual delegate allocations, the outcome in some Republican caucus states was impossible to obtain. The results reported in the appendix were collected from numerous sources. Each relevant state government or state party organization, was contacted (sometimes several times). The printed media (especially *Congressional Quarterly Weekly Report*, the *New York Times*, and the *Washington Post*) were scrutinized. The C.B.S. compendium by Warren J. Mitofsky and Catherine C. Krein, *Campaign '76: A Reference of Official Vote Returns* (New York: Arno, 1977) was used as a secondary check and, on occasion, as a primary source.

11. CS can be defined mathematically for the two-candidate race as follows: Let i and j denote two candidates. Let d_i and d_j denote the number of delegates each candidate has won, respectively, and let D be the total number of delegates to be selected during the campaign. Then CS_i, or the competitive standing of candidate i, is:

$$CS_i = \frac{d_i - d_j}{D - d_i - d_j}$$

If j is to denote any candidate other than candidate i, CS_i for the multicandidate race is:

$$CS_i = \frac{d_i - \sum_j d_j}{D - d_i - \sum_j d_j}$$

If candidate i has 50% of the delegates committed (i.e., is just at the victory point), then $CS_i = 1$. To see this, if $d_i = D/2$, then:

$$CS_i = \frac{D/2 - \sum_j d_j}{D - D/2 - \sum_j d_j} = \frac{D/2 - \sum_j d_i}{D/2 - \sum_j d_j} = 1$$

Chapter 5

1. Theodore White, *The Making of the President, 1968* (New York: Pocket Books, 1969), pp. 438–43.

2. John Aldrich, Michael Gant, and Dennis Simon, "To the Victor Belong the Spoils" (Michigan State University, 1978), mimeographed; and John Aldrich, "A Dynamic Model of Pre-Convention Campaigns" (Paper prepared for delivery to the Midwest Political Science Association, Chicago, 1979).

3. Donald Matthews, " 'Winnowing': The News Media and the 1976 Presidential Nominations," in *Race for the Presidency: The Media and the Nomination Process* ed. James David Barber (Englewood Cliffs, N.J.: Prentice-Hall, 1978).

4. The derivation of these propositions rests on the mathematical structure employed. For the explication of this structure, see sources in n. 2 above.

5. *Newsweek*, 12 January 1976, p. 21.

6. Jonathan Moore and Janet Fraser, eds., *Campaign for President: The Managers Look at '76* (Cambridge, Mass.: Ballinger, 1977), p. 36.

7. Ibid., p. 37.

8. Witcover, op. cit., pp. 649–50.

9. Philip D. Straffin, Jr., "The Bandwagon Curve," *American Journal of Political Science* 21, no. 4 (November 1977):695–710.

10. Aldrich, "Dynamic Model."

11. See Steven J. Brams, *The Presidential Election Game* (New Haven: Yale University, 1978), especially chap. 2. Brams reviews much of this literature, and cites additional sources.

12. Straffin, op. cit.

13. Ibid., p. 702.

14. Donald Collat, Stanley Kelley, Jr., and Ronald Rogowski, "Presidential Bandwagons" (Paper delivered at the Annual Meeting of The American Political Science Association, Chicago, 1976).

15. James Beniger, "Winning the Presidential Nomination: National Polls and State Primary Elections, 1936–1972," *Public Opinion Quarterly*, Spring 1976, pp. 22–38.

16. Governor Wallace was shot in an assassination attempt while campaigning in the Maryland primary in 1972. In March and April, his standing in the polls was a nearly constant 15–18%. After he was shot, his popularity stayed at about 25%. However the meaning of these figures is impossible to ascertain.

Chapter 6

1. See John Aldrich, "Candidate Behavior in the Presidential Primaries" (Paper delivered at the Meeting of the Public Choice Society, New Orleans, 1978); and idem, "A Model of the Presidential Primary Campaign" (Paper delivered at the International Conference on Applied Game Theory, June 1978, Vienna).

2. Ibid.

3. Ibid.

4. See, for example, James I. Lengle and Byron Shafer, "Primary Rules, Political Power and Social Change," *American Political Science Review*, 70 (March 1976):25–40; and Thomas Hammond, "Another Look at the Role of 'the Rules' in the 1972 Democratic Primaries," *Western Political Quarterly*, forthcoming, 1980.

5. Particularly helpful in this regard were the preprimary and postprimary reports in *Congressional Quarterly Weekly Reports*. Dennis Simon and I coded this variable independently with a high degree of agreement. I sincerely appreciate his help, especially since he worked in ignorance of the purpose or model.

6. Witcover, op. cit., p. 398, fn. 1.

7. Ibid., p. 414.

8. Moore and Fraser, eds., op. cit., p. 44.

9. Ibid.

10. Witcover, op. cit., p. 416.

11. Moore and Fraser, op. cit., p. 34.

12. *Congressional Quarterly Weekly Report*, 29 May 1976, p. 1,382.

13. Witcover, op. cit., p. 429.

14. *Congressional Quarterly Weekly Report*, 12 June 1976, p. 1,473.

15. Witcover, op. cit., pp. 192–93.

16. *Washington Post*, 21 February 1976, p. 19.
17. Witcover, op. cit., p. 328.
18. Ibid.
19. Ibid., p. 343.
20. *New York Times*, 2 June 1968, p. 31.
21. Witcover, op. cit., p. 205.
22. Ibid., p. 214.
23. Brams, op. cit. The quoted question is the title of his first chapter.

Chapter 7

1. Still the classic work demonstrating that the public has little information in general and that many voters fail to meet the basic requirements for reaching an issue-based voting decision is Campbell, Converse, Miller, and Stokes, *The American Voter*, already cited. The possibility of misperception is raised most clearly in Richard A. Brody and Benjamin I. Page, "Comment: The Assessment of Policy Voting," *American Political Science Review* 66 (June 1972):450–58; and Benjamin I. Page and Richard A. Brody, "Policy Voting and the Electoral Process: The Vietnam War Issue," *American Political Science Review* 66 (September 1972): 979–95.

2. *New York Times*, 13 February 1976, pp. 1, 36.

3. Downs, op. cit. For a review of more recent developments, see Davis, Hinich, and Ordeshook, op. cit., pp. 426–48.

4. For an overview of the literature on this point, see Riker and Ordeshook, *An Introduction*. See also Richard McKelvey and Peter Ordeshook, "Symmetric Spatial Games without Majority Rule Equilibrium," *American Political Science Review* 70 (December 1976):1,172–84; and Gerald H. Kramer, "A Dynamical Model of Political Equilibrium," *Journal of Economic Theory* 16 (1977):310–34.

5. Benjamin Page, *Choices and Echoes in Presidential Elections* (Chicago: University of Chicago, 1978).

6. Unfortunately, the relevant questions were not asked of the nation after January, in 1964. The last poll in 1968, showing Nixon doing as well as or better than Rockefeller in the fall elections, was a telling blow to the Rockefeller organization, since his highly public media blitz had emphasized his greater electability so heavily.

7. See Peter Aranson and Peter Ordeshook, "Spatial Strategies for Sequential Elections," in *Probability Models of Collective Decision Making*, ed. Richard G. Niemi and Herbert F. Weisberg (Columbus: Merrill, 1972).

8. Sidney Verba and Norman Nie present this point, especially in respect to Republican activists, in *Participation in America: Political Democracy and Social Equality* (New York: Harper & Row, 1972).

9. Brams, op. cit., especially chap. 1. The quotation is from pp. 15–17.

10. See Downs, op. cit.; also Davis, Hinich, and Ordeshook, op. cit.

11. Kenneth A. Shepsle formalized these notions by representing a candidate's "position" on an issue as a probability distribution over several options or ranges of policy positions. His formulation underlies most theoretically based discussions of ambiguity. See his "The Strategy of Ambiguity: Uncertainty and Electoral Competition," *American Political Science Review* 66 June 1972, pp. 555–68; and "Parties, Voters, and the Risk Environment: A Mathematical Treatment of Electoral Competition Under Uncertainty," in Niemi and Weisberg, op. cit., pp. 273–79. His "The Paradox of Voting and Uncertainty," pp. 252–70 in the same collection, is also relevant.

12. Brams, op. cit., chap. 1.

13. Benjamin I. Page, "The Theory of Political Ambiguity," *American Political Science Review* 70 (September 1976):742–52.

14. Witcover, op. cit., p. 402.

15. *Gallup Opinion Index*, no. 142, May 1977, p. 23.

16. I would like to thank Dennis Simon for these data.

17. Page, *Choices and Echoes*.

Chapter 8

1. I am ignoring Senator Larry Pressler of South Dakota; Benjamin Hernandez, a businessman; and Harold Stassen, who have all declared their candidacies. In addition Senator Lowell Weicker of Connecticut has already entered and dropped out of the competition. Congressman Jack Kemp and General Alexander Haig are also potential candidates about whom little has been heard recently.

2. On the rules changes related to the Winograd Commission, see *Congressional Quarterly Weekly Report*, 3 June 1978, pp. 1,392–96; and 17 June 1978, pp. 1,571–72.

3. *New York Times*, 25 February 1979, p. 17.

4. John H. Kessel, "The Seasons of Presidential Politics," *Social Science Quarterly* 58, no. 3 (December 1977):418–35.

5. Kessel, ibid., cites the research of Gerald Pomper, *Elections in America* (New York: Dodd, Mead, 1968), p. 188, for gubernatorial performance; and F. L. Grogan, "Candidate Promises and Presidential Performance: 1964–1972," (Paper delivered at the Annual Meeting of the Midwest Political Science Association, Chicago, April 21–23, 1977) for evidence of Johnson's and Nixon's performance.

Index